CURRENT THEMES
IN LINGUISTICS
Bilingualism,
Experimental Linguistics,
and Language Typologies

Edited by

FRED R. ECKMAN

University of Wisconsin–Milwaukee

**HEMISPHERE
PUBLISHING CORPORATION**

Washington   London

A HALSTED PRESS BOOK

JOHN WILEY & SONS

New York   London   Sydney   Toronto

To
Ellen and Leo

Hemisphere Publishing Corporation
1025 Vermont Ave., N.W., Washington, D.C. 20005

Distributed solely by Halsted Press, a Division of John Wiley & Sons, Inc.,
New York.

1 2 3 4 5 6 7 8 9 0   D O D O   7 8 3 2 1 0 9 8 7

Library of Congress Cataloging in Publication Data

Main entry under title:

Current themes in linguistics.

    Papers presented at a symposium, held at the
University of Wisconsin—Milwaukee, Mar. 26–28,
1976.
    Includes indexes.
    1. Linguistics—Congresses. I. Eckman, Fred. R.
P23.C87   410   77-5934
ISBN 0-470-99171-2

Printed in the United States of America

CONTENTS

PREFACE

On March 26, 27, and 28, 1976, a symposium was held at the University of Wisconsin–Milwaukee on the topics: Bilingualism, Experimental Linguistics, and Language Typologies. This volume represents the final versions of the papers presented there, with the exception of a paper by Edward Keenan, University of California, Los Angeles, which was presented at the symposium, but does not appear in this volume.

In order to expedite completion of this volume, transcripts of the discussion which followed the presentation of the papers have not been included. However, many of these comments were incorporated into the final version of these papers. For their valuable contribution to the success of the symposium, I would like to thank the invited discussants: Diana Bartley (Curriculum and Instruction, UWM), Irwin Feigenbaum (Linguistics, UWM), Ashley Hastings (Linguistics, UWM), Anita Hochster (English, University of Michigan–Flint), Greg Iverson (Linguistics, UWM), Cynthia Jumes (Social Welfare, UWM), Ken Miner (Linguistics, UWM), John Norman (Philosophy, UWM), Michael Perloff (Philosophy,

UWM), Catherine Ringen (Linguistics, University of Iowa), Robert Wachal (Linguistics, University of Iowa), Barbara Wheatley (Linguistics, UWM), and Jessica Wirth (Linguistics, UWM).

This symposium was the fifth of a series of symposia which have been held at the University of Wisconsin–Milwaukee. It is also the case that this symposium constitutes a slight deviation from the course followed by the previous four symposia, which dealt with topics that were of interest mainly to theoretical linguists and philosophers of science. While some of the papers from this symposium should be of interest to these two groups, an attempt has been made to appeal also to teachers and scholars interested in applied linguistics and language pedagogy. It is hoped that future UWM Linguistics Symposia will continue in this course and attempt to deal with topics of interest to both theoretical and applied linguists.

Fred R. Eckman

ACKNOWLEDGMENTS

Funds for this symposium were made available by grants from the following sources:

1. The Lectures Committee of the School of Letters and Science, The University of Wisconsin–Milwaukee.
2. The Bilingual/Bicultural Teacher Education Project, Department of Curriculum and Instruction, The University of Wisconsin–Milwaukee.
3. The Departments of Linguistics, Anthropology, Center for Latin America, English, Philosophy and Spanish Speaking Outreach Institute.

From all of these sources we gratefully acknowledge receipt of these grants.

I would like to thank the students of the UWM Linguistics Circle, who gave freely of their time and energy in making this symposium run smoothly. I would like to give special thanks to my colleagues, whose efforts were invaluable in the organization and administration of this conference: Gail Ardery, Irwin Feigenbaum, Robert Hanson, Ashley Hastings, Greg Iverson, Andreas Koutsoudas, Barbara Wheatley, and Jessica Wirth.

I
BILINGUALISM

1
Code-switching as a verbal strategy among bilinguals

Robert J. Di Pietro
Georgetown University

Any discussion of code-switching is best begun with a working definition of the term. I offer the following: code-switching is the use of more than one language by communicants in the execution of a speech act. There is no claim to comprehensiveness in this definition. It is intended as nothing more than a starting point for what I will have to say about it in this paper. Code-switching can be approached from many theoretical viewpoints. It is a complex phenomenon of language use that reveals the truth of an observation made over 250 years ago about the special nature of all human behavior. Giambattista Vico, an eighteenth-century thinker who launched the formal study of human institutions, noted that the objectivity of the natural sciences, with all its implications for methodology, could not apply fully to any discipline in which humans made themselves the object of study (see the exposition of Vico's views in his *New Science,* translated by Bergin and Fisch 1968). While plants, animals, and the substances that compose them exist independently of the human observer, language is made by

3

humans and has no separate existence. Since grammar and its use reside within us, our study of them must always take that fact into account.

William Mackey (1970) comes face to face with the problem of objectivity when he tries to distinguish between code-switching and code-integration in the French/English bilingualism of Canada. After observing that the grammatical code structure of each language used by bilinguals is apt to contain elements which derive from the other language (or languages) they know, Mackey finds that he must ask himself a very difficult question: when is a given element a part of the particular language the bilingual happens to be speaking and when is it an intrusion from the other language(s) in the bilingual's linguistic competence? Mackey finds his answer in how the element is shared by the community of speakers. Here is his reasoning: "If everyone uses one and only one form, that form . . . is part of the bilingual's languages" (Mackey 1970:201). The word *wrench* instead of *clef anglaise,* for example, is the usual word used by French-speaking Acadians and can be considered part of their code. Most of the time, however, the linguist can come nowhere near such certainty in judging the integration of words and expressions into one of a bilingual's codes. In a test Mackey gave French/English bilinguals, he found the word *sweater* judged sometimes as a French word and sometimes as an English word. Those who thought it was English had another word, *chandail,* which they labeled as French. Mackey's conclusion is that integration is a matter of percentages in a community and depends on what element happens to be "uppermost in the minds" of a given number of people (Mackey 1970:206). But how do we know what is uppermost in the minds of others? Only with difficulty do we arrive at an understanding of what we have in our own minds. It has been my experience that code-switching often goes unnoticed by the speakers themselves. In fact, on many occasions I have code-switched myself without realizing what I was doing. At other times, I have found myself deliberately shifting from one language to another in order to achieve some desired goal or effect. The intentional shifting of languages for strategic purposes in conversations is my major point, but first I want to make reference to some other studies of code-switching which reflect its many-sidedness.

Wakefield and associates (1975) have investigated the ways in which code-switching affects the understanding of what is being said. Using sample sentences in which a code-switch is enacted at various points, their conclusion is that switching to another language within a major syntactic constituent of a sentence renders perception of that sentence more difficult than a switch which takes place at constituent boundaries.

Anisman (1975), to cite a more extensive study, confronts two issues: what are the linguistic signs that mark a code-switch and how is code-switching correlated to social class? The conclusion reached by Anisman with regard to the first issue is that prosodic features, in this case stress-timing versus syllable-timing, may function to signal a code-switch even when the speakers appear to have remained within the confines of the same linguistic code. As far as the second issue is concerned, the vacillation between syllable-timed and stress-timed speech appeared to be correlated with his subjects' (Puerto Ricans) sense of membership within their sociolinguistic group. Here, as in Mackey's study cited above, the question of code-integration presents itself. How can we be certain that changes in prosodic features represent a code-switch? Depending on how we interpret the English spoken by these people, a shift from syllable-timing to stress-timing may be better defined as a shift in style level. Such an interpretation would not deny the correlation of language with group membership as proposed by Anisman. It does, however, lead us to require some way to distinguish code-switching from style-shifting.

In a recent work of my own (Di Pietro 1976), I discerned five stages of ethnic identity among Italian Americans based on their use of language. In surveying the sociolinguistic acculturation of Italian immigrants and their descendants in the United States over the past century, I found that code-switching behavior progresses from an initial stage in which stylized English expressions were buried within an Italian matrix, through successive stages where switching into English became more functional, to reach a final stage in which English provides the matrix and switching into Italian is conventionalized and frozen. Eddie Kuo (1974) reached a similar conclusion with regard to the Chinese living in the United States and suggests that language behavior can be a good measure of changes in patterns of ethnic identification.

According to a study by Nils Hasselmo (1970), which preceded both mine and Kuo's, people living in communities that
are in the process of becoming bilingual find themselves with
several options regarding norms of usage. They may choose to
use their original language, with borrowings from the second
one. They may also use the second language with borrowings
from the first one. Eventually they use the second language
without borrowings.

Yet another study, this time by Gumperz and Hernández-Chavez (1972) focused on the relationship between social
phenomena and the motivation to shift from one language to
another. Among the social phenomena affecting choice of
language among bilinguals, Gumperz and Hernández-Chavez cite
topic of conversation, social context, allusions to past events,
and cultural attitudes expressed. To support their belief that
code-switching reflects the social labeling applied to the
languages involved, Gumperz and Hernández-Chavez analyzed the
recorded conversations of several bilingual speakers of Spanish
and English. One of their conclusions was that English served to
introduce new information while Spanish provided stylistic
embroidering to the speakers' intent (see Gumperz and Hernández-Chavez 1972:94). Speakers also used Spanish to emphasize
their identity as Chicanos, thereby reflecting a minority status
within an English-speaking community.

As perceptive as all of the above-mentioned research is on
code-switching, there are many aspects which have so far
escaped statement. In doing my own field work, I was not
especially motivated by the desire to provide a clear definition
of when an item is a code-switch and when it has been
integrated into a grammatical system. I did not even want to
show how social factors affect the bilingual's choice of language.
Instead, my point of departure was that all people, regardless of
the languages they speak, possess certain verbal skills on which
they rely to influence the outcomes of their conversations with
others. My premise was that participation in verbal interaction is
vital to the assertion of one's personality structure. The bilingual
has every bit as much a need to do so as the monolingual. Yet,
equipped with a functional competence in two or more
languages, the bilingual is presented with alternative strategies
unavailable to monolinguals. From what I have observed, code-

switching provides the bases of these strategies. In illustration of my point, let me take an example of a code-switch supplied by Gumperz and Hernández-Chavez. A bilingual whom they identify only as "E" purportedly explained to another, labeled "M," that the recording of their conversation was to show how Chicanos can shift back and forth from English to Spanish. M responded with: *Ooo, como andábamos platicando* ('Oh, like we were saying'). According to the investigators, this switch was occasioned by the mention of the word *Chicanos* and the remembrance of past conversations (see Gumperz and Hernández-Chavez 1972:93).

My own reaction was quite different, however. M's switch to Spanish could also have been an attempt to accommodate E's explanation for the recording. Since E has said that the recording was to show code-switches, M obliges with an appropriate example. M is willing to cooperate with E and what better way could there be to illustrate the activity of code-switching than by giving an actual code-switch? The challenge is out to Gumperz and Hernández-Chavez to prove such an explanation would not be as valid as the one given by them.

There are some aspects of my own investigations into code-switching which differ from studies of Chicano bilingual behavior and perhaps have contributed to my differing conclusions. For Italian-born people and their descendants residing in the United States, the language interface seems more complex than it is for Chicanos. Involved are standard Italian, dialect Italian, and a version of Italo-American koiné. A code-switch from English to any of these varieties of Italian has its own particular effect. Here are some possibilities:

(1) Vado a comprare dell'*ice-cream.* (standard Italian, with standard English code-switch)
(2) Vado a comprare l'*aisiskríma.* (standard Italian with Sicilian American koiné switch)
(3) I'm going to buy some *gelato.* (standard English with standard Italian code-switch)
(4) I'm going to buy some *aisiskríma.* (standard English with Sicilian American koiné switch)

Example 1 above could be said by an educated speaker of standard Italian from Italy who wishes to show his American relatives that he has learned the English word for *gelato*. Example 2 could be said by the same individual to show that he has recognized the distortion of the word which is made by his American relatives and is intending to mock them. Example 3 might be said by an American of Italian descent who wants to elevate himself socially by showing that he has learned some standard Italian. The same individual might say example 4 for comic effect or ridicule. I have heard all four by different individuals and have observed the effect they have had on the other participants in the speech act.

In spite of my belief in the strategic value of code-switching, I stand ready to admit that not all instances of code-switching are for verbal maneuvering. The use of an element from another language may be totally unintentional. I once overheard an Italian girl say to her companion in a department store in Rome: *Come si dice pullover in inglese?* ('How do you say "pull-over" in English?'). This girl was clearly not aware that she was using an English word in her utterance, just as many American speakers of English are not cognizant of the fact that *pizza* is an Italian word. To be effective as a verbal strategy, a code-switch must be recognized as such. Whether or not the element in question is fully integrated, as is Mackey's concern, seems to be more a question for the analyst than it is for the speakers.

Another trait of code-switching among Italians in the United States is its rare use to display group membership. Except for those communities of Italian speakers in a few parts of the United States—Boston's North End, Brooklyn, Manhattan, and parts of California and Louisiana—Italian code-switching is no longer used for group labeling. As a child growing up in an Italian American family, I heard jokes being told in English but with the punch line delivered in Italian dialect. Much as American Jews sometimes do with Yiddish, Italian was used in my experience to draw a line of demarcation between the younger, more "Americanized" members of the family and the old-timers who remained culturally unchanged.

Among the Italian immigrants of the turn of the century, code-switching from standard Italian to dialect Italian served to consolidate those Italians who felt both alienated from their homeland and unwelcome in the new country. There are many attestations of this function of code-switching in the Italian-language theater which flourished here in the early years of this century. In a play entitled *Nofrio Locandiere* ("Nofrio, the Innkeeper") written around 1915 by Giovanni de Rosalia and performed by the *Teatro Comico di New York,* the lead character, Nofrio, is the embodiment of the poor immigrant faced with the hardships of making a living in a strange new world. In this particular play, Nofrio has managed to amass enough money to buy a small inn. With his life's savings invested in this new enterprise, he is especially concerned about its success. To his bad luck, his inn is about to become the setting of a violent confrontation between a young woman who has fled there with her lover and her irate father, who is hot on the trail of the two of them. Totò, the young man, attempts to convince Franceschina, the daughter, to flee. She, however, has become resolved to face her father's wrath. A portion of the dialog in standard Italian, with Nofrio's line in Sicilian dialect, goes as follows:

Totò: *Ma egli ti uccide!* ('But he will kill you!')
Franceschina: *Non mi importa!* ('I don't care!')
Totò: *E uccide pure me!* ('And he'll kill me, too!')
Franceschina: *Non mi importa!*
Nofrio: *Signurina, puru a mia ammazza sò patri!* ('But, Miss, your father will kill me, too!')
Franceschina: *Non mi importa!*

The code-switch to Sicilian must have brought the house down. This otherwise stereotypic play is given a very real and human touch by Nofrio's line. The code-switch puts the audience on stage and makes Franceschina's refusal to concede a symbol of the harsh treatment given all immigrants. The *Teatro Comico* still puts on performances today, but now the code-switching goes between English and Italian.

Business transactions in both Italian and English provide some other insights into how code-switching affects the performance of verbal strategies. At the meat counter of an Italian grocery store located in Washington, D.C., there is a ticket-dispensing machine with a bilingual Italian/English sign affixed to it. The sign reads: "*Si prega prendere il numero*/Please take a number." Anyone entering the store will observe that many of the clerks use both languages in their transactions with customers. The meat counter is an especially busy part of the store. Without the bilingual ticket machine democratically dispensing numbered stubs, confusion would reign over who is next to be waited on. The butcher, an elderly man who is Italian by birth, calls out the numbers in English as he prepares to serve the clientele. With each new customer, the butcher must decide which language to use. He apparently uses several clues in choosing a language. Of great importance are the many nonverbal signs given him by the customer's stance, dress, and facial expressions. Perhaps he already knows the customer. Or the customer may speak first. In any case, the butcher always accommodates the customer, not only in the transaction of merchandise but also in the choice of language.

The butcher's interactional style differs with the language being spoken. In English, he is rather matter-of-fact and formal. When he switches to Italian, however, he often carries on a light banter of jokes. If the customer is a young, attractive woman, he will engage in mild flirtations. Here is an example of an interchange he had with a young woman in Italian:

> Butcher (showing her an Italian ham): *Non è bello?* ('Isn't it beautiful?')
> Young Woman: *Sì, lo è.* ('Yes, it is, indeed.')
> Butcher: *Bello come chi se lo compra.* ('As beautiful as the one who is buying it.')

Both the butcher and the young woman know that this is part of the style of interaction and the flirtation is not to be taken seriously. Joking behavior as well as flirtations make the work go more pleasantly for the butcher, as long as he is speaking Italian.

On another occasion, the cashier at the checkout counter of the same store also attempted a lighthearted flirtation with a female customer, this time in English. To a woman writing a check in payment of her purchases, he remarked: "Be sure to put your telephone number on it. That's so I can call you when your husband's not around." Her husband, who was standing nearby, overheard the cashier and threatened to break his neck. It was quite apparent that the cashier had not learned to relate his choice of verbal strategies to his choice of language. A code-switch from Italian to English did not entail, for him, a switch in verbal strategies in the manner of his coworker at the meat counter.

The home is perhaps the most fruitful place for the study of Italian/English code-switching. With both parents working, young children are often left in the care of a grandparent who still speaks Italian. The degree of understanding between grandparent and child is not always easy to determine. The grandparent who prefers to speak Italian is often forced to code-switch to English in order to be understood by the child. The following is the dialog of a home episode in which there was either total failure to communicate or the child feigned inability to comprehend:

Grandmother: *Angela, vieni a pigliar la medicina.* ('Angela, come and take your medicine.')
Angela (age 7): What?
Grandmother: *Vieni a pigliar la medicina!* ('Come and take your medicine!')
Angela: What?
Grandmother: Come over here and take your *medicina!*
Angela: What machine?
Grandmother: Come here!!

It is not unusual for parents to switch to Italian in order to discuss topics that they wish to keep from their small, supposedly monolingual English-speaking children. To counter this adult bilingual strategy, children often develop a receptive competence in Italian. They never make this ability to understand known to their parents, so that they may continue to listen in on taboo topics. One mother suspected that her little boy, aged 5, had indeed acquired the ability to understand her conversations in Sicilian. She decided to test him by not engaging in the usual switch back to English when speaking directly to him. Interrupting a conversation in Sicilian between his mother and grandmother, the child called to his mother from the basement, in English: "Can I bring my car-case up?" The mother continued to speak Sicilian and said to him: *"Li puoi acchianari tutt'e dui"* ('You can bring both of them up!). The son, forgetting that he isn't supposed to understand Sicilian, answered: "I can't. One of them belongs to Mary [his sister]." The mother pushed on in Sicilian: *"Iddu Maria carri avi?"* ('So

Mary has cars?'). Still unaware of the implications of the missing code-switch, the son remarked: "Sure, some of the cars belong to her and some are mine." As a result of this interchange, the mother realized that her little boy had understood all the intimate things she had been freely discussing with adult members of the family in Sicilian. Another form of prophylaxis would have to be found to keep intimacies from reaching young ears.

A third strategic use of code-switching, more precisely a rendition of the same message in both languages, was engaged in by a mother who gave some candy to the grandmother for distribution to the children. The mother said first in Sicilian: "*Kissu è pi tutt'e dui!*" and then loudly, in English: "That's for both of them!" The English version was intended to be overheard and to serve as a warning to the children that the candy was to be divided equally between them.

Our understanding of the ways bilinguals use their languages is still very rudimentary. As long as we linguists continue to focus all our attention on the grammatical artifact and the changes it undergoes in various settings, we will never develop an adequate theoretical framework for discussing bilingual verbal strategies. Examining code-switching will inevitably add to our general knowledge of how we communicate with each other. The definition I gave at the outset of this paper describes only the surface manifestations of code-switching. I offered nothing more than a timid invitation to probe the depths of its use.

REFERENCES

Anisman, Paul H. (1975) "Some aspects of code-switching in New York Puerto Rican English," *Bilingual Review* II/1-2:56-85.

Bergin, T. G. and M. H. Fisch (1968) *The New Science of Giambattista Vico.* Ithaca, N.Y.: Cornell University Press.

Di Pietro, Robert J. (1976) Language as a marker of Italian ethnicity. *Studi Emigrazione* (Rome, Italy), 42:202-218.

Gumperz, J. J. and E. Hernández-Chavez (1972) "Bilingualism, bidialectalism and classroom interaction," in C. B. Cazden, V. P. John and D. Hymes (eds.), New York: Teachers College Press.

Hasselmo, Nils (1970) "Code-switching and modes of speaking," in Glenn G. Gilbert (ed.), *Texas Studies in Bilingualism,* pp. 179-210. Berlin: De Gruyter.

Kuo, Eddie C. (1974) "Bilingual pattern of a Chinese immigrant group in the United States," *Anthropological Linguistics* 16/3:128-140.

Mackey, W. F. (1970) "Interference, integration and the synchronic fallacy," *G.U.R.T.*, monograph no. 23, pp. 195-223, Washington, D.C.: Georgetown University Press.

Wakefield, James A., Peggy E. Bradley, Byong-Hee Yom and Eugene B. Doughtie (1975) "Language-switching and constituent structure," *Language and Speech* 18/1:14-19.

2
Culture and language
as factors in learning and education

Wallace E. Lambert
McGill University

It is difficult to dislodge deep-seated beliefs. The one I would like at least to loosen somewhat is the belief that culture and language have profound influences on cognitive processes. The trouble is that it makes awfully good common sense to say that people from different cultural or linguistic backgrounds think differently, and it even makes fairly good social-scientific sense. For instance, some time ago the anthropologist Levy-Bruhl (1910) presented a certain type of evidence to support the idea that the thinking of "primitive peoples" differed in substance and structure from that of more "civilized" man. Although this thesis has been thoroughly criticized over the years, especially by other anthropologists, it has been difficult to devise decisive empirical counterdemonstrations so as to eradicate its influence within the behavioral sciences (see Cole et al. 1971). In the case of language, the ethnolinguists Sapir (1921) and Whorf (1941) presented an equally attractive argument for language's influence on thought, and although disputed by many, it has also proved resistant to empirical counterproofs (see Carroll and Casagrande 1958).

Over and above the difficulties we all have in defining culture, language, and thought, I have come to question the notion that culture or language affect basic cognitive structures and the related notion that culture affects the structure of personality. I was impressed early in my training with Kroeber's (1948) principle of the "psychic unity" of mankind, so much so that now I am persuaded that similarities among ethnolinguistic groups are much more prominent than differences, that cultural and linguistic backgrounds do not reach down to the basic structures of thought or personality, that variations of thought and personality within cultural or national groups (as reflected, for example, in socioeconomic background differences) are much greater than between-group variations, and that few if any modal personality or modal cognitive profiles of any substance are likely to turn up in cross-cultural or cross-national research.

This statement is perhaps too enthusiastic and too strong in view of the important debates on the subject that are just getting underway. To be fair, it should be said that there actually are no good grounds yet available for deciding one way or the other. In the domain of language, for example, the Piaget school argues for the independence of language and thought while the Vygotsky school argues for an interdependence. In the domain of culture's influence, there is a socially significant debate going on between those who argue that certain cultural or linguistic groups are "deficient" relative to others and those who hold that it is a question of "differences" rather than "deficiencies." And now both of these points of view are challenged by a third that questions whether there are any real deficiencies or differences (Cole et al. 1971; Cole and Bruner 1971). It is to be hoped that these debates will stimulate research that in time will help us decide among the alternatives, but until then I believe it helps us to grapple better with the issues involved if we regard with a robust skepticism any claims about cultural or linguistic influences on the basic structures of thought or of personality. There is, of course, no debate about the influence of culture and language on the content of thought or the expression of personality, but these matters, captivating as they are in their own right, are much less socially significant than the one we are concerned with here.

My own early skepticism has been strengthened by personal

research experiences where cultural and linguistic contrasts were expected to emerge, but didn't. It started with a large-scale, cross-national study Otto Klineberg and I conducted some years ago on children's conceptions of foreign peoples (Lambert and Klineberg 1967). Anthropologists helped us select ten world settings that would likely provide cultural contrasts in the ways children view themselves, their own national or ethnic group, and foreign groups. For example, through interviews we solicited the views of large numbers of children in such supposedly diverse settings as Japan, Brazil, Israel, South Africa, Turkey, France, Canada, and the United States. Instead of cultural or national contrasts, what emerged from this study was a large and consistent set of age changes in children's conceptions of the world which were essentially the same from one setting to another. There were some differences that appeared to be cultural in nature, but it would have been very difficult in our investigation to disentangle the influences of social class, types and amounts of schooling, amounts of travel experience, and the like from what seemed to be differences attributable solely to cultural setting. In this instance, then, we were expecting cultural differences; we gave them ample opportunity to show through; but few if any unambiguous ones did.

It happened again when I tried to investigate cultural differences between Canada's two main ethnic groups, the French Canadians and English Canadians (Lambert 1970). Here the research involved between-group comparisons of attitudes; various aspects of social perception; indices of achievement motivation, and competitiveness; and values associated with child training. Again, the major outcome was a pattern of similarities between the two ethnic groups, and the few contrasts that did turn up, as in the case of child-training values (Lambert, Yackley and Hein 1971), cannot be attributed to cultural factors in any simple direct way. They could, in fact, be due as much to differences in social class, education, religion, and the like as to ethnic background. At McGill we are still probing for reliable and unambiguous cultural differences among ethnic groups in Canada, and there is much work yet to do, particularly in making sure that we select comparison groups and testing procedures which will permit real cultural differences to show through. Nonetheless, when a serious attempt was made to find cultural differences where they might most be expected in the Canadian setting, few if any turned up.

One further research experience impressed me, this one conducted by my brother and Leigh Minturn (Minturn and Lambert 1964), who were interested in the varieties of ways mothers bring up children and how upbringing affects personality. In collaboration with anthropologists they chose six cultural settings which, according to the anthropological literature, would be likely to provide the maximum in contrasts. Their investigation called for one- to two-year residences in each of the six cultural settings during which time detailed observations and interviews were to be carried out. The major outcome in this study was also unanticipated:they found very few instances of unambiguous cultural differences in styles of mothering. Instead, the styles of mothering that did emerge seemed to depend on conditions such as the number of persons living within a particular space, the amount of time available after required work to be with children, and so forth. What struck me was that mothers from such diverse settings as southern India, the Philippines, Mexico, and the United States could be so much alike in their associations with their children when account is taken of the environmental exigencies placed on them as parents, exigencies that could turn up in any form in any cultural setting.

These then are some personal experiences that have probably enhanced the bias in my thinking. Bias or not, it was nonetheless reassuring to read a recent article by Michael Cole and Jerome Bruner (1971), who take a very similar point of view. As they examined the claim that children of minority groups suffer from some sort of intellectual deficit, they were far from convinced. In fact, they argued that the information so far available "casts doubt on the conclusion that a deficit exists in minority group children, and even raises doubts as to whether *any* nonsuperficial differences exist among different cultural groups" (Cole and Bruner 1971:868; emphasis in original article). A similar idea has recently come from a less technical and less academic source, namely, Richard Hoggart, the Assistant Director-General of UNESCO (Hoggart 1973), who from his own experiences has developed a faith in cross-cultural communication and understanding because of the "common qualities, the ribs of the universal human grammar" that link all men and because of "common experience" and "common sorrows which above all link us."

There is then the beginnings of an argument to be made against cultural or linguistic differences and their putative impingement on the structures of personality and cognition, and in time the argument may become convincing enough to disturb deep-seated beliefs to the contrary. But until that time arrives, the argument for most people will remain academic. It is this dilemma that intrigues me, namely, that people's beliefs can become so pervasive and so deeply rooted that no attention is given to evidence which might support or contradict the beliefs held. A researcher confronted with this inconsistency might be well advised to drop the topic and move on to other research matters, but I feel that it is more productive to focus squarely on the beliefs themselves and to try to understand their workings—in this case, to examine people's beliefs about the influence of culture and language and to try to understand how such beliefs affect people's lives, the lives of both ethnic majority and ethnic minority groups. Perhaps with our focus on belief systems, we can better understand the practical importance of cultural and linguistic backgrounds in learning and education and see more clearly ways of ameliorating the learning experiences of young people from "different" backgrounds.

Let's start then with the working hypothesis that most people believe that cultures differ in basic ways and that cultural and linguistic backgrounds shape our personalities and our modes of thought. Beliefs of this sort are rooted in the early socialization of children. For instance, our own cross-national research on children's views of foreign peoples (Lambert and Klineberg 1967) indicates that, from infancy on, young children are puzzled about who they are, where the limits of one's own family or community or nation lie, and what criteria should be used to differentiate in-groups from out-groups. Parents, it turns out, become the crucial teachers of children by providing answers to these questions, and what parents typically do (regardless of their "cultural" background) is to draw contrasts for the child between the child's own ethnic group and various other, usually quite distinctive, foreign peoples. This parental training in contrasts among ethnic groups uses the own group as a reference point and typically the own group is stereotyped and presented in a more favorable, "better-than" light than the comparison groups. Through early education in group contrasts, then, children are likely to pick up the idea that other peoples are different, strange, generally less good, and less dependable. Through schooling, these early-developed beliefs are usually strengthened by training in civics, history, and social studies classes to the extent that there are contrasts drawn between one's own nation and own social system and those of the "distinctive" others in foreign settings, and to the extent that this is done with an ethnocentric bias. Thus, education within the family and within the school typically contributes to a belief that one's own national or cultural group is special, and this is done with the best of aims, that is, of socializing the child, or preparing him to take on constructive roles in his own community and society.

The perception of cultural differences is enhanced as well by people's tendencies to link cultures with specific languages or dialects. These linguistic differences are concrete and real, and, to the extent that cultural or national differences are more apparent than real, the languages associated with particular ethnic groups take on all the more social significance—as though the language differences are used in people's thinking to verify the link between a culture and a particular use of language. It is not difficult, therefore, to understand why linguistic minority groups often demand and fight for the right to use their own language as a working or learning language instead of a national or international language that might well be of more practical or utilitarian value. In my view this becomes a powerful emotional issue because the group's identity is associated with its distinctive language, and this linguistic distinctiveness becomes an enormously precious personal characteristic which dominates that group's system of beliefs. Because culture and language become linked in people's thinking, the more one questions the reality of differences in culture, the more important the distinctiveness of the language becomes.

We can start, then, with the proposition that linguistic distinctiveness is a basic component of personal identity for members of an ethnic group—that ethnicity and language become associated in people's thinking, the thinking of those outside a particular ethnic group as well as those within the group. With these assumptions about people's belief systems as a reference point, we may go on to discuss certain socially relevant questions about culture, language, and learning that a group of us at McGill are trying to answer:

1. Do people's beliefs about culture and language affect the learning process? More specifically, do beliefs about a particular ethnolinguistic group influence learners in their attempts to master that group's language?
2. Is there any basis to the belief that in becoming bilingual or bicultural one dulls his cognitive powers and dilutes his identity?
3. Should minority groups try to maintain their ethnolinguistic identities and heritages in the North American setting?

These questions are interdependent. The first suggests a need to test whether beliefs are really important for the learning process, specifically whether people's beliefs about a particular cultural group affect their efficiency in attempts to learn that group's language. The first question also prompts us to explore how the beliefs of members of ethnic minority groups influence their willingness to maintain their own distinctive language. In other words, the first question requires us to examine the ways beliefs about a cultural group get associated with the language spoken by that group and, through such an association, affect the language-learning process. The second question concerns the sacredness of the language–culture link by exploring the not-uncommon belief that in becoming bilingual and bicultural (that is, violating the one language–one culture rule), one deteriorates his cognitive powers and the clarity of his cultural identity. The answer to the third question depends on the answers to the other two. Depending on the veridicality of the belief that bilingualism and biculturalism are debilitators, and on the importance of beliefs about language and culture in the learning process, we would approach the adjustment problems of ethnolinguistic minority groups in quite different ways. Our major goal, then, is to pose questions that will suggest appropriate ways of helping America's ethnolinguistic minority groups who, more than most others, may become victims of belief systems, other people's as well as their own.

1. DO BELIEFS ABOUT A PARTICULAR ETHNOLINGUISTIC GROUP AFFECT THE EFFICIENCY OF LEARNING THAT GROUP'S LANGUAGE?

Robert Gardner and I first became interested in people's beliefs about foreign groups in the context of learning and teaching foreign languages (see Gardner and Lambert 1972). How is it, we asked ourselves, that some people can learn a second or foreign language so easily and so well while others, given what seem to be the same opportunities to learn, find it almost impossible? With this as a start, we began to wonder about the more general question of what it is to have a knack for languages. To say that one has to have "an ear for languages" is to give an excuse rather than an answer, since it is too easy to transfer mysteries to biology, either as the source of one's linguistic difficulties or as the source of one's linguistic genius. Perhaps the knack for languages lies in a profile of abilities or aptitudes that develop differently from person to person, some profiles favoring the language-learning process more than others. This idea makes good sense, but there is likely something more to it than aptitudes. Everyone or almost everyone learns his native language painlessly, so why would not everyone have at least a minimally adequate aptitude profile? And history makes it clear that when societies want to keep two or more languages alive, and learning more than one is taken for granted, everyone seems to learn two or more as a matter of course.

As social psychologists we believed that there was something more involved. We expected that success in mastering a foreign language would depend not only on intellectual capacity and language aptitude but also on the learner's perceptions of and beliefs about the other ethnolinguistic group, his attitude toward representatives of that group, and his willingness to identify enough to adopt the distinctive aspects of the behavior, linguistic and nonlinguistic, that characterize that other group. The learner's motivation for language study, it follows, would be determined by his attitudes and readiness to identify and by his orientation to the whole process of learning a foreign language.

We saw many possible forms the student's orientation could take, two of which we looked at in some detail: an "instrumental" outlook, reflecting the practical value and advantages of learning a new language, and an "integrative" outlook, reflecting a sincere and personal interest in the people and culture represented by the other group. It was our hunch that an integrative orientation would sustain better the long-term motivation needed for the very demanding task of second-language learning, and here we had in mind students in North American contexts studying the popular European languages. For the serious student who in time really masters the foreign language, we saw the possibility of a conflict of identity or alienation (we used the term *anomie*) arising as he became skilled enough to become an accepted member of a new cultural group. His knowledge of the language and the people involved would both prepare him for membership and serve as a symptom to members of the other group of his interests and affection. Thus the development of skill in the language could lead the language student ever closer to a point where adjustments in allegiances would be called for.

In our early studies with English-speaking Canadians in Montreal, we found support for such a theory: achievement in French, studied as a second language at the high school level, was dependent upon linguistic aptitude and verbal intelligence on the one hand, and quite independent of aptitude, on a sympathetic set of beliefs toward French people and the French way of life. It was this integrative orientation that apparently provided a strong motivation to learn the other group's language. In the Montreal setting, students with an integrative orientation were more successful in second-language learning than those who were instrumentally oriented.

A follow-up study (Gardner 1960) confirmed and extended these findings, using a larger sample of English Canadian students and incorporating various measures of French achievement. In this case it was difficult to dissociate aptitude from motivational variables since they emerged in a common factor that included not only French skills stressed in standard academic courses but also those skills developed through active use of the language in communication. Apparently, in the Montreal context, the intelligent and linguistically gifted student of French is more likely to be integratively oriented, making it more probable that he could become outstanding in all aspects of French proficiency. Still in the same study, the measures of orientation and desire to learn French emerged as separate factors, independent of language aptitude, and in these instances it was evident that they played an important role on their own, especially in the development of expressive skills in French. Further evidence from the intercorrelations indicated that this integrative motive was the converse of an authoritarian ideological syndrome, opening the possibility that basic personality dispositions may be involved in language-learning efficiency. The integrative motive, incidentally, is not simply the result of having more experience with French at home. Rather it seems to depend on the family-wide attitudinal disposition.

The same ideas were tested out in three American settings (communities in Louisiana, Maine, and Connecticut) with English-speaking American high school students learning French. Although each community has its own interesting patterns of results, the role played by attitudes toward one's own group and toward foreign groups emerged again as an important influence on the learning process.

Attitudes of this sort also affect the language learning of French American young people in these settings as it affects the ways they adjust to the bicultural demands made on them. For example, it became evident in our investigation that the attitudes of French American adolescents toward their own ethnolinguistic group and toward the American way of life can influence their development of linguistic skills in French and English, leading in some instances to a dominance of French over English, in other cases of English over French, and in still others bilingual competence. The outcome seems to be determined, in part at least, by the way the young French American handles the conflicts of allegiances he is bound to encounter. For instance, we found in Louisiana that positive attitudes of French American teenagers toward the French American culture, coupled with favorable stereotypes of the European French, were highly correlated with expressive skills in French. Other types of outlook, however, seem to restrict the potential development of these young people. Thus, a very strong pro-French attitudinal bias or an exceptionally strong motivation and drive to learn

French do not automatically promote outstanding competence in the French language. Nor does a strong pro-American outlook assure proficiency in English.

Certain modes of adjustment were especially instructive in the sense that they provided the young French American with models of how best to capitalize on his bicultural heritage. In Louisiana, for example, students who had very favorable attitudes toward their own cultural group and who also had a good competence in English were outstanding on various measures of proficiency in French. This pattern suggests that French Americans who are content and comfortable with both facets of their cultural and linguistic heritage are psychologically free to become full bilinguals. In Maine we noted a somewhat different type of adjustment, one of equal interest:French American students with a strong instrumental orientation toward French study and who receive parental encouragement to do well in French demonstrate outstanding skills in various aspects of French and feel assured of their competence in both French and English. Realizing that "instrumental" has a quite different meaning for students learning their own language, this family-supported instrumental approach offers the French American a real chance of being both French and American.

To test further these notions, we wondered whether they would apply in more foreign settings and this led us to the Philippines where a foreign language, English, has become not only a second national language but also the medium of instruction from the early grades on and an essential language for economic advancement and success. For the Philippine study we had to shift attention from French to English and from France to the United States. It also meant reworking the content of many of our measures and changing our expectations about student reactions, for in this case the language being offered has enormous instrumental value. The results of this investigation brought to light certain cross-nationally stable relationships and certain others that are tied to particular cultural contexts. For example, we found that Filipino students who approach the study of English with an instrumental orientation and who receive parental support for this outlook were clearly successful in developing proficiency in the language. Thus, it seems that in settings where there is an urgency about mastering a second language—as there is in the Philippines and in North America for members of linguistic minority groups—the instrumental approach to language study is extremely effective. Nevertheless, for another subgroup of Filipino students, an integrative orientation toward the study of English had a striking effect on proficiency, especially the audiolingual aspects. This cross-cultural support for the importance of motivational and attitudinal dispositions strengthens greatly our confidence in the basic notions we started with. But still the Philippine investigation changed our perspective on the instrumental–integrative contrast. We see now that the typical student of foreign languages in North America will profit more if he is helped to develop an integrative outlook toward the group whose language is being offered. For him, an instrumental approach has little significance and little motive force. However, for members of ethnic minority groups in North America as well as for those living in nations that have imported prestigious world languages and made them important national languages, the picture changes. Learning a second language of national or worldwide significance is then indispensable, and both instrumental and integrative orientations toward the learning task must be developed. The challenge for these minority groups or those who import languages is to keep their own linguistic and cultural identity alive while mastering the second language, and in this regard various findings indicate that becoming bilingual does not mean losing identity. In fact, we are now convinced that striving for a comfortable place in two cultural systems may be the best motivational basis for becoming bilingual, which in turn is one's best guarantee for really belonging to both cultures.

These investigations make it very clear that beliefs about foreign peoples and about one's own ethnicity are powerful factors in the learning of another group's language and in the maintenance of one's own language.

2. IS THERE ANY BASIS TO THE BELIEF THAT BECOMING BILINGUAL OR BICULTURAL DULLS COGNITIVE POWERS AND DILUTES IDENTITY?

Effects on Cognition

The technical literature on the consequence of becoming bilingual and/or bicultural stretches back to the turn of the century and is still growing. In the early literature (1920s and 1930s), we find a generally pessimistic outlook on the effects of bilingualism, but since the 1960s there is a much more optimistic picture emerging. Bilingualism and biculturalism, as one might expect, generate much emotional and political steam and this often clouds whatever facts are available. In general, the researchers in the early period expected to find all sorts of problems, and they usually did: bilingual children, relative to monolinguals, were behind in school, retarded in measured intelligence, and socially adrift. One trouble with most of the early studies was that little care was taken to check out the essentials before comparing monolingual and bilingual subjects. Thus, social-class background, educational opportunities, and the like were not controlled, nor was much attention given to determining how bilingual or monolingual the comparison groups actually were. But even though there are grounds to worry about the adequacy of many of these studies, an overwhelming trend in the outcomes is instructive: the largest proportion of these investigations concluded that bilingualism has a detrimental affect on intellectual functioning, a smaller number found little or no relation between bilingualism and intelligence, and only two suggested that bilingualism might have favorable consequences on cognition.

With this picture as background, Elizabeth Anisfeld (then E. Peal) and I started an investigation on the bilingual-monolingual topic in 1962 in the Canadian setting (Peal and Lambert 1962). We, of course, had strong expectations of finding a bilingual deficit as the literature suggested, but we wanted to pinpoint what the intellectual components of that deficit were in order to develop compensatory education programs. We argued that a large proportion of the world's population is, by the exigencies of life, bound to be bilingual, and it seemed to us appropriate to help them, if possible.

We were able in our first investigation to profit from most of the shortcomings of earlier research, making us feel relatively confident about the results (see Lambert and Anisfeld 1969). What surprised us, though, was that French–English bilingual children in the Montreal setting scored significantly ahead of carefully matched monolinguals both on verbal and nonverbal measures of intelligence. Furthermore, the patterns of test results suggested to us that the bilinguals had a more diversified structure of intelligence as measured, and more flexibility in thought.

For someone who doesn't really believe that language influences thought, these results, suggesting the possibility that bilingualism—a double-language experience—might affect the structure and flexibility of thought, came as a double-barreled surprise. But one investigation rarely has enough weight to change the course of events, even though an important follow-up study (Anisfeld 1964) confirmed the 1962 conclusions. What was needed was confirmation from other settings and from studies using different approaches.

Since then confirmations have started to emerge from carefully conducted research around the world, from Singapore (Torrance et al. 1970), Switzerland (Balkan 1970), South Africa (Ianco-Worrall 1973), Israel and New York (Ben-Zeev 1972), western Canada (Cummins and Gulutsan 1973), and, using a quite different approach, from Montreal (Scott 1973). All of these studies (and we found no others in the recent literature to contradict them) indicate that bilingual children, relative to monolingual controls, show definite advantages on measures of "cognitive flexibility," "creativity," or "divergent thought." Sandra Ben Zeev's study, for example, involved Hebrew–English bilingual children in New York and Israel, and the results strongly support the conclusion that bilinguals have greater "cognitive flexibility." In this case, the term means that bilinguals have greater "skill at auditory reorganization" of verbal material, a much more "flexible manipulation of the linguistic code," and are more advanced in "concrete operational thinking" as these were measured in Ben Zeev's investigation. Anita Ianco-Worrall's study involved Afrikaans–English bilingual children in Pretoria, South Africa, and it lends equally strong support for a somewhat different form of cognitive flexibility, an advantage over monolingual controls in separating word meaning from word sound. The conclusion is drawn that the bilinguals were between two and three years advanced in this feature of cognitive development, which Leopold (1939-49) felt to be so characteristic of the liberated thought of bilinguals. Ianco-Worrall also found good support for a bilingual precocity in realizing the arbitrary assignment of names to referents, a feature of thinking which Vygotsky (1962) believed reflected insight and sophistication.

The recent study by Sheridan Scott (1973) involving French–English bilinguals in Montreal is perhaps the most persuasive. She worked with data collected over a seven-year period from two groups of English Canadian children. One group had become functionally bilingual in French during the time period because they attended experimental classes where most of the instruction was conducted in French. The other group had followed a conventional English-language education program. At the grade 1 level, the two groups were equated for measured intelligence, socioeconomic background, and parental attitudes toward French people. In fact, had the opportunity been presented to them, it is likely that most of the parents in the control group would have enrolled their children in the experimental French program, but no such opportunity was available since it was decided in advance to start one experimental class per year only (see Lambert and Tucker 1972).

Scott was interested in the effect becoming bilingual would have on the cognitive development of the children, in particular, what effect it would have on the children's "divergent thinking," a special type of cognitive flexibility. The term was apparently introduced by Guilford (1950, 1956) to characterize a cognitive style that contrasts with "convergent thinking." Convergent thinking is measured by tests that provide a number of pieces of information which the subject must synthesize to arrive at a correct answer; thus, the information provided funnels in or converges on a correct solution. Divergent thinking provides the subject a starting point for thought—"think of a paper clip"—and asks the subject to generate a whole series of permissible solutions—"and tell me all the things one could do with it." Some researchers have considered divergent thinking as an index of creativity (e.g., Getzels and Jackson 1962) while others suggest that until more is known it is best viewed as a distinctive cognitive style reflecting a rich imagination and an ability to scan rapidly a host of possible solutions.

Scott was interested, among other things, in whether bilingualism promotes divergent thinking. Her results, based on a multivariate analysis, show a substantial advantage for the bilingual over the monolingual children on the divergent thinking tests, and in this investigation one can examine the year-by-year development of the advantage. Her study opens up many interesting possibilities for more in-depth analysis of the bilingual's thought processes.

There is, then, an impressive array of evidence accumulating that argues plainly against the common sense notion that becoming bilingual, that is, having two strings to one's bow or two linguistic systems within one's brain, naturally divides a person's cognitive resources and reduces his efficiency of thought. Instead, one can now put forth a very persuasive argument that there is a definite cognitive advantage for bilingual over monolingual children in the domain of cognitive flexibility. Only further research will tell us how this advantage, assuming it is a reliable phenomenon, actually works:whether it is based on a better storage of information by bilinguals, whether the separation of linguistic symbols from their referents or the ability to separate word meaning from word sound is the key factor, whether the bilingual contrasts of linguistic systems aid in the development of general conceptual thought, or whatever. In any case, this new trend in research should give second thoughts to those who have used the notion of bilingual deficit as an argument for melting down ethnic groups. It is also to be hoped that it will provide a new insight to those ethnolinguistic groups who may also have been led to believe in the notion of a likely deficit attributable to bilingualism.

One feature of the studies just reviewed merits special attention:all the cases reported (those in Singapore, South Africa, Switzerland, Israel, New York, western Canada, Montreal) dealt with bilinguals using two languages, both of which have social value and respect in each of the settings. Thus, knowing Afrikaans and English in South Africa, Hebrew and English in New York and Israel, or French as well as English for English-speaking Canadian children would in each case be adding a second, socially relevant language to one's repertory of skills. In no case would the learning of the second language portend the dropping or the replacement of the other as would typically be the case for French Canadians or Spanish Americans developing high-level skills in English. We might refer to these as examples of an additive form of bilingualism and contrast it with a more subtractive form experienced by many ethnic minority groups who, because of national educational policies and social pressures of various sorts, are forced to put aside their ethnic language for a national language. Their degree of bilinguality at any point in time would likely reflect some stage in the subtraction of the ethnic language and its replacement with another. The important educational task of the future, it seems to me, is to transform the pressures on ethnic groups so that they can profit from an additive form of bilingualism; as we'll see in the final section, projects with these aims run up against beliefs and attitudes of another sort.

Effects on Identity

What about the notion that becoming bilingual and bicultural subtracts, through division, from one's sense of personal identity? Here too, there are signs in the recent literature of interest in this topic, but there are still only a few studies to draw on. Three, however, do bear on the issue of the identity of bilinguals, and all three are encouraging in their outcomes.

The first is the study, mentioned earlier, of French Americans in communities in New England and Louisiana (Gardner and Lambert 1972) and their ways of coping with a dual heritage: some oriented themselves definitely toward their French background and tried to ignore their American roots; others were tugged more toward the American pole at the expense of their Frenchness; and still others apparently tried not to think in ethnic terms, as though they did not consider themselves as being either French or American. These three types of reactions parallel closely those of Italian American adolescents studied earlier by Child (1943). To me these ways of coping characterize the anguish of members of ethnic groups when caught up in a subtractive form of biculturalism, that is, where social pressures are exerted on them to give up one aspect of their dual identity for the sake of blending into a national scene. We will return to these three reaction styles later when we can contrast them with a fourth style which reflects an additive form of biculturalism that also turned up in our study of French Americans. The important point here is that identities are fragile and they can, through social pressures, be easily tipped off balance.

Identities need not be so disturbed, though, as the study of Aellen and Lambert (1969) showed. In this case we were interested in the adjustments made by adolescent children of

English-French mixed marriages in the Montreal setting. We examined the degree and direction of the offspring's ethnic identifications as well as a selected set of their attitudes, values, and personality characteristics.

The children of these mixed marriages come in contact with and are usually expected to learn the distinctive social and behavioral characteristics of the two cultures represented in their families. The question is whether the demands made on them necessarily generate conflicts, whether the experience with two cultures possibly broadens and liberalizes such children, or whether some combination of both outcomes is typical. In addition to the cultural demands made on them, the children of mixed ethnic marriages may face other difficulties to the extent that their parents, as suggested by Gordon (1966) and Saucier (1965), may have married outside their ethnic group because of personal instability and immaturity. Much of the previous research suggests that persons who intermarry in this way often have relatively strong feelings of alienation, self-hatred, and worthlessness, and are disorganized and demoralized. Mixed ethnic children might well find it difficult to identify with their parents if these characteristics are typical or representative. Still, the offspring could develop understanding and sympathy for parents with such an outlook. On the other hand, people may intermarry in many instances because they have developed essentially healthy attitudes and orientations which are nonetheless inappropriate within their own ethnic group, making intermarriage with a sympathetic outsider particularly attractive. They may have become, like Park's marginal man, "the individual with the wider horizon, the keener intelligence, the more detached and rational viewpoint... always relatively the more civilized human being" (Park 1964:376). In that case, their children might be particularly well-trained in tolerance and openmindedness, especially since the children themselves are likely to feel that they, unlike their parents, are automatically members of both ethnic groups. The purpose of the Aellen and Lambert 1969 investigation was to examine both these possibilities as objectively as possible by comparing groups of adolescent boys of mixed French-English parentage with others of homogeneous background, either French or English. All groups in the comparison were similar as to age, socioeconomic class, intelligence, and number of siblings.

It was found that the profile of characteristics of the boys with mixed ethnic parentage is a healthy one in every respect when comparisons are made with groups from homogeneous ethnic backgrounds; they identify with their parents, especially with their fathers, as well as the comparison groups do; they relate themselves to and identify with both ethnic reference groups, this being particularly so for those in a French academic environment; they show no signs of personality disturbances, social alienation, or anxiety; nor do their self-concepts deviate from those of the comparison subjects; they see their parents as giving them relatively more attention and personal interest, and their attitudes toward parents are as favorable as those of the comparison groups; they seek out distinctively affectionate relationships with peers; their general attitudinal orientations are similar to those of the comparison groups while their specific attitudes toward both English and French Canadians are relatively unbiased; their values show the influence of both ethnic backgrounds as do their achievement orientations, which are less extreme than those of the comparison groups. Rather than developing a divided allegiance or repressing one or both aspects of their backgrounds, as has been noted among the offspring of certain immigrant groups (Child 1943), they apparently have developed a dual allegiance that permits them to identify with both their parents and to feel that they themselves are wanted as family members. One of the mixed ethnic boys summed up this finding by saying: "I respect both my parents, and I respect their origins." One might argue that the concern of the parents of mixed ethnic adolescents to "include" their children is exaggerated, a symptom of tension and value conflict, but such an interpretation is negated by the apparent success these parents have had in passing on a sense of being wanted. There are, however, many features of this pattern of results that need further study.

This profile sketch is more pronounced for the mixed ethnic subjects who are part of the French Canadian high school environment. These young people may be more susceptible to the English Canadian culture than those attending English Canadian schools would be to French Canadian culture because of the Canadian cultural tug of war, which seems, at least until recently, to be controlled by the more powerful and prestigious English Canadian communities (see Lambert 1967).

Two general modes of adjustment to a mixed ethnic background became apparent. In one case, these young men incorporate both ethnic streams of influence, which are either modified by the parents before they are passed on to their children or are tempered by the adolescents themselves, so that they are less extreme than those represented by either of the major reference groups. A tendency to amalgamate both cultural streams of influence is suggested by the contrasts noted between the ethnically mixed groups and the homogeneous groups, for example, the unbiased ethnic identifications of the former, their perceptions of parents as being inclusive, their favorable attitudes toward both English and French Canadians, and their less extreme achievement values. In the other case, they tend to adapt their views to the predominant features of the academic-cultural environment in which they find themselves. This form of adjustment is suggested by the tendency of the mixed ethnic groups to line up with the respective homogeneous groups with whom they attend high school, for example, their choices of the values they hope to pass on to their own children, the personality traits they see as undesirable, and their judgments of the relative attractiveness of English Canadian or French Canadian girls.

This illustration provides hope for biculturality in the sense that offspring of mixed ethnic marriages appear to profit from the dual cultural influences found in their families. Rather than cultural conflicts, we find well-adjusted young people with broad perspectives who are comfortable in the role of representing both of their cultural backgrounds. We also have here an illustration of the additive form of biculturalism; the boys studied were caught in the flow of two cultural streams and were apparently happy to be part of both streams.

There was a similar type of outcome in the investigation, mentioned earlier, conducted by Richard Tucker and myself (Lambert and Tucker 1972) concerning the English Canadian children who took the majority of their elementary schooling via French and who after grades 5 and 6 had become functionally bilingual. Here we were able to measure on a yearly basis their self-conceptions and their attitudes toward English Canadian, French Canadian, and European French ways of life. The attitude profiles of the children in the Experimental French program indicate that by the fifth grade important affective changes had occurred. The children state that they enjoy the form of education they are receiving and want to stay with it; their feelings toward French people have become decidedly more favorable; and they now think of themselves as being both French and English Canadian in personal makeup. It is this apparent identification with French people—those from Canada and those from Europe—that raises the question of biculturalism. Has the program made the children more bicultural? It is difficult to answer this question because the meaning of *bicultural* is so vague. It is certain that the children now feel they can be at ease in both French and English Canadian social settings and that they are becoming both French and English in certain regards, but not becoming less English as a consequence. It is certain too they have learned that in classes with European French teachers they should stand when a visitor enters while they need not stand in classes that are conducted by English Canadian or French Canadian teachers. We wonder how much more there is to being bicultural beyond knowing thoroughly the languages involved, feeling personally aligned with both groups, and knowing how to behave in the two atmospheres. Are there any deeper personal aspects to cultural differences? That is, does culture actually affect personality all that much or is it perhaps a more superficial and thinner wrapping than many social scientists have suggested?

The attitudes of the parents at the start of the project were basically friendly and favorable, although marked with very little knowledge about the French Canadian people around them. These parents wanted their children to learn French for essentially integrative reasons—getting to know the other ethnic group and their distinctive ways—but they did not want them to go so far as to think and feel as French Canadians do, in other words to lose their English Canadian identity. How will they interpret the attitudes of their children who by grade 5 come to think of themselves as being both English Canadian and French Canadian in disposition and outlook? Some may see this as a worrisome sign of identity loss, but we believe they will come to interpret their children's enjoyment in having both English Canadian and French Canadian friends and both types of outlooks as a valuable addition, not a subtraction or cancellation of identities.

As we see it, the children are acquiring a second social overcoat, which seems to increase their interest in dressing up and reduces the wear and tear placed on either coat alone. Our guess is that the children are beginning to convince any worried parents that the experience is, in fact, enriching and worthwhile.

Of course, the parents cannot share fully their children's experience of their development of a dual identity. Nevertheless, in the few noticeable cases where the divergence of views between parents and children has become very apparent, even those parents give the impression that they are pleased that their children are being prepared to take their place in a new type of multilingual and multicultural society and to help shape its development. As parents, they can easily take pride in the fact that they have gone out of their way to help in this special type of preparation.

These studies suggest to us that there is no basis in reality for the belief that becoming bilingual or bicultural necessarily means a loss or dissolution of identity. We are aware of the possible pressures that can surround members of ethnolinguistic minority groups and make them hesitant to become full-fledged members of two cultural communities. At the same time, though, we see how easy and rewarding it can be for those who are able to capitalize on a dual heritage. The question of most interest, then, is how in modern societies these possibilities can be extended to ethnolinguistic minority groups, which is the major issue of the section to follow.

3. SHOULD MINORITY GROUPS TRY TO MAINTAIN THEIR ETHNOLINGUISTIC IDENTITIES AND HERITAGES IN THE NORTH AMERICAN SETTING?

In order to suggest an answer to this question, it seems to me that we need first to examine in more detail the types of conflicts ethnolinguistic groups in North America can encounter in their attempts to adjust to the bicultural demands made on them. Through this exploration we hope to be able to discern which factors in the society lead to crises of allegiances and which provide opportunities for a comfortable bicultural identity. To this end, we will start with the case of French Canadians and their continuing struggle to survive as an ethnic group. Perhaps through a brief survey of Canadian research we can get perspective on the general problems faced by ethnic minorities.

A series of investigations was started in 1958 with French Canadian (FC) and English Canadian (EC) residents of Montreal, a setting with a long history of interethnic group tensions. The research technique employed in these studies, referred to as the "matched-guise" procedure, has groups of subjects drawn from various age and social class levels of the EC and FC communities give their impressions or evaluations of the personality characteristics of speakers who represent their own and the other ethnic group. Thus, groups of EC and FC subjects are asked to estimate or judge the probable personality traits of a number of speakers, say 12, presented to them on tape. Half of the speakers use French and half use English while reading a standard translation-equivalent passage. Listeners are kept in the dark about the fact that each speaker they hear is a balanced French–English bilingual; the reactions elicited by each speaker's two linguistic guises are later matched up and compared statistically (see Lambert 1967, Giles 1971a). The procedure has proved instructive and useful as a means of investigating social tensions in bicultural or multiethnic settings such as Quebec (see Lambert 1970), Israel (Lambert, Anisfeld and Yeni-Komshian 1965), and Great Britain (Giles 1971b).

The early research showed that EC college students evaluate the personality of speakers more favorably when the speakers use their EC rather than their FC linguistic guise. Furthermore, and somewhat surprising, FC students showed the same tendency, in a more exaggerated form; that is, they too rated the EC guises of speakers much more favorably than the FC guises (Lambert 1967). Apparently, then, both ECs and FCs attribute different status and different degrees of respect to those who represent the EC and FC communities in French Canada.

But there are in Quebec various forms of French currently in use, and each of these is also given its own position in the status hierarchy. For example, Chiasson-Lavoie and Laberge (1971) recently found evidence of a linguistic insecurity among working class FCs in Montreal. D'Anglejan and Tucker (1973) also report on a similar type of language sensitivity, which shows itself in an overattention to correctness of speech among working-class FCs and a marked preference for European-style French by FCs of various regional and occupational backgrounds. Thus, FCs tend to react, as minority groups often do, by downgrading their own characteristic modes of behavior, including speech.

These sociolinguistic phenomena also affect the fate and durability of social contact between members of various ethnic and linguistic groups. For instance, the status relations and role expectations of the two or more people involved in social interaction are likely to be colored by the inferences each actor makes of the others, inferences that are based to an important extent on speech styles (Giles 1971c, 1972).

The dilemmas are not merely those of college-age people in the FC community, for youngsters also get involved, and in this case too there are no signs of amelioration when 1960 and 1970 research is compared. In 1962 Elizabeth Anisfeld and I (Anisfeld and Lambert 1964) examined the reactions of ten-year-old FC children to the matched guises of bilingual youngsters of their own age reading French and English versions of a standard passage and found that the FC guises of the speakers were rated more favorably than the EC guises on a whole series of traits.

Currently, Sylvie Lambert (1973) has taken a further and more extensive look at the ten-year-old FCs' self-views. Her results, collected in 1972, suggest that FC ten-year-olds downgrade representatives of their own ethnolinguistic group to a marked degree in comparison with representatives of the European French (EF) community, and on a selection of traits related to social attractiveness (e.g., interestingness, amusingness, sureness of self), they evaluate their own group less favorably than ECs. What is particularly instructive about this study is that it included the views of FC schoolteachers, and it was found that FC elementary schoolteachers have essentially the same profiles of stereotypes as the ten year olds. The social implications of these trends and the changes noted over a ten-year period are enormous.

All told, these research findings indicate that little has been done in North America to help ethnolinguistic minority groups maintain respect in their linguistic and cultural heritage so that they can become full-fledged bicultural members of their national society. There are, however, several recent developments in American society that hold out a new and exciting type of hope. These developments, in fact, constitute another instance where the United States has an opportunity to set an outstanding example of what can be done for ethnic minority groups. The first development is a new perspective, generated it seems by the critical self-analysis of collegiate activists in the 60s, on what it means to be American. It was American collegiates who demanded national respect for minority groups of every variety, including black Americans and American Indians. As a nation, these young people argued, we have no right to wash out distinctive traditions of any minority group since their ways of life, relative to the so-called American way of life, are in many respects admirable.

The second development, which may have stemmed from the first, takes the form of a national willingness to help minority groups. One way this willingness to help manifests itself is in new educational laws that provide extensive schooling in Spanish for Spanish Americans in America's large urban centers, in the passage of the Bilingual Education Act, and in new laws passed in states such as Massachusetts that provide schooling in any number of home languages whenever a group of parents request it.

The third development is a new direction in psycholinguistic research which, although only now getting underway, indicates that the minority-class American can perhaps most easily become fully and comfortably American if his Spanish, Polish, Navajo, or French roots are given unlimited opportunity to flourish. For example, the research of Padilla and Long (1969; see also Long and Padilla 1970) indicates that Spanish American children and adolescents can learn English better and adjust more comfortably to the United States if their linguistic and cultural ties with the Spanish-speaking world are kept alive and active from infancy on. Peal and Lambert (1962) came to a similar conclusion when they found that FC young people who are given opportunities to become bilingual are more likely than monolinguals to be advanced in their schooling in French schools, to develop a diversified and flexible intelligence, and to develop attitudes that are as charitable toward the other major Canadian cultural group as their own. A similar conclusion is drawn from the recent work of Lambert and Tucker (1972) where EC youngsters are given most of their elementary training via French. These children too seem to be advanced, relatively, in their cognitive development, their appreciation for French people and French ways of life, and their own sense of breadth and depth as Canadians.

In view of these sympathetic and supportive new developments, is it now possible to assist the minority-class American to become fully and comfortably bilingual and bicultural? Is it now possible to counteract and change the reactions of ethnically different children in the United States so that they will no longer feel different, peculiar, and inferior whenever they take on their Spanish, Portuguese, Polish, Navajo, or French styles of life as a temporary replacement for the American style?

Asking ourselves these questions prompted us to start a community-based study in northern Maine (Lambert, Giles and Picard 1973). The setting for the investigations was Maine's St. John Valley area, an American peninsula that protrudes into the Quebec and New Brunswick provinces. The closest "Anglo" community is nearly 50 miles to the south of Madawaska, center of the St. John Valley. The ties are much closer on a personal, social, and cultural level with French New Brunswick and Quebec than with the rest of the state of Maine. The total Valley region is made up of approximately 70 to 75 percent French Canadian descendants with the local language still a strong part of the way of life.

The research questions that shaped the investigation took the following form:

1. How do America's ethnolinguistic groups adjust to the bi-cultural demands made on them? Is it typical for French Americans in New England, for example, to reject their ethnolinguistic affiliations and identify more closely with the majority English-speaking culture? What is the developmental nature of changes that take place in their ethnic identity? In psycholinguistic terms, would the typical French American evaluate speakers of English more favorably than speakers of one of the various forms of French?

2. Does participation in a bilingual education program influence children's attitudes toward the various forms of French, and if so, in what direction?

To provide at least partial answers to these questions, different subgroups of people living in Maine, some from the Valley region and some from outside, some French American and others not, were asked to listen and give their subjective reactions to a variety of speech styles as presented by adult native speakers of one or another of the styles. The speech styles decided on were: European French (EF); middle class French Canadian (mcFC); lower class French Canadian (lcFC); middle class Madawaskan French (mcMF); lower class Madawaskan French (lcMF); middle class Madawaskan English (mcME); and middle class nonregional English (nrE).

Three groups of listeners were decided on so that we could examine age changes in the reactions of native French Americans. In the first study, attention was directed to the evaluative reactions of two groups of college students, one French American and the other comprising non-French Americans who live outside the St. John Valley. In the second study, our focus was on French American high school students from the Valley region, and in the third study, on French American ten-year-olds, some of them with training in French (i.e, via French) for four years under the Title VII Bilingual Program, and others without such a program of training in French.

The listeners in the three studies were required to evaluate each speaker separately by rating him or her on bipolar adjectival trait scales (e.g., good–bad, wise–foolish, and so on). The traits finally used were selected after preliminary testing in the Valley schools and colleges that permitted us to identify those personality qualities seen as valuable and worthwhile by each age group. The details of these investigations are available elsewhere (Lambert, Giles and Picard 1973) but the general outcomes are particularly pertinent.

1. *Do French American young people typically reject their French affiliation and identify more closely with the majority English-speaking culture?*

Considering the findings of all three studies, this matter can be examined developmentally. There is substantial evidence to suggest that at the age of ten, the typical French American youngster from Maine's St. John Valley region who follows a conventional all-English curriculum in public school rejects his

French ethnicity and orients himself to the English-speaking American as a model. The ethnic allegiances that he does have are apparently limited to his own ethnolinguistic group, the lower class, local French community, but even in this instance his affiliations are ambivalent and potentially self-effacing. The influence of European French as a model appears to be minimal at this age, and the English Canadian speakers are perceived more favorably than are French Canadians.

By adolescence, however, a different ethnic orientation seems to develop. Thirteen- to seventeen-year-old French Americans from the Valley also appear to orient themselves toward the English-speaking American model, but other factors come into play which tend to reduce this model's impact. For instance, European French people are seen to be as competent (e.g., intelligent, determined, and confident, etc.) and as attractive socially as Americans, judging from the reception given to nrE and mcME speakers. Also in the eyes of the adolescent, the middle class version of the local French dialect (mcMF) has assumed an advantage over the working-class counterpart (lcMF) in the sense that it is judged as favorably as the English models or the EF in terms of social attractiveness.

College students in the Valley region appear to have equally sympathetic attitudes toward European and local forms of French as toward English. That is, English no longer has a pre-eminent position in the hierarchy. This finding is of special interest because it could mean that the French American elite who go on to college have developed an understanding and appreciation for both aspects of their biculturality. This possibility will be checked out carefully with follow-up research, as it has both theoretical and social importance (see Gardner and Lambert 1972). At any rate, we find that college students judge speakers of the mcMF and EF styles to be as competent as speakers of the various English styles. Stated otherwise, European French and educated local French are considered by the French American college students to be as appropriate and respected media of social interaction as English.

These results contradict the commonly held belief that with time members of America's ethnic minority groups become assimilated, which often is taken to mean forgetting about the old country and old country ways (including language) and becoming "American." In this community we have evidence for an increase through the age levels in appreciation for old country ways in the sense that European and local versions of French are given the same degree of respect as English by college students. It could be that for these young people being "American" implies being French or being ethnic, no matter what variety.[1]

2. *How do non-French Americans from northern Maine react to the various styles of French, particularly the local variety?*

Unfortunately, we have only the reactions of the college sample from the first study discussed above to draw on for an answer. Limited as this base is, the results show clearly that college students living in northern Maine who are not part of the French American community also indicate that the mcMF and EF speech styles of French are as acceptable and valuable in their eyes as are the nrE or mcME of English. This subgroup of informants was sensitive to social class differences and showed this by downgrading the lower class variety of local French. The fact that members of the larger American culture share the evaluative norms of the French American population of northern Maine must be seen as a most favorable and optimistic sign, one that makes it all the more necessary that this finding be verified through replications of the same type of study with other than college students and in various regions of New England.

3. *Does experience in a bilingual education program influence French American children's attitudes toward the French and English languages?*

The findings from our third study certainly suggest that substantial changes are made by French instruction in the children's attitudes toward their two languages. It was found that the No Program children were strongly Anglo-oriented in their evaluative reactions whereas the children with experience in the bilingual education program were, in contrast, much more favorably disposed toward French. Indeed, the Program children's outlook toward French was much more like the older age groups studied, except that they did not rate mcMF as favorably as the high school and college age students did and they had a more favorable orientation toward Canadian-style French than did the older age groups. Judging from the attitudes of the older subjects, one might anticipate that in time the mcMF style would naturally attain more prestige for these children. Of course, the natural development of favorable attitudes toward the local version of French could be jeopardized if the bilingual program in any way belittled the local variety in comparison with the two imported styles—the European and the Canadian. The point is that the planners of bilingual programs should keep prevailing adult preferences in mind, and our evidence is that this community favors European and the educated form of local French.

The results of our third study also suggest that the Program children may have been made overenthusiastic and slightly biased toward French, which is in contrast to the more balanced bicultural outlook of the college group investigated. But we have to keep in mind that there is a major difference in the educational experiences of the two groups. The ten year olds in the bilingual program are being schooled in part through French, and the value of being French is unmistakably introduced to the children via the program. The older students have never had such an experience; they followed a conventional all-English program of schooling designed for American students, and it is much less likely that they would be literate in French. We can, then, easily understand the enthusiasm of the Program children.

Nevertheless, those responsible for such programs must keep overall goals clearly in mind and aid the children in ultimately making a two-language and two-culture adjustment. My own bias is that a bilingual education program, to be helpful and constructive, should attempt to develop the full potential of ethnolinguistic minority groups so that members can become fully American at the same time as they remain fully French, Polish, or whatever. There is an accumulation of evidence that children can very easily become comfortably bicultural and bilingual, and that from this base they can enhance their sense of personal well-being, their sense of social justice, and their tolerance and appreciation of human diversity (see Gardner and Lambert 1972, Lambert and Tucker 1972).

The results of these pilot studies should, then, be heartening to all those involved in the local bilingual education program, since it seems clear that such programs can have a powerful influence on the fate of the cultural and linguistic identities of young members of ethnolinguistic minority groups. Equally satisfying is the realization that the St. John Valley community as a whole, even those who are not members of the minority group, react favorably to the educated version of local French as they do to the European version, making both forms of French as respectable media of communication as English.

Encouraging as these studies are, they are only a start, and we are currently redoing this type of research in other New England communities. But in my mind there are grounds enough here to answer Question 3 in the following way: North American ethnolinguistic groups should be encouraged from as many sources as possible to maintain their dual heritage. Not only are they America's richest human resource, but we are beginning to see where conflicts of allegiances are likely to arise and how these groups can be helped to attain a comfortable bilingual and bicultural way of life by being themselves, making their potential value to the nation all the greater. In my mind, there is no other way for them to be comfortable, for to substract one of their heritages would be to spoil their chances of adjustment. In other words, I don't think they will be able to be fully American unless they are given every possibility of being fully French, Portuguese, Spanish, or whatever as well. And to the extent that this can be done, the United States will be a greater nation and a more interesting one.

This ends up being a long paper and I apologize. But I needed all these words to present my personal view of how culture and language affect the learning and education process. I had first to redirect the reader's thinking from what he or she might have expected by the title and to present my reasons for skepticism about the conventional treatment of cultural and linguistic influences on thinking and learning. I don't believe culture and language per se actually affect the form or structure of thought. But most people believe that they do have this effect, and it was to these types of beliefs, held by national groups as well as ethnolinguistic minority groups, that attention was directed. First I tried to demonstrate how influential these beliefs about ethnicity are in the learning process, especially the learning of an ethnic group's language, and in the case of ethnic group members, the maintenance of one's own language. Then I examined persistent and nasty beliefs about the disturbances and confusions attendant on bilingualism and biculturalism and found these beliefs, to my way of thinking, to be false. And because they appear false to me I wanted to re-examine the plight of America's ethnolinguistic minorities with a view of changing people's beliefs about the worthwhileness of giving America's minority groups a real chance to survive and flourish.

NOTE

1. We are aware, of course, that in these studies we have not systematically controlled for the social class and educational potential of the three age groups brought into comparison (the ten year olds, the adolescents, and the college students). Replications of these studies should therefore include young adults in the community who have not had the opportunity of college training to determine if this favorable outlook toward French is general. It would also be valuable to compare the St. John Valley region with other French American communities to determine if these outlooks are shared by French Americans.

REFERENCES

Aellen, C. and W. E. Lambert (1969) "Ethnic identification and personality adjustment of Canadian adolescents of mixed English-French parentage." *Canadian Journal of Behavioral Science* 1:69–86.

d'Anglejan, A. and G. R. Tucker (1973) "Sociolinguistic correlates of speech styles in Quebec," in R. Shuy (Ed.), *Social and ethnic diversity.* Washington, D.C.: Georgetown Unversity Press.

Anisfeld, E. (1964) A comparison of the cognitive functioning of monolinguals and bilinguals. Unpublished Ph.D. dissertation, McGill University.

——— and W. E. Lambert (1964) "Evaluational reaction of bilingual and monolingual children to spoken language," *Journal of Abnormal and Social Psychology* 69:89–97.

Balkan, L. (1970) *Les effets du bilinguisme français-anglais sur les aptitudes intellectuelles.* Bruxelles: Aimav.

Ben-Zeev, S. (1972) The influence of bilingualism on cognitive development and cognitive strategy. Unpublished Ph.D. dissertation, University of Chicago.

Carroll, J. B. and J. B. Casagrande (1958) "The function of language classifications in behavior," in E. Maccoby, T. Newcomb and E. Hartley (eds.), *Readings in Social Psychology.* New York: Holt, Rinehart and Winston.

Chiasson-Lavoie, M. and S. Laberge (1971) "Attitudes face au français parle à Montréal et degrès de conscience de variables linguistiques," in R. Darnell (ed.), *Language Diversity in Canada.* Edmonton, Alberta: Linguistics Research, Inc.

Child, I. L. (1943) *Italian or American? The Second Generation in Conflict.* New Haven: Yale University Press.

Cole, M. and J. S. Bruner (1971) "Cultural differences and inferences about psychological processes," *American Psychologist* 26:867-876.

———— J. Gay, J. A. Glick and D. W. Sharp (1971) *The Cultural Context of Learning and Thinking.* New York: Basic Books.

Cummins, J. and M. Gulutsan (1973) Some effects of bilingualism on cognitive functioning. University of Alberta, Edmonton. Mimeographed.

Gardner, R. C. (1960) Motivational variables in second-language acquisition. Unpublished Ph.D. dissertation, McGill University.

———— and W. E. Lambert (1972) *Attitudes and Motivation in Second-Language Learning.* Rowley, Mass.: Newbury House Publishers.

Getzels, J. W. and P. W. Jackson (1962) *Creativity and Intelligence.* New York: Wiley.

Giles, H. (1971a) "Our reactions to accents," *New Society* (October 14):713-715.

———— (1971b) "Patterns of evaluation to RP, South Welsh and Somerset accented speech," *British Journal of Social and Clinical Psychology* 10:280-281.

———— (1971c) A study of speech patterns in social interaction: Accent evaluation and accent change. Unpublished Ph.D. dissertation, University of Bristol.

———— (1972) Communicative effectiveness as a function of accented speech. Unpublished research report, University College, Cardiff.

Gordon, A. I. (1966) *Intermarriage.* Boston: Beacon Press.

Guilford, J. P. (1950) "Creativity," *American Psychologist* 5:444-454.

———— (1956) "The structure of intellect," *Psychological Bulletin* 53: 267-293.

Hoggart, R. (1973) *On Culture and Communication.* Don Mills, Ontario: Oxford University Press.

Ianco-Worrall, A. D. (1973) "Bilingualism and cognitive development," *Child Development* 43:1390-1400.

Kroeber, A. L. (1948) *Anthropology.* New York: Harcourt Brace Jovanovich.

Lambert, S. (1973) The role of speech in forming evaluations: A study of children and teachers. Unpublished master's thesis, Tufts University.

Lambert, W. E. (1967) "A social psychology of bilingualism," *Journal of Social Issues* 23:91-109.

_____ (1970) "What are they like, these Canadians? A social-psychological analysis," *The Canadian Psychologist* 11:303-333.

_____ and E. Anisfeld (1969) "A note on the relationship of bilingualism and intelligence," *Canadian Journal of Behavioral Science* 1:123-128.

_____, M. Anisfeld and G. Yeni-Komshian (1965) "Evaluational reactions of Jewish and Arab adolescents to dialect and language variations," *Journal of Personality and Social Psychology* 2:84-90.

_____, H. Giles and O. Picard (1973) Language attitudes in a French-American community. *International Journal of the Sociology of Language*, No. 4, 1975.

_____ and O. Klineberg (1967) *Children's Views of Foreign People: A Cross-National Study*. New York: Appleton-Century-Crofts.

_____ and G. R. Tucker (1972) *Bilingual Education of Children: The St. Lambert Experiment*. Rowley, Mass.: Newbury House Publishers.

_____, A. Yackley and R. N. Hein (1971) "Child training values of English Canadian and French Canadian parents," *Canadian Journal of Behavioral Science* 3:217-236.

Leopold, W. F. (1939-49) *Speech Development of a Bilingual Child*, 4 vols. Evanston, Ill.: Northwestern University Press.

Levy-Bruhl, C. (1966) *How Natives Think*. New York: Washington Square Press; originally published, 1910.

Long, K. K. and A. M. Padilla (1970) Evidence for bilingual antecedents of academic success in a group of Spanish-American college students. Unpublished research report, Western Washington State College.

Minturn, L. and S. Lambert (1964) *Mothers of Six Cultures*. New York: John Wiley.

Padilla, A. M. and K. K. Long (1969) An assessment of successful Spanish-American students at the University of New Mexico. Paper presented to the annual meeting of the AAAS, Rocky Mountain Division, Colorado Springs.

Park, R. E. (1964) "Personality and cultural conflict," in R. E. Park, *Race and Culture*. Glencoe, Ill.: The Free Press; originally published in *Publication of the American Sociological Society* 25 (1931):95-110.

Peal, E. and W. E. Lambert (1962) "The relation of bilingualism to intelligence," *Psychological Monographs* 76:1-23.

Sapir, E. (1921) *Language*. New York: Harcourt Brace Jovanovich.

Saucier, J. F. (1965) *Psychiatric Aspects of Interethnic Marriages*. McGill University. Mimeographed.

Scott, S. (1973) The relation of divergent thinking to bilingualism: Cause or effect. Unpublished research report, McGill University.

Torrance, E. P., J. C. Gowan, J. M. Wu and N. C. Aliotti (1970) "Creative functioning of monolingual and bilingual children in Singapore," *Journal of Educational Psychology* 61:72-75.

Vygotsky, L. S. (1962) *Thought and Language*. Cambridge, Mass.: The M.I.T. Press.

Whorf, B. L. (1941) "The relation of habitual thought to behavior and to language," in L. Spier, A. I. Hallowell, and S. S. Newman (eds.), *Language, Culture and Personality*. Menasha, Wis.: Banta.

3

The acquisition of relative clauses in French and English: Implications for language-learning universals

Amy Sheldon
University of Minnesota

The goal of research in child language acquisition is to create a general theory of language acquisition. To accomplish this, child language research must compare acquisition across languages in order to discover which principles and strategies of language learning are universal and which are developed to process the particular language that is being learned. While it has often been claimed that there are behavioral universals in learning

This research was funded by a grant from the *Conseil des Arts du Canada* and was assisted by a McMillan travel award from the University of Minnesota. Grateful acknowledgment is made for the assistance provided by Guy Simard at the *Université du Québec à Rimouski* in facilitating this research. A special word of thanks is owed to the following people for their cooperation: The Commissioner of the School Board of Rimouski, the teachers and principal at the St. Agnès school, the sisters at *La Jardin de la Nature,* the chairperson of the Nursing Department of the *CEGEP de Rimouski,* and the children and nursing students who participated in the experiments. Research assistance was provided by Jacinthe Boudreau, Suzanne Chenard, Diane Garneau, Danielle Godbout, and Danielle Stanek. Statistical assistance was given by Paul Desjardins and Steven Froman. I would like to thank Catherine Ringen and Gerald Sanders for their comments and suggestions on this paper.

language (Bever 1970; Chomsky 1965; McNeil 1970; Slobin 1971), we know very little about what these are. Because we know little about what governs language acquisition, we can make few reliable predictions about the order and pattern of acquisition.

Our knowledge of universal and language-specific principles of language learning should be of particular value in understanding the course of learning a second language. Many of the errors that second-language learners make are predictable. The question is: why are they made? To what extent are they due to interference from the native language, and to what extent are they due to language-independent factors? Clearly we cannot claim that the source of the learner's difficulty is due to interference unless we have ruled out the possibility that it is a function of language-independent factors.

If we find evidence for universal principles in language learning, then we would expect that in those situations where these principles are relevant, the order of acquisition and the kinds of errors that are made in learning any language will be the same whether the language is learned as a first or second language. Thus, we would expect that certain difficulties that second-language learners have will be the same as those that they faced in learning their native language. For this reason, investigating the principles that children use in learning their native language can contribute to our understanding of the role of universal and language-specific factors in second-language learning.

The results of cross-language research into what language learners find difficult, and why, should be of interest to teachers in a bilingual setting. The results can shape realistic expectations in teachers. They can create a positive and informed attitude toward learner errors, and they can be of use in developing appropriate reading and teaching materials.

This paper discusses language acquistion in English and French. It reports on the outcome of a study of the acquisition of subject and object relative clauses by monolingual French-speaking children between the ages of 4 and 10 years in Rimouski, Québec. Their language behavior is compared with the behavior of monolingual English-speaking children between 4 and 8 years who had been tested previously in the United States

(Sheldon 1974; Legum 1975). The results of both these studies are discussed within the framework of principles and strategies that have been proposed to account for language learning in English. I intend to show how these principles and strategies are also relevant to the explanation of language learning in French. I will claim that certain of these strategies are in fact universal and that their use is not a function of the fact that these children are learning English, or French, or any SVO language, for that matter. Note that we cannot falsify the claim that the acquisition of relative sentences is governed by universal principles and that there will be a common order of development across languages unless we test acquisition in more than one language. The French study brings evidence to bear on this claim.

This study investigated a universal principle that Slobin (1971:352) proposed to account for language learning, which can be formulated as an empirical claim in the following way:

> A sentence with an interruption or rearrangement of linguistic units will be more difficult to process than a sentence that does not contain an interruption or rearrangement.

Sheldon (1974) investigated the evidence for this claim in a study in which four- and five-year-old English-speaking children were tested on their ability to comprehend sentences with relative clauses. They were given four types of relative sentences, which are shown in Table 1 (sentences 1, 2, 4, 5). Slobin's universal can be interpreted in the form of two hypotheses that make predictions about the acquisition of relative clauses. The first is the Interruption Hypothesis, which claims that nested clauses (i.e., sentence-internal clauses) are more difficult to process than non-nested clauses (i.e., sentence-final clauses). Thus, in English and French, sentences with relative clauses that modify subject NPs (sentences 1 and 2: SS, SO) should be harder to comprehend and process than sentences that have relative clauses that modify object NPs (sentences 4 and 5: OS, OO) because the subject relative in the former is nested inside of the main clause and interrupts it. The second hypothesis is the Word Order Hypothesis, which claims that a surface sequence in which the underlying word order has been preserved is easier to

TABLE 1. Types of relative sentences that were tested
in French and English

Subject relatives

(1) Subject NP relativized (SS):

Le lion qui pousse le cheval fait tomber la vache.
The lion that pushes the horse knocks down the cow.

(2) Object NP relativized (SO):

Le lion que le cheval pousse fait tomber la vache.
The lion that the horse pushes knocks down the cow.

(3) Object NP relativized, relative clause subject postposed (SO'):

Le lion que pousse le cheval fait tomber la vache.
The lion that the horse pushes knocks down the cow.

Object relatives

(4) Subject NP relativized (OS):

Le lion fait tomber la vache qui pousse le cheval.
The lion knocks down the cow that pushes the horse.

(5) Object NP relativized (OO):

Le lion fait tomber la vache que le cheval pousse.
The lion knocks down the cow that the horse pushes.

(6) Object NP relativized, relative clause subject postposed (OO'):

Le lion fait tomber la vache que pousse le cheval.
The lion knocks down the cow that the horse pushes.

---

process than one in which the underlying word order has not
been preserved. According to this hypothesis, sentences in which
the object NP is relativized (sentences 2 and 5: SO, OO) will be
harder than sentences in which the subject NP has been relativized (sentences 1 and 4: SS, OS).[1]

Slobin (1971:354) cites evidence that appears to support
these hypotheses from studies that investigated the use of
relative clauses by English-speaking children between the ages of
two and five years. In these studies sentences with object
relatives (i.e., sentence-final) were produced earlier than sentences with subject relatives (i.e., sentence-internal). In addition,
sentences with subject relatives were more difficult to imitate
than sentences with object relatives. However, the positive data
that he presents for this universal in regard to relative clauses

consists solely of elicited or spontaneous production data. It is well known that correct imitation is not a reliable indication of how a sentence is understood or if it is understood at all. Spontaneous production data is also of limited use, at best, in providing insight into the speaker's linguistic competence or comprehension ability. It could be a function of the sample size, and sometimes reflects nothing more than pragmatic factors involved in communication. For example, Limber has shown this very nicely. He made recordings of spontaneous speech from children between the ages of two and four years and from adults in a variety of activities. He found that for *both* children and adults the majority of subject NPs were personal pronouns, demonstrative pronouns, and names. The fact that it is not possible to have restrictive relative clauses modifying such NPs explains why we don't find them in spontaneous speech. Pronouns and names appeared much less frequently in object position and this correlated with the higher proportion of object NP modification. Clearly, one cannot make reliable inferences about the speaker's linguistic or receptive competence on the basis of production data alone. For this reason, the English and French studies are an investigation of how children understand relative sentences. To test comprehension they were required to act out the relative sentence with toy animals.

The results of Sheldon (1974) did not confirm Slobin's predictions about the difficulty of interruption or the difficulty of word-order rearrangement for the language processor. That is, children's performance on sentences with internal relative clauses did not differ from their performance on sentences with final relative clauses. And they did not make more errors on sentences which had the object NP relativized than they made on sentences which had the subject NP relativized. Instead, it was found that sentences in which the identical NPs have the same grammatical function in their respective clauses (SS and OO) were significantly easier to understand than sentences in which the identical NPs have different functions (SO and OS). The results of this study are shown in Table 2 part A. These results were replicated with a group of 10 subjects whose mean age was 4.6 (Sheldon 1974).

The Parallel-Function Hypothesis was proposed to account for these facts. This hypothesis claims that in a complex sentence, if

TABLE 2. Percentage of correct answers by age group

	Sentence type					
Age group	SS	SO	OS	OO	SO$'$	OO$'$
A. English relative sentences—3.0 possible						
4.0 $(N = 11)$	33.0%	6.0%	18.0%	45.3%		
4.9 $(N = 11)$	48.3	24.3	30.3	54.6		
5.2 $(N = 11)$	75.6	21.3	39.0	51.6		
Average percent correct $(N = 33)$	52.3%	17.1%	29.1%	50.5%		
B. English relative sentences—5.0 possible						
6.1 $(N = 15)$	68%	18.6%	17.2%	48.0%		
7.0 $(N = 18)$	72	23.2	41.0	67.6		
8.1 $(N = 14)$	80	31.4	47.0	57.0		
Average percent correct $(N = 47)$	73.3%	24.4%	35.0%	57.5%		
C. French relatives—4.0 possible						
4.2 $(N = 16)$	73.50%	9.00%	15.75%	32.75%	3.25%	6.25%
5.2 $(N = 16)$	81.25	12.50	15.75	36.00	0	6.25
6.2 $(N = 16)$	93.75	12.50	11.00	31.25	1.75	0
7.6 $(N = 16)$	81.25	7.75	31.25	29.75	0	3.00
8.6 $(N = 16)$	72.00	7.75	36.00	70.25	0	3.00
9.9 $(N = 16)$	78.25	54.00	67.25	61.00	9.50	20.25
Average percent correct $(N = 96)$	80.00%	17.25%	29.50%	43.50%	2.41%	6.54%

Sources: Part A, Sheldon 1974. Part B, Legum 1975.

coreferential NPs have the same grammatical function in their respective clauses, then that sentence will be easier to process than one in which the coreferential NPs have different grammatical functions. The grammatical function of the relativized NP will be interpreted to be the same as its antecedent. Independent support for a parallel-function constraint can be found in

English studies of pronominal coreference (Maratsos 1973), in relative clause comprehension using a picture identification task and different types of relative sentences (Brown 1971), and in a study of the development of relativization (Ferreiro et al. 1976).

In addition, Legum (1975) conducted a study of the comprehension of relative sentences using the same toy-moving task with monolingual English-speaking children between the ages of six and eight years, in an attempt to replicate the results of Sheldon (1974). The results of his study are shown in Table 2, part B. Legum found that there was no reliable effect of age; that is, the performance of children in the six-year-old group did not differ significantly from that of children in the seven- and eight-year-old group, F (2, 41) = 3.12, $p > .05$. There was no significant main effect for embedding, $F < 1$; that is, performance on sentences with nested relative clauses (SS and SO) was not significantly different from performance on sentences with final relative clauses (OS and OO). Performance on parallel-function relative sentences (SS and OO) was significantly better than performance on nonparallel-function sentences, again at greater than the .001 level of significance. These results replicate the finding of Sheldon with younger English-speaking children. They support the Parallel-Function Hypothesis, and they do not support the Interruption Hypothesis. They indicate that the parallel-function constraint operates in acquisition as late as eight years. The only difference between the younger group (Sheldon) and the older group (Legum) is in how their performance was affected as a function of which NP is relativized. Sentences with relativized subjects (SS and OS) were significantly easier than sentences with relativized objects (SO and OO), $p < .001$. The younger group showed no difference in performance on sentences in which the subject or object NP were relativized, although there was a trend in the five-year-old group in favor of sentences with relativized subjects. Thus, the variable or word order in the relative clause appears to be an age-related factor. It does not play a role in younger children's comprehension of English, but it is relevant to older children. Figure 1 is a graphic representation of the performance of the younger and older English groups.

These findings demonstrate that the Parallel-Function Hypothesis is crucial for the explanation of certain facts about the

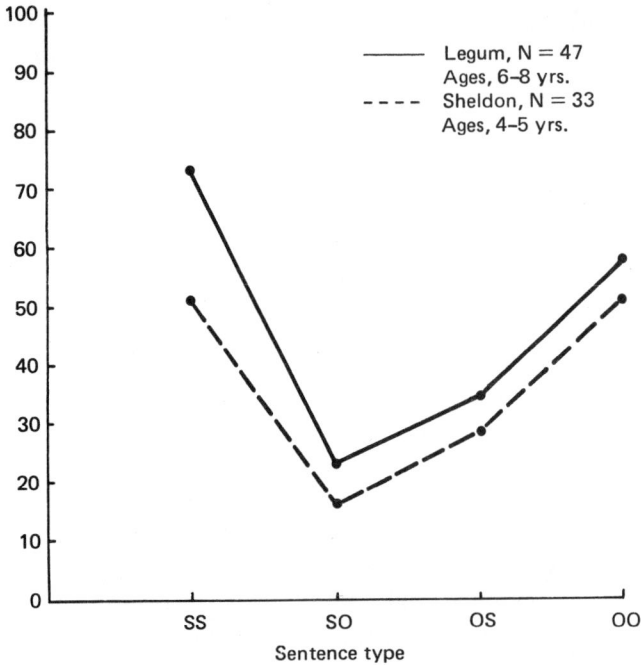

FIG. 1. Percentage of correct answers by age: English.

acquisition of relative clauses in English, and that this effect is independent of the age of the language learner. The question that arises is whether a parallelism constraint is language specific or whether it plays a role in the acquisition of other languages. An answer to this question was sought in a study of the acquisition of French. The participants in this study, monolingual speakers between the ages of four and ten, living in Rimouski, Québec, were tested by means of the same toy-moving procedure that was used in Sheldon (1974) and Legum (1975). Examples of the types of sentences that were used are in Table 1.

The French sentence types differ from the English in two respects. First, the French relative pronoun varies in its form according to the function of the NP that is relativized. The form for relativized subjects is *qui* and the form for relativized objects is *que*. Because the French relative pronoun contains the grammatical information that is necessary to correctly assign a function to the relativized NP, which the English relative marker *that* does not, it is possible that French children would learn these sentences faster or in a different order than children learning English. In fact, we would expect that they would not use a parallel-function heuristic for assigning NP function, since it isn't necessary.

Another difference between English and French is that French has an optional rule of subject postposition, which places the subject NP in a *que* relative clause behind the verb. Thus in Table 1, sentence types (2) and (3) are paraphrases and types (5) and (6) are paraphrases.

Slobin has proposed another developmental universal which is relevant to the acquisition of the French type of relative sentences (sentences (3) and (6), Table 1). He claims (1971:350) that

> Sentences deviating from standard word order will be interpreted at early stages of development as if they were examples of standard word order.

I will label this claim the Preferred Word-Order Hypothesis.[2] Since the standard word order in French is SVO, this principle predicts that in French-type relatives—sentences (3) and (6)—the NP that follows the verb will be understood as the receiver of the action and not the agent. Thus, sentence types (3) and (6) should be acquired late according to this principle because word order in the relative clause is *que V S*. On the other hand, because the French relative sentences have a morphological indication of which NP is relativized, it is possible to interpret the correct function of the postverbal NP. If attention to morphological cues takes precedence over the Preferred Word-Order principle, the French learners would have no difficulty with sentence types (3) and (6).

The results of the French study are shown in Table 2, part C. What we find is that French children are ignoring the morphological cues and instead are assigning functional relationships by means of other heuristics, which are also being used by children learning English.

Considering sentence types (1), (2), (4) and (5), which correspond to the English types, an analysis of variance indicated that performance on the parallel-function relatives (SS and

OO) was significantly better than performance on the non-parallel-function relative sentences (SO and OS), F (5, 90) = 2.86, p < .05. A post hoc analysis of variance indicated that performance on the parallel-function object relative sentence type (OO) is significantly better than performance on the nonparallel-function object relative sentence type (OS), F (5, 90) = 9.73, p < .01. There was a significant interaction between the ease of parallel-function object relatives and age, however. A Tukey standardized range test was performed on the consecutive means of the parallel-function object relative (OO). It indicated that the level of performance of the eight-year-olds was significantly better than the performance of the seven-year-olds. A Tukey test was also performed on the consecutive means of the nonparallel-function object relative (OS). It indicated that performance on this sentence type does not increase significantly until one year later, in the ninth year. At this time performance on the nonparallel-function subject relative (SO) also improves dramatically. Performance across these four sentence types—SS, SO, OS, OO—begins to level out in the ninth year, showing a general mastery of these kinds of sentences at that time.

As in Sheldon (1974), a control test was administered after the relative sentence test. The purpose of this test was to determine the extent to which performance on the relative-sentence task was due to the meaning of the sentence, the procedure of acting out two propositions, the length of the sentence, or preferred toy-moving strategies, such as using the first toy that is picked up to perform both actions in the sentence. This test consisted of the coordinate structure counterparts to the relative sentences. The children had to act them out in the same fashion as the relative sentences. Examples of these sentences are in Table 3.

Only the youngest group of subjects were tested on this task. Their performance is shown in Table 4. The results are essentially the same as those for the English subjects in Sheldon (1974). There is no difference in performance across the four types of coordinate sentences, but there is a difference in performance across the different types of relative sentences. Not only is there no difference in the order of difficulty among the coordinate sentences, but they are much easier than the relative

TABLE 3. Control test: Coordinate structure counterparts
to the relative sentences

---

(1) Identical subjects (SS)—Parallel function:

Le lion pousse le cheval et *le lion* fait tomber la vache.
The lion pushes the horse and *the lion* knocks down the cow.

(2) Subject of first clause identical to object of second clause (SO):

Le lion pousse le cheval et la vache fait tomber *le lion.*
The lion pushes the horse and the cow knocks down *the lion.*

(3) Object of first clause identical to subject of second clause (OS):

Le lion pousse *le cheval* et *le cheval* fait tomber la vache.
The lion pushes *the horse* and *the horse* knocks down the cow.

(4) Identical objects (OO)—Parallel function:

Le lion pousse *le cheval* et la vache fait tomber *le cheval.*
The lion pushes *the horse* and the cow knocks down *the horse.*

---

sentences. This is additional evidence that it is the structure of the relative sentences that is the source of difficulty.

We can conclude from the results of the relative-sentence test, therefore, that a parallel-function constraint is operating in the acquisition of French relative sentences. It is interesting to note

TABLE 4. Percentage of correct answers by age group

		Sentence type			
Age group	*N*	SS	SO	OS	OO
A. French coordinate sentences—4.0 possible					
4.2 (*N* = 15)		85%	88%	83%	83%
B. English coordinate sentences—3.0 possible					
4.0 (*N* = 8)	8	58.3%	58.3%	54.3%	71.0%
4.9 (*N* = 11)	11	60.6	66.6	60.6	66.6
5.2 (*N* = 11)	11	88.0	66.6	75.6	85.0
Average percent correct (*N* = 30)	30	70.0%	64.3%	64.3%	74.3%

Source: Part B, Sheldon, 1974.

that the factor of parallel-function plays a role in the adult French speaker's comprehension of the sentence types also. A control group of 16 monolingual French speakers, who were nursing students at the *Collège d'enseignement général et professionel de Rimouski,* was tested on the same sentences, using the same toy-moving task. To make the task more difficult they heard each sentence only once, whereas the children, on the other hand, had the sentence repeated as often as necessary. The mean age of the adult subjects was 19.6. The results of the experiment are shown in Table 5. An analysis of variance indicated that the adults performed significantly better on the parallel-function sentence types (SS and OO) than on the nonparallel-function types (SO and OS), $F (1, 62) = 9.00, p <$ .01. The importance of this finding is that it shows that adults also do not always pay attention to the morphology of *qui* and *que* but sometimes use a parallel-function heuristic instead. Apparently, the parallel-function heuristic is a childhood strategy that persists into adulthood, although it is used to a much lesser degree by adults than by children.[3]

While the factor of parallel function plays a role in the acquisition and use of French relative sentences, it clearly doesn't account for the whole story. There is additional evidence that French-speaking children are ignoring the morphology of the relative pronoun. This is shown by their performance on sentence types (3) (SO′) and (6) (OO′), which have postposed subject NPs in the relative clause. When we compare performance on sentence type (3) (SO′) to its counterpart type (2) (SO), and sentence type (6) (OO′) to its counterpart type (5) (OO), we see a big difference in the level of performance (see Table 2). An analysis of the errors indicates that sentence type (3), *le lion que pousse le cheval* . . . (SO′), was being interpreted as if it were an SS sentence type (1): *le lion qui pousse le*

TABLE 5. French adult performance: Percentage of correct answers

	Sentence type					
	SS	SO	OS	OO	SO′	OO′
$N = 16$	98.4%	89%	89%	98.4%	89%	82.8%

cheval. . . . In addition, the OO′ sentence type (6), . . . *la vache que pousse le cheval,* was interpreted as if it were an OS sentence type (4): . . . *la vache qui pousse le cheval.* This is evidence that children are not paying attention to morphology but are depending on standard word order to interpret a sentence. Sentence types (3) (SO′) and (6) (OO′) have postposed subject NPs in the relative clause. The missing NP in these sentences can be correctly reconstructed only if the listener pays attention to and correctly identifies the relative pronoun. Only 3 out of 96 children in this study were successful on these sentence types, and they were almost ten years old. In order to rule out the possibility that the children didn't use the morphological differences between *qui* and *que* because they couldn't hear them and therefore fell back on using a word-order heuristic, I tested the two youngest groups for their perception of a phonemic difference between *qui* and *que* in a minimal pair test. While 9 out of 15 children in the four-year-old group responded randomly, only 2 out of 15 in the five-year-old group responded randomly. On the basis of the five-year-olds' performance, we can assume that older children would have had no trouble on this task. We can conclude that even though most children in this study could hear a difference between *qui* and *que,* when presented as a minimal pair, they were either unable to identify the grammatical function of *qui* and *que* in the sentences, or they did not use that information when it was present in the sentences to process them. Instead, they used a heuristic of relying on the standard word order of French and invariantly interpreted the NP that followed the subordinate clause verb as if it were the underlying object. The evidence from French indicates that Slobin's Preferred Word-Order Hypothesis is a possible candidate for a language-learning universal.

The French-speaking child's preference for interpreting any NVN sequence as the standard French order of agent-action-object has been noted by Sinclair and Bronckart (1972). They presented children from three- to six-years-old with sequences of two nouns and a verb in all the possible orders of combination, for them to act out with dolls. As children got older they increasingly interpreted the first noun as the agent and the second noun as the object-acted-upon no matter where the verb occurred in the sequence. The tendency to interpret the first noun as the agent increased with age. In fact, more six-year-olds interpreted the sequence *boite–ouvrir–garçon* as 'the box opens the boy' than did younger children.

The reliance of children on word order rather than morphology has also been observed in other languages. Word order in Russian is more flexible than in English or French. Russian is also a more highly inflected language. Slobin (1966) reports that Russian children adopt a fixed order and learn morphological markers late. Roeper (1972) reports that German children prefer an ordering of indirect object before direct object. Sentences with the order of direct before indirect object were often understood as if the order was indirect before direct, even though the article in German is inflected for the grammatical function of the NP. When asked to imitate sentences with the NPs in the order of direct object before indirect object, children tended to switch the articles in their imitation, placing the article for the indirect object with the first NP and the article for the direct object with the second NP.

There is evidence for Slobin's generalization from English too. The preference that English-speaking children have for interpreting the first NP in a sentence as the logical subject has been noticed in studies of the passive in child language. Children have difficulty understanding full passive sentences because they interpret them as being active sentences. Thus, a sentence like *the girl is pushed by the boy* is understood as *the girl pushes the boy* (Bever 1970; Beilin and Spontak 1969; Fraser et al. 1963; Turner and Rommetveit 1967). The presence of passive markers in the sentence is ignored. It is not the case that children respond randomly, which one might expect if they were paying attention to the passive markers. Instead, they systematically prefer the active interpretation, despite the passive markers in the sentence.

Children will also interpret object cleft sentences such as *it's the lion that the giraffe kicks* to mean *the lion kicks the giraffe*. But they have no trouble understanding subject cleft sentences correctly, such as *it's the lion that kicks the giraffe* (Bever 1970, Sheldon 1972). Children will interpret object questions, in which the questioned object NP appears in surface subject position, such as *who did John see?* as meaning *who saw John?* But they will have no trouble with subject questions, such as *who saw John?* (Ervin-Tripp 1970).

In addition, children learn the *John is eager to please* type of complement construction earlier than the *John is easy to please* construction (Cromer 1970, Kessel 1970). In the example *John is easy to please,* though *John* is in the surface subject position, it is not the underlying subject of the sentence; rather, it is the underlying object.

In general then, linguistic constructions that constitute an exception to SVO word order in English are hard to learn because they are interpreted as examples of standard word order. What this suggests is that children will develop strategies that work for the general case before they develop strategies that work for the exceptions. Sentences that are exceptions to the general case are also exceptions to the strategies that they have developed for processing these general cases. Because children persist in using strategies for processing the predominant word order inappropriately on sentences that are exceptions to the predominant word order, they will have difficulty learning the exceptions. This difficulty that the French children have in decoding sentence types (3) and (6) (the *que* relatives with postposed subjects) indicates that rules that create surface structures that constitute linguistic exceptions, in this case the postposition of the underlying subject, are learned relatively late. Only after children can deal with *que* relatives that have the subject before the verb—sentence types (2) and (5)—can they handle the exception.

One might also expect that sentences that children learn late will also be harder for adults to process. While this expectation is borne out in the case of the nonparallel-function sentences (SO and OS), which were harder for both children and adults, it is not the case that French adults have more difficulty with the relative sentences that have postposed subjects (SO' and OO'). The results of their performance on this task shows no significant difference on sentence types (3) and (6) (SO' and OO' types with postposed subjects) as compared to types (2) and (5) (SO and OO types that do not have the subject inverted). We can account for the difference between the adults and children if we assume that the adults have the rule of subject postposing, and that they are effectively using the morphological cues present in these sentences to process the inversion. The children do not have the rule, and they are relying on word order to process these sentences. If the child doesn't have this rule, then sentences with the inversion are not part of their relative clause system. This would make their relative clause system more like that of the English child than the adult French speaker. This supports the hypothesis that at certain stages children's languages are more like each other than they are like the adult language they are learning.

There are other ways in which the behavior of the French- and English-speaking child are alike. One interesting outcome of the relative clause test in English with the four- and five-year-olds (Sheldon 1974) was that there was much less improvement on the object relatives than there was on the subject relatives. In the French study also, performance on the object relatives was not high. A tabulation of the errors that were made by each child indicated that they were responding to the object relatives in a consistent fashion. At each age level, the object relatives, which follow the main clause, were interpreted as modifying the main clause subject NP, rather than the main clause object NP. That is, given sentence (5), *the lion knocks down the cow that the horse pushes,* the children made the lion knock down the cow and the horse push the lion. This response was found in both French and English. We can explain it if we assume that the children have a rule of Extraposition from NP which moves an internal relative clause to the end of the main clause, and that they over-rely on this rule to interpret any relative clause at the end of the main clause as if it had been part of the subject in deep structure and was transported by the Extraposition rule to sentence-final position. The reason why their performance on object relatives is so low is because they are associating all relative clauses with the main clause subject NP. I have called this the Extraposition strategy (Sheldon 1974). It is being relied upon heavily by children as old as ten years. What is interesting about this finding for both English and French children is that it shows another way in which child languages are more like each other than they are like the adult language being learned. Both adult English and French speakers prefer to associate a relative clause with the adjacent NP whenever possible, even in cases where it can be associated with either NP, as in:

(1) A guy was dating my sister who lives in Montreal.
(2) Un garçon sort avec ma soeur qui vit à Montréal.

Because most adults do not interpret object relative clauses as being extraposed, they do not find this sentence ambiguous, in English or in French.

Since the use of the Extraposition strategy by both English and French children indicates the systematic avoidance of continuous constituents and the favoring of discontinuous constituents, the French acquisition data, like the English data, falsifies Slobin's claim that children will use strategies of speech perception which prohibit interruption of linguistic units.

French and English children are alike in another aspect. A frequent mistake that was made on subject relatives by both groups is what I call an "adjacency error." Children would interpret a sentence like (1), *the lion that pushes the horse knocks down the cow,* such that the lion pushes the horse and the horse knocks down the cow. In doing this, they were apparently using a strategy that I call the Adjacency strategy (Sheldon 1977), which is as follows:

> In parsing a noncompound sentence, starting from the left, group together as constituents of the same construction two adjacent NPs (i.e., not separated by other NPs) and an adjacent, noninitial verb that has not already been assigned to a clause. Interpret the first NP as the subject of the verb and the second NP as the object of the verb.

This strategy accounts for why children segmented the sequence, in sentence (1), *the lion pushes the horse,* as one clause, and the sequence that spans the clause boundary, *the horse knocks down the cow,* as another actual clause. Users of this strategy would ignore the relative pronoun. Thus, the use of this strategy in subject relatives accounts for the child's inability to find the boundary where the relative clause ends and the main clause resumes. This strategy is relied on until quite late by both English and French children. Notice that it will correctly parse the OS relative type (4). Between the ages of seven and nine, when children's performance on the OS sentence type gets better, we also find an increased generalization of this strategy to sentences where it shouldn't apply (e.g., to SS and SO sentence types).

Adjacency errors have been noted in two other studies of relative clauses. In a study of the comprehension of written relative clauses, Quigley et al. (1974) found that most deaf subjects between the ages of ten and eighteen make adjacency errors on subject relatives. There was no change in the strength of this response between ten and eighteen years. Hearing subjects between eight and ten years also made the same mistake. In a picture-cued comprehension task, Brown (1971) found that three- to five-year-olds also made adjacency errors on subject relatives.

There is evidence that an adjacency strategy is over-relied on in interpreting other types of sentences also. Tavakolian (1975) asked three- to five-year-old English-speaking children to act out sentences with two conjuncts in which the subject of the second conjunct was missing. When given a sentence like *the horse jumps over the duck and bumps into the rabbit,* they would make the horse jump over the duck, and the duck bump into the rabbit. Adjacency errors were also found on sentences with *in order to* complementizers. For example, on a sentence like *the rabbit jumps over the duck to bump into the horse,* they would make the rabbit jump over the duck and the duck bump into the horse.

To summarize the results of the French study, I have shown that despite the difference between French and English relative sentences, French children like English children have difficulty in assigning the correct function to the relativized NP. In attempting to do this, I am claiming that both English and French children rely on the Parallel-Function strategy. Not only does this partly account for the order of acquisition of subject and object relative sentences, it also accounts for many errors that were made. Secondly, both French and English children have difficulty in finding the NP that the relative clause modifies. In attempting to find an antecedent for the relative pronoun in object relatives, they over-relied on the Extraposition strategy. They preferred to associate all modifiers with the main clause subject, or sentence-initial NP, despite the fact that adult speakers in both languages prefer to associate modifiers with the adjacent NP. We cannot assume, therefore, that there will be differences in children's languages because there are differences in adult languages.

Slobin's claim about the putative universal difficulty of inter-ruptions, that is, of nested clauses, makes false predictions about the child's difficulty with French relative sentences as well. On the other hand, the French data support Slobin's Preferred Word-Order Hypothesis since children will try to interpret functional relations in clauses in terms of the predominant word order of the language. That is equivalent to saying that children over-rely on their strategies for processing the predominant word order, with the consequence that rules that change order are learned late.[4]

The French data also add to the growing body of evidence that language processors will over-rely on an Adjacency strategy to incorrectly segment adjacent surface sequences as actual constituents of a clause. Since the overuse of strategies for parsing sentences accounts for a number of the mistakes that were made, apparently learning a language involves—at least—learning to restrict the use of these strategies in those cases where they do not apply.

The French study is one step in the line of testing the universality of language-learning principles and strategies that were proposed to account for language acquisition in English. It replicates the main findings of the English studies using another language that had some differences as well as some similarities in the relative clause system. But the French results are stronger than a replication. They provide more evidence than we had with the English data alone to claim that these results are not due to the particular language that the children are learning but that they are due to the fact that the children are learning relative clauses. Since we now know that these results are not language specific, we have a basis for making the strongest possible claim, namely, that these same principles and strategies that found support in English will also account for the order of acquisition of relative sentences and the errors that language learners make on these constructions across languages. I am making the following hypotheses:

I. The Parallel-Function strategy is a language-independent processing heuristic.

II. All languages will have an Adjacency strategy for parsing sentences. The functional relations of the elements in the clause will be interpreted in terms of the predominant, language-specific word order.

III. Reliance on word order takes precedence over reliance on morphology.[5]

While it is possible that the results of the English and French studies are due to the fact that they are related languages, the crucial test of the universality of these principles is with a language that is unrelated to them, for example, an SOV language like Japanese. I think that an investigation of learners of such a language would be a fruitful avenue for future research.

In conclusion, although language-learning research is still in its infancy, so to speak, it is useful to measure the distance that has been traveled. Nelson Brooks made the following statement in his book on language learning in 1964:

> A discussion of learning is not complete without some remarks about error, which bears a relationship to learning resembling that of sin to virtue. Like sin, error is to be avoided and its influence overcome, but its presence is to be expected.

What I have shown here, however, is that we have a lot to learn from learner errors. They supply important data in the construction of a theory of language acquistion.

NOTES

1. This principle is relevant if we assume that *that* is analyzed as a relative pronoun and the relativized NP has been fronted.
2. Note that it is questionable whether there is a difference between this claim and his prohibition on the rearrangement of word order. It seems that what is at stake in both of these claims is that children will have difficulty processing sentences that violate the predominant surface word order in the language. I will not pursue this issue further here.
3. There is an important methodological point to be made here. Developmental psychologists compare the performance of children to a control sample of adults in order to avoid what Limber calls the "double standard of attributing gaps in children's performance to some developmental deficit, but tacitly assuming alternative explanations when those same gaps occur in the speech of a presumed fluent, mature individual."

I think the same methodological moral applies in second language learning research, and in teaching too. The errors in the performance of bilingual children should be compared to the errors in the performance of monolingual children, and the gaps in the performance of the adult second-language learner should be compared to those of native speakers, whose language processing powers should not be taken for granted. If adults had difficulty comprehending sentences with singly embedded relative clauses in French, what types of sentences might they have trouble with that we thought were too easy to justify investigation?

4. The implications that this hypothesis has for second-language learners deserves to be studied.

5. This statement is consistent with Slobin's statement (1966:134) that "all of the world's languages make use of order in their grammatical structure, but not all languages have inflectional systems." Rūķe-Draviņa (1972:265), also, arrives at a similar conclusion in a diary study of the production of nominal, adjectival, and verbal inflections in Latvian, through the child's fourth year.

REFERENCES

Beilin, H. and G. Spontak (1969) Active-passive transformations and operational reversibility. Paper presented at the Society for Research in Child Development, Santa Monica, Calif.

Bever, T. G. (1970) "The cognitive basis for linguistic strucutres," in J. R. Hayes (ed.), *Cognition and the Development of Language*. New York: John Wiley.

Brooks, N. (1964) *Language and Language Learning*. New York: Harcourt Brace Jovanovich.

Brown, H. D. (1971) "Children's comprehension of relativized English sentences," *Child Development* 42:1923–1926.

Chomsky, N. (1965) *Aspects of the Theory of Syntax*. Cambridge, Mass.: The M.I.T. Press.

Cromer, R. F. (1970) "Children are nice to understand. Surface structure clues for the recovery of a deep structure," *British Journal of Psychology* 61:397–408.

Ervin-Tripp, S. (1970) "Discourse agreement: How children answer questions," in J. R. Hayes (ed.), *Cognition and the Development of Language*. New York: John Wiley.

Ferreiro, E., C. Otheuin-Girard, H. Chipman and H. Sinclair (1976) "How do children handle relative clauses?" *Archives de Psychologie* 44:172.

Fraser, C., U. Bellugi and R. Brown (1963) "Control of grammar in imitation, comprehension and production," *Journal of Verbal Learning and Verbal Behavior* 2:121–135.

Kessel, F. S. (1970) "The role of syntax in children's comprehension from ages six to twelve," *Monographs of the Society for Research in Child Development* 35:6, serial no. 139.

Legum, S. (1975) "Strategies in the acquisition of relative clauses," *Proceedings of the Fifth Annual California Linguistics Association Conference.*

Limber, J. (1976) "Unraveling competence, performance, and pragmatics in the speech of young children," *Journal of Child Language* 3(3):309-318.

Maratsos, M. (1973) "The effects of stress on the understanding of pronominal coreference in children," *Journal of Psycholinguistic Research* 1:1-8.

McNeil, D. (1970) *The Acquisition of Language.* New York: Harper and Row.

Quigley, S. P., N. L. Smith and R. B. Wilbur (1974) "Comprehension of relativized sentences by deaf students," *Journal of Speech and Hearing Research* 17:325-341.

Roeper, T. (1972) "Theoretical implications of word order, topicalization and inflections in German language acquisition," in C. A. Ferguson and D. I. Slobin (eds.), *Studies in Child Language Development.* New York: Holt, Rinehart and Winston.

Rūķe-Draviņa, V. (1972) "On the emergence of inflection in child language: A contribution based on Latvian speech data," in C. A. Ferguson and D. I. Slobin (eds.), *Studies of Child Language Development.* New York: Holt, Rinehart and Winston.

Sheldon, A. (1972) "The acquisition of relative clauses in English," University of Texas Ph.D. dissertation. Bloomington: Indiana University Linguistics Club publication.

_____ (1974) "On the role of parallel function in the acquistion of relative clauses in English," *Journal of Verbal Learning and Verbal Behavior* 13(no. 3):272-281.

_____ (1976) "Speakers' intuitions about the complexity of relative clauses in Japanese and English," *Papers from the Twelfth Regional Meeting, Chicago Linguistic Society.* Chicago: University of Chicago Linguistics Society.

_____ (1977) "On strategies for processing relative clauses: A comparison of children and adults," *Journal of Psycholinguistic Research* 6:4.

Sinclair, H. and J. P. Bronckart (1972) "S.V.O. A linguistic universal? A study in developmental psycholinguistics," *Journal of Experimental Child Psychology* 14:329-348.

Slobin, D. I. (1966) "The acquisition of Russian as a native language," in F. Smith and G. A. Miller (eds.), *The Genesis of Language.* Cambridge, Mass.: The M.I.T. Press.

_____ (1971) "Developmental psycholinguistics," in W. O. Dingwall (ed.), *A Survey of Linguistic Science.* College Park: University of Maryland Linguistics Program.

Tavakolian, S. (1975) The structural analysis of complex sentences and the determination of functional relationships by preschoolers. University of Massachusetts. Manuscript.

Turner, E. A. and R. Rommetveit (1967) "The acquisition of sentence voice and reversibility," *Child Development* 38:649-660.

4

Decreolization and second-language acquisition

William Washabaugh
The University of Wisconsin–Milwaukee

INTRODUCTION

Decreolization is an extraordinary variety of second-language acquisition.[1] That is, the movement of a Creole language toward the standard language dominating the Creole community is unlike any other kind of second-language learning. It is social rather than individual; it is temporally hyperextended. In sum, decreolization is the acquisition of a standard language over a very long period of time by a whole group of people. These facts account for the extraordinary character of decreolization.

As an extraordinary process, decreolization is theoretically important. In any behavioral science, the study of the extraordinary case can lead to a clearer understanding of ordinary cases. For example, for the psychologist, the schizophrenic displays in raw form the same tensions which the average sane man hides. Thus the study of the extraordinary schizophrenic will shed light on the personality dynamics of the ordinary and normal man. In linguistics, Creole languages and the decreolization of Creoles are the extraordinary cases the study of which can make the normally opaque processes of second-language learning transparent.

Decreolization is theoretically significant, then, because a clearer view of decreolization promises greater insight into second-language acquisition. But I contend that we have not yet arrived at a clear view of the dynamics of decreolization. First I will show that decreolization involves multidimensional variation rather than bidimensional variation, as is often suggested. Second, the motivation or stimulus for change in decreolization is a complex of forces and not simply a desire to acquire a more standard language. Finally, and most importantly, variation and change in decreolization is constrained by surface structures rather than by deep structure categories.

In order to argue each of these points, I will outline Bickerton's (1971) oft-emulated analysis of variation in the form of the pre-infinitival complementizer in Guyanese Creole. In the course of the outline, Bickerton's principles for the analysis of decreolization will become clear. It is these principles which are in need of revision. First I present evidence for the multidimensionality in decreolization. Then I concentrate on the issue of constraints on variation in decreolization. My general aim is to show that one must avoid excessively rationalistic theoretical biases in order to recognize the proper constraints on variation in decreolization.

BICKERTON ON *Fi-Tu* VARIATION

In this section I outline Bickerton's (1971) analysis of the variation in the form of the pre-infinitival complementizer in Guyanese decreolization. The intent of this presentation is to make clear the principles which Bickerton employs in analyzing decreolization. I follow this presentation with an account of my own replication of Bickerton's analysis, using data from another and quite distant part of the Caribbean. The intent of the replication is to show that Bickerton has many right answers;

but, as I point out later, he has the right answers for the wrong reasons.

In his study of Guyanese Creole (hereafter GC) Bickerton discovered that the pre-infinitival complementizer *fi* or *fu* was variably replaced by the standard complementizer *tu*. For example, in Guyana one could hear (1) and (2) as well as (3) and (4):

(1) faama na noo wat tu do
    'The farmers don't know what to do'
(2) mi ga tu ripeer am dis kotin
    'I have to repair it during this harvest'
(3) hooptong piipl-dem na noo wa fu (fi) duu
    'The people from Hopetown don't know what to do'
(4) mi ga fu (fi) go bak go ripeer am
    'I have to go back and repair it'

Seeing that the variation between *fi* and *tu* was not random, Bickerton presented two models which could account for the patterns in the variation between *fi* and *tu*. The first model, the "variable rule model," is descriptively adequate but involves the unwarranted assumption that rules of language may be inherently variable. The second "wave model" is both descriptively adequate and theoretically orthodox. According to this "wave model" the more standard form *tu* replaces the more Creole *fi* progressively, starting first in one complementizer environment and then proceeding to others. The environments which constrain the replacement of *fi* by *tu* depend on the deep structure properties of the verb phrases in which the complementizer appears. Specifically, three deep structure configurations of the verb phrase are significant in constraining variation in the replacement of *fi*: (1) the structure of complements after inceptive and modal verbs (+INCEP); (2) the structure of complements after desiderative verbs (+DES); and (3) the structure of adverbial complements of purpose, together with all other types of complements (−INCEP, −DES). These complement types are listed in the order of their increasing inhibition of the replacement of *fi* by *tu*. That is, for each individual speaker, regardless of where he stands on the decreolization continuum, *tu* will appear in a (+INCEP) environment before it appears in a

(+DES) environment, and it will appear in a (+DES) environment before it appears in a (−INCEP, −DES) environment. Moreover, for any individual, the frequency of the use of *tu* will be greater in a (+INCEP) environment than in a (+DES) environment, and greater in a (+DES) environment than in a (−INCEP, −DES) environment.

Bickerton found that this prediction of the ordering of environments was supported by the data with the result that speakers could be arranged in the order of their increasingly general use of *tu*. That order of acquisition of *tu* is implicational in character. That is, the presence of a *tu* in any of the three environments for any speaker requires that *tu* appear also in all environments and for all speakers above and to the left of that environment as shown in Table 1. The implicational ranking of speakers represents the developing polylectal grammar with respect to this one morphological unit.

Replication of Bickerton's Analysis

Bickerton's implicational scaling of Guyanese Creole *fi* variation can be replicated with data from the English Creole of Providence Island, Colombia. Providence Island is a volcanic island 17 square kilometers in size, located 110 miles from the coast of Nicaragua in the western Caribbean. The population numbers about 3,000 persons divided into 550 families and

TABLE 1. An abstract implicational scale of *fu-tu* variation, adapted from Bickerton (1971:476)

Speakers	+INCEP	+DES	+INCEP, −DES
1	F	F	F
2	T/F	F	F
3	T	F	F
4	T	T/F	F
5	T	T	F
6	T	T	T/F
7	T	T	T

Legend: F = *fu*, T = *tu*.

TABLE 2. Implicational scale of
variation in *tu* use

Speakers	+INCEP	+DES	−INCEP, −DES
1	−	−	Ⓧ
2	−	Ⓧ	−
3		−	−
4	−	−	−
5	−		−
6		−	−
7	−	Ⓧ	−
8		−	−
9	X	−	
10	X	−	Ⓧ
11	X	X	X
12	X	X	X
13	X	X	X
14		X	−
15	X	X	X
16		X	−
17	⊝		X
18	X	X	X
19	X	⊕	X
20	+	X	X
21	X	X	X
22		+	−
23	X	X	X
24	X	X	X
25	Ⓧ	+	−
26	+	+	+

Legend: + = categorical use of *tu*, X =
variable use of *tu*, − = categorical use of *fi*;
scalability = 89.9 percent.

living in 14 communities scattered around the perimeter of the
island. It is governed by Colombia, but inhabitants are by and
large monolingual speakers of Caribbean English (Wilson 1973).

Tables 2 and 3[2] show the results of my replication of
Bickerton's analysis of Guyanese *fi* variation with data from
Providence Island Creole (hereafter PIC). The environments in
which *fi* or *tu* appeared in PIC were coded as either (+INCEP),
(+DES), or (−INCEP, −DES). Coding judgments were based

TABLE 3. Frequency scale of variation in
tu use

Speakers	+INCEP		+DES		−INCEP, −DES	
1	0/4	0%	0/5	0%	1/8	(13)%
2	0/5	0	2/5	(40)	0/5	0
3		0	0/3	0	0/15	0
4	0/5	0	0/5		0/8	0
5	0/5	0			0/3	0
6	0/1		0/2	0	0/7	0
7	0/3	0	4/10	(40)	0/4	0
8			0/2	0	0/6	0
9	2/5	40	0/2	0	0/1	
10	3/6	50	0/2	0	2/27	(7)
11	5/12	42	1/7	14	1/11	9
12	10/19	53	2/9	(22)	9/35	26
13	2/6	33	2/7	29	2/24	8
14			1/3	33	0/9	0
15	12/42	(29)	10/25	40	6/42	14
16			1/2	50	0/3	0
17	0/3	(0)	1/1		4/8	50
18	2/3	67	4/6	67	4/10	40
19	4/6	67	7/7	(100)	2/4	50
20	10/10	100	14/17	82	30/47	64
21	24/32	75	21/23	(91)	13/19	68
22			2/2	100	0/2	0
23	12/13	92	9/10	90	19/20	(95)
24	14/15	93	14/15	93	6/9	67
25	14/16	(88)	32/32	100	21/21	100
26	2/2	100	11/11	100	6/6	100

mainly on the directives given in Bickerton (1971). Table 2 presents an implicational scaling of speakers based on the categorical presence or absence of, or variability in the use of, *tu*. The scalability of Table 2 is 89.9 percent. Deviations are circled.

The raw frequencies and percentages which appear in Table 3 present the numerical results of the codings. The data are presented in the form of ratios of the observed frequency of the use of *tu* to the sum of the observed frequencies of *tu* use plus *fi* use. An inspection of these frequencies will show that they too are patterned implicationally. The highest frequencies appear in the most favorable environments and progressively lower frequencies appear in the less favorable environments. The seven deviations are circled.

Features of Bickerton's Analysis

It should be apparent from the foregoing discussion that in his analysis of *fi–tu* variation Bickerton has made the following three assumptions: (1) that variation in decreolization is bidirectional (see also Bickerton 1973:20); (2) that the *fi* replacement process applies to just the pre-infinitival complementizer; and (3) that variation in the replacement of *fi* is constrained by the deep structure configurations of the verb phrases in which the complementizer stands.

But there is a good deal of evidence to support alternative principles: (1a) that decreolization involves multidirectional variation; (2a) that *fi* replacement applies to the lexical item *fi*; and (3a) that variation in *fi* replacement is constrained by features of surface structure.

DIRECTIONALITY OF VARIATION
IN DECREOLIZATION

The multidirectionality of variation in decreolization can be made apparent by distinguishing three different categories of variation in the complementizer in PIC. There is type-1 variation, such as the variation between *fi* and *tu*. We will also call this vertical variation. In PIC, vertical variation occurs during the slow acquisition of the near-standard (acrolectal) *tu* replacing the stigmatized creole (basilect) complementizer *fi*. There is a type-2 variation, which is indicative of social pressure not so much to acquire the acrolect as to avoid the basilect. The variation between *fi* and ∅ in PIC is often such a variation indicative of avoidance of the basilect. Sentences (5) through (15) illustrate the variety of linguistic environments in which *fi* is optionally deleted.

(5) wen im mek kom in ah jos dok
    'When he tried to come in, I just ducked'

(6) an i staat draa bakwe
    'And he started to move backwards'
(7) ai waan im brienz aal laik mi
    'I would like to see him fool someone like me'
(8) yu memba wan taim jan did sen mi go an wok
    'You remember one time John sent me to go and work'
(9) iz aal i waan du ron
    'All he wants to do is run'
(10) im keri tu pikni dong de pass skuul
    'He brought two kids down there to attend school'
(11) dem ken get wan a di buot bring dong di paip
    'They can get one of the boats to bring down the pipe'
(12) an jou waaka den tel mi waz di fos wan get pan di spat
    'And Joe Walker they tell me was the first one to get to
    the spot'[3]
(13) evri die in sen di likl gyal go go sii if di bwai fat
    'Every day she sent the little girl to go and see if the boy
    was fat'
(14) ai gwain marrid tu i gyal, man
    'I am going to marry the girl, man'
(15) him no waan mi men go chap it aut
    'He didn't want me to go chop it (the field) out'

The occasions for the use of a $\emptyset$ complementizer are not rare. In my data corpus, for all possible opportunities to use a pre-infinitival complementizer a $\emptyset$ form was used 46 percent of the time.[4] A type-3, or horizontal, variation is exemplified by *fi* and *fə*. There is a good deal of phonological variation in PIC which cannot be attributed to the progressive acquisition of standard forms. The pre-infinitival complementizer can appear as *fi* or *fə*, or *tu* or *tə*; the past tense marker varies among *me, mê, mẽn, bẽn, wẽn*; prepositions *pan* ('upon') and *fam* ('from') may appear as *pãn, pã,* or *pa* and *fõ* or *fa* (see Edwards and Rosberg 1970:308–314).

There are three major social motives which account for these three classes of variation: (1) pressure to acquire the acrolect, (2) pressure to avoid basilectal forms, and (3) pressure to use a casual style of speech in informal situations.

The strongest motive for variation in PIC is the desire to avoid basilectal features of speech. Note that this is not the same motive as the desire to acquire a standard variety of English. Actually, most islanders give no sign of having a strong desire to acquire a standard variety of English. In fact, there are social pressures working against the imitation of Standard English. Strong feelings are generated against persons, whether adults or children, who try to use more standard speech than is customary. Islanders say that such *yankin'* or *speakin'*, as it is called, is a sign that speakers think themselves too good for the island. Children learning English in school cannot practice that English outside the classroom without being criticized by their peers. In short, in Providence Island society, there are not only pressures to avoid basilectal features of speech, but also very strong pressures to avoid too rapid an acquisition of Standard English.

Given the social stigmatization of basilectal features of speech, much variation in decreolization turns out to be the result of the progressive acquisition of a second language accomplished in a reverse natural manner. The natural or most frequent process of second-language acquisition is incorporation of words, sounds, and grammatical patterns from the language to be acquired. Decreolization reverses this pattern. Providence Island speakers alter their speech by avoiding basilectal words and sounds and grammatical patterns. This is especially true of basilectal speakers who are isolated from acrolectal speakers and acrolectal models of speech. Such speakers respond to social pressure by avoiding basilectal features in their speech and by replacing them with any forms which seem to them to be more acrolectal. Since these speakers lack models for imitation, the replacements they select are often far from standard.[5] The project of recognizing and incorporating Standard English forms of speech is probably more frequent and more successful among speakers of mesolectal varieties (varieties midway between basilectal Creole and the near-standard acrolect). Such speakers tend to be at higher socioeconomic levels on the island.

The negative character of the social pressure for language change accounts for the *fi-∅* avoidance variation in the form of the pre-infinitival complementizer. Such *fi-∅* avoidance variation in turn must have an influence on the patterns of *fi–tu* vertical variation. Bickerton's analysis, implying that variation is largely a product of pressure to *acquire* rather than a produce of pressure to *avoid*, is likely to miss the complexity of this relationship between *fi*, $\emptyset$, and *tu* forms.

The second motive, the need for a casual variety of speech, also accounts for some of the *fi*-$\emptyset$ variation and also for the horizontal variation noted above. As in most other languages, speakers of Providence Island Creole apply fast speech rules of phonological weakening and deletion as well as other natural rules of morphological deletion in a casual variety of speech.

Most studies of decreolization have ignored the existence of such stylistic variation. Some (DeCamp 1968:7, Bickerton 1973:20) have even argued that all stylistic variation is another facet of vertical variation. They claim that casual speech is formed by switching to a basilectal variety while careful speech is simply more mesolectal or acrolectal. It is implied that individuals speaking at one stage of the basilect–acrolect continuum cannot manipulate the elements of that stage more and less carefully.

A cursory study of talk about talk on Providence Island shows that there is more to decreolization than vertical variation. On Providence Island speakers have words to refer to two distinct dimensions of talk. The poles of one dimension are called *broad talk* and *speakin'*; these terms refer to the vertical continuum ranging from basilet to acrolect—Standard American English is called *deep talk*. The poles of the horizontal dimension are called *bad* or *brawlin' talk* and *sweet talk*.[6] Someone using *bad* or *brawlin' talk* speaks fast, weakens or deletes consonants, centralizes vowels, and is often hard to understand. Someone who talks *sweet* is easy to understand because he speaks clearly and with maximally distinct sounds.[7]

THE UNIT OF DECREOLIZATION

Bickerton's analysis of *fi* variation in GC was confined to just the complementizing function of *fi*. Bickerton says that "it is not the formative *tu* as such but *tu* as complementizer that is perceived as nonstandard" (1971:482). But a proper analysis of *fi* in PIC must include both the complementizing function and the two prepositional functions of *fi*. Variations in all three functions of *fi* must be considered in this analysis since all three uses of *fi* vary in PIC as a result of the same social pressure. In other words, the social pressure to avoid basilectal speech applies to the lexical item *fi* rather than to just one grammatical function of that lexical item.

As we have seen, the PIC complementizer *fi* varies with *tu*. The frequency of the use of *fi* is highest among the lower socioeconomic groups and lowest among the upper socioeconomic groups. As shown in sentences (16) and (17), the *fi–tu* variation is not fully constrained by selectional restrictions.

Besides variation in the complementizer function of *fi*, the prepositional uses of *fi* also exhibit variation. The possessive constructions in sentences (18) through (21), all of which were used by the same speaker in telling one story, reveal the nature of the variation in the genitive prepositional function of *fi*.

(16) ai mek fi stan op bot ai had tu fal back
     'I tried to stand up but I had to fall back'
(17) jan riez di prais fi get di fish tu sen san andres
     'John raised the price to get the fish to send to San Andres'
(18) yu get auta mai yaad
     'You get out of my yard'
(19) ai put fi mi haan pan it
     'I put my hand on it'
(20) nau hiz faada draun an a buot
     'Now his father drowned on a boat'
(21) im se se mi gwain ded tuu, siem iz fi im pupa
     'He said that he was going to die too just like his papa'

Again there are no firm selectional restrictions on this variation.

Still a third variation is found in the dative prepositional use of *fi*. Sentences (22) and (23) show that the variation here is between *fi* and *for*.

(22) di plien waz tu kom for im
     'The airplane was supposed to come for him'
(23) de de luk fi mi wid gon
     'They are looking for me with a gun'

The quantitative analysis of *fi* variation presented later in this paper will deal with just the replacement of the *fi* complementizer. Elsewhere (Washabaugh 1974:133) I have reported that a speaker's progress in replacing the *fi* complementizer is significantly correlated with his progress in replacing the *fi* genitive preposition.

CONSTRAINTS ON VARIATION
IN DECREOLIZATION

In his analysis of *fi* replacement, Bickerton assumes that deep structure constraints properly account for the patterns of variation. In this section I argue that this analysis is overly simple. Rather than one single set of constraints, there must be varieties of constraints to deal with the different dimensions of variation. Moreover, the constraints on *fi* replacement are surface structure ones rather than deep structure.

Any selection of environmental constraints on variation must be a principled selection. That is, each constraint must be accompanied by an explanation for its proposed effect. The sole test of the adequacy of a constraint cannot be just the empirically discovered effect of that constraint on the patterning of variation. Such a method cannot insure the truth of the final analysis. Rather, constraints should be deduced from linguistic or metalinguistic principles. Arguments should accompany the proposal of each constraint to explicate the deductive reasoning through which they are posited. For example, Labov (1972:106) suggests that a consonant immediately proceeding the copula in English inhibits the application of the copula contraction rule. The reason for the inhibition is that the juxtaposition of a preceding consonant and a contracted copula forms a consonant cluster. Since a consonant cluster is a marked syllabic form, there is a tendency to avoid it. Thus, he argues, contractions will occur less frequently where a consonant precedes the copula. Every proposal of an environmental constraint should be accompanied by a similar explanation.

The environmental constraints on *fi* replacement presented by Bickerton are not well supported or well presented. First, those deep structure constraints cannot be applied consistently. The inconsistency lies in the instructions for identifying the deep structure configurations of the complements introduced by each *fi–tu*. Bickerton claims that desiderative and similar "psychological" verbs are typically followed by a complementizer in an NP object complement clause. He, therefore, suggests that in coding data for analysis, one should code all complementizers after desiderative verbs as (+DES) since *waan* is a desiderative verb, or as (−INCEP, −DES) since the complement following *waan* is an adverbial complement of some sort. The specific instructions are to code the verb, but in following the specific instructions the coder will wrongly assign the *fi* complement in (24) to the category (+DES):

(24) ah waan it fi kieri it huom
     'I want it so that I can bring it home'

From this one example we can see that the result of the coding instructions will be that the (+DES) category will contain cases in which *fi* introduces both object complements and adverbial complements. This method of coding verbs instead of directly coding clauses by their deep structure characteristics seems contrary to Bickerton's original aim of establishing categories with a basis in deep structure.

A second difficulty with Bickerton's constraints has to do with the definition of the third constraint on *fi–tu* variation, (−INCEP, −DES). The very statement of this constraint shows that it is not well argued or supported by sound reasoning. Rather it is a wastebasket category into which will fall all instances of *fi* complements not appearing after inceptive or desiderative verbs. This category will include not only adverbial complements expressing purpose (Bickerton 1971:477) but also subject complements, reduced relative clauses, and clauses used as object of preposition. Empirical fit of data, not independent justification, is the only reason for Bickerton's having postulated such a category as (−INCEP, −DES).[8]

A third difficulty is that Bickerton presents no arguments to support his selection of deep structure complement configurations as the constraint on *fi* variation. His rationalist linguistic biases have led him to simply assume that speakers in a post-Creole community can identify deep structure configurations and mark formatives to match them because such Creole speakers are like all other second-language learners who have an ability to formulate general and proper hypotheses about the linguistic data to which they are exposed. All second-language learners have this ability because second-language learning is identical in form to first-language learning (Bickerton 1975); and there can be no doubt that first-language learners have an ability to construct grammatical systems of maximally general rules.

As sound as this reasoning seems, it hides a controversial point. Within this reconstructed logic is the view that the acquirer of a second language has an ability to *instantly* discern the proper and most general environment in which to apply newly acquired forms and processes. If not *instantly,* then at least in a span of time no greater than the time needed by a child to refine his generalizations about his first language.

But, contrary to this reasoning, speakers in a post-Creole community are not able to uncover the proper and most general environments for newly acquired forms and processes as quickly as the first-language learner. Such Creole speakers seldom have the same pressing need as a first-language learner for speedy acquisition of the target language. Moreover, the Creole speakers, unlike the first-language learner, rarely have the immediate access to a model of the language to be acquired. In short, while the process of first-language acquisition and decreolization might be formally the same, the actual activation of these processes is probably quite different. I hypothesize that in decreolization there is likely to be a lengthy period in which the adult fails to identify the proper and most general linguistic environments for use of forms or application of processes. During that long period, placement of newly acquired forms will be guided by less than general surface structure environments.

To attempt to constrain variation in decreolization by deep structure categories is to ignore all the variation during this long period in which the incorporation of new forms proceeds with less than maximal generality. Such an overly simplified analysis must involve an ignoring or mishandling of a great deal of variation. The variation which is missed is not individual and idiosyncratic variation, but socially shared and, because of the slowness of decreolization, long standing. In short, to try to account for all variation in decreolization by deep structure constraints requires that one ignore a great deal of socially shared, long-term variation. This forcing of data into the theory is not unlike the trimming by Procrustes of his victims to fit his bed.

A "LEXICAL DIFFUSION MODEL" OF VARIATION IN DECREOLIZATION

The alternative to Bickerton's deep structure constraints on *fi* variation is linguistically and psychologically more plausible, that is, surface structure and lexical constraints on variation. Speakers, desiring to replace their stigmatized *fi* forms, turn to whatever acrolectal models are available and find in those models a complementizer *tu*. The speakers' problem is to discover where the *tu* is placed in the target language and to incorporate that *tu* into similar positions in his own sentences. A number of psychological learning strategies give him the answers to this problem.

Strategy 1—Replace *fi* with *tu* after those target-language verbs which are most strongly associated with *tu*. The speaker will first recognize that certain verbs are immediately and regularly followed by *tu* in the target language. The speaker will key in on those same verbs in his own speech as the sites for replacing *fi* with *tu*. Those verbs which are distantly and less regularly followed by *tu* in the model will be more difficult to recognize and therefore slower to condition a replacement of *fi* by *tu*. Finally, those basilectal verbs which are not shared by the acrolect will be the last to condition replacement of *fi* by *tu*.

For example, there are verbs in English which are regularly and immediately followed by *tu*, for example, *start, try,* and the modals *have* and *got*. Since these same verbs are found in the basilect they will be the first verbs to condition *fi* replacement. Other English verbs are irregularly followed by *tu* and often stand at some distance from *tu* in the surface structure, for example, *want, tell, come,* and *go*. Though I have no data on English surface structure regularities for each of these verbs, I suggest that they are ordered here according to their average frequency of appearance with *tu* their average proximity to *tu* in discourse. Finally, the English target does not contain certain verbs as they are regularly used in the basilect, for example, *fiil, nuo, raada, mek*.

When these verbs are used by a PIC speaker as in sentences (25) through (28), they inhibit *fi* replacement.

(25) ah fiil fi piipi
'I want to pee'
(26) ah mek fi stan op
'I tried to stand up'
(27) ah raada fi liv hiir
'I prefer to live here'
(28) ah nuo fi hangl dem
'I know how to handle them'

The contention that lexical items constrain *fi–tu* variation is parallel to the claims made by Chen and Wang (1974), Chen and Hsieh (1971), and Hsieh (1970, 1972a, 1972b), with regard to lexical diffusion in phonology. Though the lexical diffusion hypothesis has been applied thus far only to phonological variation, there is every reason to expect that it can also apply to syntactic variation. To a limited extent other analyses of syntactic variation have employed lexical constraints.

Bolinger (1972:18f.), for one, shows that lexical items are major constraints on the deletion of the *that* complementizer in English. Bickerton (1975) suggests that the verb *start* is unique in acquiring the *-ed* past tense marker in GC. Thus, lexical constraints are already used sporadically in analyses of syntactic variation. I am proposing lexical items as primary rather than exceptional contraints on the replacement of the *fi* complementizer.

The "lexical diffusion model" proposed here explains certain patterns of variation in decreolization. Specifically, it handles the sort of variation which must occur in the speech of individual speakers who have failed to recognize the most general and therefore deep structure environments for *fi* replacement. Presumably at some point after *fi* replacement has occurred with most verbs, the Creole speakers will come to recognize the underlying regularity of *fi* replacement. Only then are they able to arrive at a generalization to match that recognition. Only at that point would one say that *fi* replacement continues according to deep structure constraints.

A second learning strategy allows the speaker to replace *fi* despite a lack of knowledge of a target language.

Strategy 2—Delete *fi* wherever it can be deleted.

Actually, speakers may activate Strategy 2 for either of two reasons, to avoid the stigmatized *fi* or to produce a casual unmarked utterance. The conditions under which the deletion for either reason can occur are similar. The function of the complementizer *fi* is to mark an embedded sentence; *fi* can be deleted wherever such a marking is redundant. First, it can be deleted after those verbs which are regularly assumed to dominate an embedded sentence (Bolinger 1972:19). Two such verbs in PIC which regularly dominate an embedded sentence are *gwain* and *waan*. Second, *fi* can be deleted if it stands immediately adjacent to the matrix verb. The rationale for this hypothesis is that speakers naturally tend to segment a sentence after the matrix verb in expectation of an embedding. This natural perceptual process is a listener's strategy for comprehending complex sentences. If the embedded sentence is also syntactically marked by a complementizer, then that complementizer is redundant and subject to deletion, especially in less careful speech. However, where the complement is separated from the main verb, the *fi* may be more necessary as a signal to the listener of a forthcoming embedded sentence.

A QUANTITATIVE STUDY OF *Fi* VARIATION

Tables 4 through 6 illustrate the regularity of *fi* variation after twelve different verbs.[9] Arranged in the order of their favoring of *fi* replacement, those verbs are: *staat* ('start'), *biigin* ('begin'), *trai* ('try'), *hav* ('have'), *gat* ('got'), *laik* ('like'), *waan* ('want'), *tel* ('tell'), *kom* ('come'), *go* ('go'), *fiil* ('want'), *nuo* ('know').

It should be apparent that there is a correlation between this ordering of verbs and Bickerton's deep structure categories, (+INCEP), (+DES), (−INCEP, −DES). However, the correlation is loose. A close examination of these twelve verbs along with a few other significant verbs shows that Bickerton's categories are simply covariates of the significant criteria of variation, which are lexical items.

TABLE 4. Implicational scale of *tu* use after twelve verbs

Speakers	staat	biigin	trai	hav	gat	laik	waan	tel	kom	go	fiil	nuo
1							−	(X)				
2			−				−			. −		
3	X		−				−	−	−	−		−
4			−				−			−		
6							−	−				
8	+		−									
17							−					
10				X			−	−	−			
15	+		X	X			X	−		−		
11	(X)		(−)	X		(−)	X					
13				X			X		X	−		
9				X			−					
12				X	X		−	−	−	−	−	
18				X			−					
20			+	+	X	X	X	X	X	−		
16	+						X					
21	+		+	(X)		+	X			X		
26			+	+			X					
7				(−)			X					
24		(−)	X	X				X		X		
19				X	X		X					
23	+		+	X			X	(+)	(+)			
25			+	(X)	+							

Legend: + = categorical use of *tu*, X = variable use of *tu*, − = categorical use of *fi*; scalability = 90 percent.

First, the verb *trai* is a desiderative verb, yet it outranks the modals *hav* and *gat* in favoring *fi* replacement. Second, the desiderative verb *nuo*, as in (28), is outranked by verbs which are (−INCEP, −DES). A number of other desiderative verbs, which are unfortunately rarely used, show a similar inhibiting affect of the *fi* replacement rule. The verb *mek* always appears with *fi*. Similarly, *fiil* and *raada* always appear with *fi*. The fact that these verbs, which are roughly synonymous with *waan* and *trai*, are more conservative, is clear evidence that the true constraints on *fi*-*tu* variation are lexical not deep structure constraints.

A major advantage of this analysis is that all the deletions of

TABLE 5. Frequency scale of *tu* use after twelve verbs

Speakers	staat	biigin	trai	hav	gat	laik	waan	tel	kom	go	fiil	nuo
1				0%			0%	33%				
2				0			0			0		
3	44%						0	0	0	0		0
4				0			0	0				
6							0	0				
8	100						0					
17				0			0					
10				40			0	0	0			
15	100		71	23			7	0		0		
11	17		(0)	33		(0)	25					
13				33			29		20			
9				50				0				
12				53		50	0	0	0	0	0	
18				67				0				
20			100	100	88	50	(22)	28	(50)	0		
16	100						43					
21	100		100	(71)		100	44			(50)		
26			100	100			50					
7				0			50					
24		0	75	93				50		50		
19				50		33	(60)					
23	100		100	83			67	(100)	(100)			
25			100	(88)		100						

fi are taken into account in computing the frequencies in Table 5. That is, the frequencies of the use of *tu* are computed by the ratio of the frequency of the use of *tu* to the frequency of possible uses of *tu*. The frequency of possible uses of *tu* is determined by adding the frequency of uses of *tu* to the frequency of the use of ∅ and the frequency of the use of *fi*. The frequency of the use of *tu* after *waan*, which especially favors deletions, is significantly affected by this consideration of deletions.

Table 7 presents the pattern of deletion of the complementizer. The frequencies shown in this table are computed from the ratio of the frequency of actual deletions to the frequency of possible deletions of *fi*.

The (±FORMATIVE) environment is the major constraint on complementizer deletion. A (−FORMATIVE) environment

TABLE 6. Raw frequency scale of *tu* use after twelve verbs

Speakers	staat	büigin	trai	hav	gat	laik	waan	tel	kom	go	fiil	nuo
1				0/4		0/1	0/10	1/3		0/1		
2	0/1			0/5	0/1		0/7			0/2		0/1
3	4/9			9/39			0/6	0/3	0/5	0/3	0/2	
4	0/1			0/5	0/1		0/8	0/1		0/2		
6	1/1			0/1			0/6	0/2		0/1		
8	0/2						0/8					
17						1/1	0/4			0/1		
10	1/1			0/3			0/6	0/3	0/2	0/1		
15	3/3		5/7	2/5		0/1	3/41	0/4	0/1	0/5		0/1
11	1/6	1/1	0/2	3/9		0/3	1/4	0/1				
13	0/1			2/6		0/1	2/7	1/1	1/5	0/5	0/1	
9			0/1	2/4	0/1		0/1	0/2				
12			0/1	10/19		1/2	0/6	0/4	0/3	0/2	0/2	
18			1/1	2/3			0/1	0/4		0/1		
20			3/3	10/10	15/17	1/2	2/9	2/7	2/4	0/2	0/1	
16	2/2						3/7	0/1				
21	5/5		2/2	20/28	1/1	2/2	14/32	0/1		1/2		
26			5/5	2/2			1/2					
7	0/1			0/3			3/6			0/1		
24		7/7	3/4	14/15		1/1	1/1	1/2	0/1	1/2		0/1
19	1/1			2/4	1/1	1/3	6/10					
23	6/6	1/1	4/4	5/6		1/1	2/3	2/2	3/3	1/1		
25			10/10	14/16		19/19	1/1					

TABLE 7. Frequency scale for complementizer
deletion in four environments

Speakers	−FORMATIVE	+FORMATIVE	*gwain*	*waan*
2	93%	20%	100%	86%
1	92	44	100	70
3	85	08	100	100
7	85	0	100	88
5	78	17	100	100
9	74	04	93	83
13	70	23	100	85
15	67	00	100	100
4	67	75	100	
11	63	17	94	100
10	63	40	100	75
8	57	100	100	40
6	55	57	100	40
14	53	33	100	43
17	52	18	100	78
12	52	07	75	71
19	52	18	100	00
18	49	31	100	56
16	43	00	100	40

significantly favors deletion of the complementizer while a
(+FORMATIVE) inhibits deletion. An analysis of variance test
shows that the difference between the mean frequencies of
deletion in these two environments is significant beyond the .01
level of probability.[10] Table 7 also shows that the two verbs
gwain ('going') and *waan* ('want') both favor deletion of the
complementizer. *Fi* is deleted almost categorically after *gwain*.
After *waan* the complementizer is deleted at an overall average
of 74 percent.[11] Most often the zero form, $\emptyset$, appears immediately after *gwain* and *waan* with no formative intervening. The
effect of these two lexical items is subordinate to the effect of
the major constraint (+FORMATIVE).[12]

THE (±FORMATIVE) CONSTRAINT AS COVARIATE

The lexical diffusion model presented here has a variety of
advantages. First, it offers a descriptively adequate account of

variation in *fi* replacement. Second, it explains why Bickerton's wave model was so clearly supported by the data despite the fact that it implies questionable assumptions about decreolization. Third, it also explains why certain constraints in Bickerton's disgarded variable rule model were empirically significant.

One of the constraints in the variable rule model was a (±FORMATIVE) constraint. According to that constraint, the presence of any number of formatives between the matrix verb and the complementizer inhibits the application of the *fi* replacement rule. The lexical diffusion model explains the effect of this (±FORMATIVE) constraint as a covariate of lexical constraints. That is, a (−FORMATIVE) environment is correlated with a high frequency of *fi* replacement because the closer the complementizer stands to the verb the more strongly it will be associated with that verb in the mind of the speakers.

Moreover, speakers will make this association even more quickly if in Standard English the complementizer stands close to the verb and if that complementizer cannot be deleted, as in the case of *have, got, begin,* and *start.* Speakers are likely to use *tu* first and most frequently after just those verbs linked to the complementizer *tu* by such strong associations.

This (±FORMATIVE) environment is just a covariate of the major constraint on variation, which is the lexical character of the verb. Relative distance of the complementizer from the verb would have little meaning unless the effect of the distance were a stronger or weaker association with the verb. Distance in itself cannot explain *fi* replacement. Distance is simply a factor of the association with the matrix verb. It is the matrix verb, primarily its lexical character, which is the major constraint of variation. Furthermore, we have seen that there are a number of verbs which are regularly followed immediately by a complementizer— *fiil, mek, nuo, raada,* etc.—which are late in being associated with *tu.* The reason for this failure of association is simply a lack of the use of such verbs in the matrilect or acrolect.

CONCLUSION

This investigation has shown that *fi* variation in PIC is quite complex. I have shown that the lexical item *fi* may be either replaced or deleted and that the motives for the two processes may be quite different. The replacement of *fi* with *tu* occurs gradually in the speech of Providence Islanders, but still the replacement is systematic. There are specific lexical constraints which favor or inhibit this gradual replacement of *fi*. Variation in the deletion of *fi* is constrained by the proximity of the *fi* to the verb in surface structure, and also by the lexical character of the verb.

These findings demonstrate one simple fact about decreolization: speakers in a post-Creole community make use of a variety of cognitive abilities in patterning their speech. Any analysis of decreolization which implies that complex variation is organized by a single language-specific ability will oversimplify the situation. Specifically, analyses which assume that regularities in decreolization are due to a specific innate language acquisition ability will fail to see that speakers also make use of a variety of more general cognitive abilities such as the ability to make associations and to apply innovations by analogy.

The rationalist assumption that all linguistic regularities must be explained by a specific linguistic ability is an oversimplification. If there is any such specific linguistic ability, it always functions in conjunction with other more general cognitive or psychological abilities. The need to invoke such general cognitive abilities to explain facts about synchronic language structure may not seem so pressing. But to explain facts of language acquistion and language change, linguists (Reber 1973, Kiparsky 1972) are finding it necessary to consider the role of such general abilities.

A fortiori, in explaining decreolization and any less extraordinary cases of second-language acquisition, linguists must open their eyes to the fact that speakers make use of general psychological strategies. Speakers in a post-Creole community start by focusing on basilectal words, not grammatical units, as the first units to be replaced. They discover more acceptable replacement words by inspecting models of the target language. They make the replacements in their speech first and fastest in those linguistic environments which stand out as the clearest parallels to the environments in which acceptable words are used most often in the target language. If speakers lack a clear model of the target language, they will delete the stigmatized word first and fastest where it is perceptually redundant. These general psychological strategies will carry speakers well along into the replacement process and only then will their specific language acquisition ability lead them to formulate hypotheses about the most general environments for replacing stigmatized units of the basilect.

NOTES

1. The suggestion that decreolization is an extraordinary variety of second-language acquisition is one of many very productive hypotheses in Bickerton (1975). This particular hypothesis, though it is in need of more thorough investigation, helps to spotlight the theoretical importance of Creole languages.

2. Tables 2 and 3 illustrate the patterning of *fi* variation for 26 speakers. The data on *fi* variation for most speakers derives from my interviews of these speakers, recorded on a Uher 4000 Report-L tape recorder, and from interviews recorded on a Sony TC-110 cassette recorder by three local men. Each of these men were trained in the use of the recorder as well as in the method of interviewing by which candid conversation was elicited. I have tested for the possibility that the use of different interviewers introduced a bias into the quantitative study of *fi* variation. Analysis of variance tests show that there is no significant difference in the mean frequencies of either *fi* replacement or complementizer deletion in material recorded by local interviewers versus material recorded by myself.

    Speakers range in age from 10 years to 87 years and live primarily in Old Town and Bottomhouse. No social parameters are used to segment these speakers into groups since, as R. Day (1972:108) says, "Decreolization apparently cuts through or transcends the various social groupings in the speech community." The total recording time for the interviews averages forty minutes for each speaker.

3. I am grateful to J. Edwards for supplying the recording of this sentence.

4. This mean was computed for a sample of 20 speakers from the ratio of the frequency of deletion of the complementizer to the frequency of possible deletions in those two environments. This latter frequency was computed by adding the frequency of the use of ∅, *tu,* and *fi.* As indicated, the mean frequency of deletion is .462. The standard deviation of that mean is .144.

5. The following narrative illustrates this point. The narrator is discussing the relative propriety of the progressive particles *da* and *de.* She argues that *de* sounds fine, but that *da* is thoroughly improper.

    ... yu da iit? If dem waan se it bad iz we dem waan, bot mi no hiir dem se so ... Yeh man, "yu da iit," wat kaina taak dat? Som piipl fa san andres taak so.

Wan taim mieri gan san andres wen i da smal laik dat likl bwai de, wen im kudn taak. Wen im gan dong de im me staat taak, "yu da iit." Im tuu simpl an ma biit im and biit im til im get bak huom. Dat taim hiir im, "yu da iit yu nuo." Im me tuu simpl . . . Yeh "yu de iit" beta, bot "yu da iit?"

Translated: "You are eating?" If they want to say it as bad as they want, but I don't hear them talking so . . . Yes man, "you are eating," what kind of talk is that? Some people from San Andres talk so. One time Mary went to San Andres when she was small like that little boy there, when she couldn't talk. When she went there she started to say "you are eating." She was too simple and mama beat her and beat her till she got back home. That time hear her, "you are eating you know." She was too simple . . . Yes, "you are eating" is better, but "you are eating?"

6. Edwards and Rosberg (1976) refer to *bad talk* as *patois. Sweet talk* is regularly used to refer to basilectal speech on Providence Island. It would be difficult to imagine anyone using *sweet talk* to refer to any form of *speakin'*. The meaning of *sweet talk* actually varies slightly from individual to individual. For some *sweet talk* means an archaic basilect, for others it means humorous talk, for others it means talk with a particular intonational contour.

7. An anecdote might clarify this distinction. I accompanied a mesolectal but *bad talking* young man on a hike up a mountainside one day. We saw a farmer working a field some 300 yards below. My companion called down, "We yu da gro?" Note that my companion selected this basilectal speech for this unusual speech event; the hearer, not aware of my presence, would have been confused by acrolectal forms. What is significant about this event is that my friend pronounced *da* with a clear stop rather than with his customary affricated stop, and with a very low vowel rather than with his usual centralized vowel. He displayed for me his ability to manipulate basilectal speech in a very careful fashion. His communication across a great distance requires careful speech; his communication across a bottle of beer requires less than careful speech.

8. Patricia Nichols (1975) has presented evidence from Gullah to show that the pre-infinitival *fi* complementizer derives historically from a purposive construction. Since the original use of *fi* indicated purpose, purposive constructions in Gullah are the last constructions in which the form of the *fi* is varied. In her view *fi* variation is patterned, not so much because (+INCEP) verbs and (+DES) verbs favor replacement, but because (+PURPOSIVE) verbs inhibit replacement.

Nichols's analysis is more acceptable than Bickerton's for two reasons: (a) she recognizes that decreolization proceeds by a progressive replacement, with different degrees of inhibition, of Creole forms, rather than by a progressive acquisition of standard forms. However, Nichols's analysis presents a difficulty; she implies that historical factors account for synchronic regularities in decreolization, that is, that the etymology of *fi* in purposive constructions accounts for the greater inhibition of *fi* replacement in purposive complements. In general, it is not possible to use such historical evidence to support a synchronic analysis.

9. A number of different uses of the complementizer are not included in this particular analysis. The use of *fi* in "obligative constructions" (Washabaugh 1975:128–130) is not included since variations in its form is probably independent of most other factors. The uses of *fi* where "tense movement" (Washabaugh 1974:69–72) has applied are not included. Though "tense movement" does not directly affect the form of the complementizer, nevertheless the result of this transformation is that a tense morpheme is placed immediately before the complementizer. The form of that morpheme is the major constraint on the form of the complementizer. The use of *fi* in reduced relative constructions is not included here since the verb controlling the complementizer in reduced relative clauses is always deleted. Those cases where *fi* appears as a complementizer-preposition with a nonfinite verb as object (Washabaugh 1975) are excluded and so also are the instances where *fi* introduces adjective and NP subject complements. In both these latter cases it is difficult to determine the role of the matrix verb in constraining the form of *fi*.

10. The distribution of the frequencies used in this analysis-of-variance test, and in all other tests of variance in this study, was normalized by the arc sine transformation.

11. For 20 speakers *waan* was followed by $\emptyset$ with a mean frequency of .738 with a standard deviation of .274.

12. Controlling for the effect of *gwain* in tests for the significance of the (±FORMATIVE) constraint does not seriously affect the results of those tests.

REFERENCES

Bickerton, D. (1971) "Inherent variability and variable rules," *Foundations of Language* 7(4):457–492.

_____ (1973) "The structure of polylectal grammars," in R. Shuy (ed.), *Report of the Twenty-Third Annual Round Table Meeting on Linguistics and Language Studies* Washington, D.C.: Georgetown University Press.

_____ (1975) *Dynamics of a Creole System*. Cambridge: Cambridge University Press.

Bolinger, D. (1972) *That's That*. The Hague: Mouton.

Cedergren, H. and D. Sankoff (1974) "Variable rules: Performance as a statistical reflection of competence," *Language* 50:333–355.

Chen, M. and H. Hsieh (1971) "The time variable in phonological change," *Journal of Linguistics* 7:1–13.

_____ and W. Wang (1974) Sound change: Actuation and implementation. Paper presented at the Fifth International Conference on Historical Linguistics, Edinburgh.

Day, R. (1972) Patterns of Variation in Copula and Tense in Hawaiian Post-Creole Continuum. Unpublished Ph.D. dissertation, University of Hawaii.

DeCamp, D. (1968) "Diasystem versus overall pattern: The Jamaican syllabic nucleus," in E. Atwood (ed.), *Studies in the Language, Literature, and Culture of the Middle Ages and Later.* Austin, Texas: University of Texas Press.

Edwards, J. and M. Rosberg (1976) "Conversation in a West-Indian taxi," *Language in Society* 4:295-322.

Fasold, R. (1970) "Two models of socially significant linguistic variation," *Language* 46(3):551-563.

Hsieh, H. (1970) The Development of Middle Chinese Entering Tone in Pekinese. Unpublished Ph.D. dissertation, University of California at Berkeley.

_____ (1972a) "Lexical diffusion: Evidence from child language acquisition." *Glossa* 6(1):89-104.

_____ (1972b) On the bidirectionality of phonological rules. University of California at Berkeley, mimeographed.

Jakobovits, L. (1968) "Second language learning and transfer theory: A theoretical assessment," *Language Learning* 19(1):55-86.

Kiparsky, P. (1972) "Explanation in phonology," in S. Peters (ed.), *Goals of Linguistic Theory.* Englewood Cliffs, N.J.: Prentice-Hall.

Labov, W. (1972) *Language in the Inner City: Studies in Black English Vernacular.* Philadelphia: University of Pennsylvania Press.

Nichols, P. (1975) The *for*-complement. Stanford University, mimeographed.

Reber, A. (1973) "On psycholinguistic paradigms," *Journal of Psycholinguistic Research* 2(4):289-319.

Washabaugh, W. (1974) Variability in Decreolization on Providence Island, Colombia. Unpublished Ph.D. dissertation, Wayne State University.

_____ (1975) "On the development of complementizers in creolization," *Working Papers on Language Universals* 17:109-140.

Wilson, P. (1973) *Crab Antics.* New Haven: Yale University Press.

II
EXPERIMENTAL LINGUISTICS

5

Semantic anomaly: Linguists' intuitions versus interpretation in context

Maija S. Blaubergs
Kenneth H. Jarrett
University of Georgia

Early psycholinguistic investigations were based on a linguistic theory in which syntax was central and isolated from semantics, Chomsky's transformational generative grammar (Chomsky 1957). In these investigations, competence was central and isolated from performance, which was conceived of primarily as interference with the expression of the underlying competence. Years of investigation provided little support for the model of competence being tested, and the conflicting findings that emerged finally resulted in the recognition of the importance of semantics for a model of language (Greene 1972). Moreoever, several recent experiments have focused directly on the relative psychological reality of competence versus performance models. Baker and Prideaux (1973) found that error frequencies in transforming sentences were not related to a formal generative grammar but were related to a performance model. Ferris (1970) found that subjects judged sentences which violated Chomsky's selectional rules as permissible, that is, grammatical. Ferris argued for the transferral of selectional rules either to a semantic component or to a performance theory of language. Further, if linguistic rules are considered as providing a model of competence (and are viewed as productive), one would not expect the results Kypriotaki (1973) obtained in eliciting the pronunciation and pluralization of nonsense words: subjects were inconsistent in the strategies they used and generally unpredictable in their deviations from linguistically predicted responses. Finally, in a direct test of the compatibility of linguists' judgments with those of naive language users, Spencer (1973) found that naive subjects agreed fairly well with each other as to the acceptability of sentences but agreed with the linguists' intuitions regarding acceptability on only half of the sentences presented. Thus, there is considerable evidence from naive language users to indicate that there is little psychological reality to models of competence as proposed by linguists.

Several trends in psycholinguistics have emerged as a result. First, psycholinguists are focusing on the interaction between syntax and semantics (e.g., Hutson 1973). Linguistic theories have also emerged in which syntax is no longer central, for example, "generative semantics" (Lakoff 1971). Second, aspects of performance such as processing strategies (e.g., Blaubergs 1973) and individual differences in language acquisition (e.g., Ingram 1974) are being investigated. A parallel trend in linguistics involving variation in competence is the study of register shift and idiolects. Third, psychologists are formulating models of language which are not based directly on linguistic theory and which incorporate context as a central concept (e.g., Olson 1970; Schank 1972).

These three trends, comprising a shifting perspective in psycholinguistics, are discussed here in relation to the interpretation of anomalous sentences. In Chomsky's theory, anomaly was contrasted with grammaticality, as in the now classic sentence, *Colorless green ideas sleep furiously*. The semantic theory formulated by Katz and Fodor (1963) to accompany Chomsky's model was concerned with the identification of anomaly. A grammatical, but anomalous, sentence would be rejected in the semantic component as uninterpretable. However, to the extent that anomaly coincides with metaphor, several theorists have attempted to explain the interpretability of sentences identified as anomalous by linguistic theory. Bickerton (1969), Matthews

(1971), and Thomas (1969) all attempted to explain metaphor within the confines of transformational generative grammar. Bickerton suggested the "marking" of a lexical item to permit its metaphorical use; for example, *green* is marked for the attribute "fertile," and *thumb* is an agent of fertility whereas *ears* are not, and thus *green thumb* is a metaphor while *red thumb* and *green ears* would be anomalous. Matthews criticized the circularity of Bickerton's suggestion, that is, the metaphor has to be recognized before such marking can be determined, and the marking determines the item's availability as a metaphor. Matthews further suggests that given the proper context, almost any deviant sentence can be interpreted as metaphorical, for example, *green ears* is not anomalous in *The sailor's profanity curled the seminarian's green ears.* Both Matthews and Thomas suggest that metaphors break the same selectional restriction rules as anomalous sentences, but that in metaphor the violation is intentional and the sentence interpretable. Clearly, the model of language involved would have to include performance as well as competence.

Reddy (1969) is critical of linguistic attempts based on selectional restriction violations to explain metaphor. His criticism in part is based on his claim that even sentences with concrete, nonanomalous interpretations can be interpreted as metaphors in an appropriate context. Thus, in the explanations of metaphor that go beyond adapting a competence model to including performance factors, the interpretation of metaphor is related to context. In a model of language that combines syntax and semantics, competence and performance, the identification of anomaly may well be replaced by interpretability. Further, interpretability may well be affected by context.

Two pilot studies based on this viewpoint are presented below. In the first experiment the interpretability of sentences violating linguistic rules was investigated. In the second experiment the differing degrees of interpretability for the same sentences in different contexts was investigated.

EXPERIMENT I

In a previously reported study (Blaubergs 1974), 15 graduate students were asked to place each of 15 sentences into one of three categories. The three categories were identified as follows:

(A) Those sentences that don't make any sense at all, that cannot be interpreted, for example, *Procrastination drinks duplicity;*

(B) Those sentences that have a metaphorical interpretation or that can be understood by extending the usual meaning of some part of the sentence, for example, *The volcano burped;* and,

(C) Those sentences that may appear nonsensical, for example, *John thinks with a fork,* yet in appropriate context can be understood, for example, *How do you eat potatoes? John thinks with a fork.*

For the third category, the subjects were asked to provide an appropriate context that would make the sentence understandable. The sentences all involved hypothetical linguistic rule violations (selectional restriction and/or strict subcategorization rules). In over half the judgments (138/225), the anomalous sentences were classified as interpretable (categories B or C). Further, the results indicated that some subjects can interpret sentences that other subjects classify as uninterpretable and that linguistics classify as anomalous. Also, the contexts provided by different subjects varied. Spencer (1975; personal communication) has questioned whether or not such contexts might also vary in appropriateness for the same subjects.

The second study investigated whether or not subjects show agreement in the degree of acceptability of various contexts for the interpretation of linguistically anomalous sentences.

EXPERIMENT II

Eight sentences for which subjects provided contexts in Experiment I were used in this study. Thirty students, adults ranging in age from 17 to 45 years, none with any formal training in linguistics, were given a booklet of the eight sentences. Each page contained one sentence with five contexts for each sentence. Subjects were asked to rank-order the degree of interpretability that each context provided for each of the sentences. The contexts used included those provided by the subjects in the first study and additional nonsensical ones to insure that each group of contexts included at least one which was invalid. The results were analyzed using the Freidman Two-Way Analysis of Variance of Ranks. The F values for the eight sentences were: 88.43, 45.97, 64.08, 89.31, 73.39, 94.76, 76.85, and 55.79. For all sentences, the F was significant at at least the $p < .001$ level, indicating that for each sentence, subjects agreed among themselves as to the suitability of the contexts, ranking those contexts similarly. It may also be inferred from the results that a variety of contexts may aid in the interpretability of the same linguistically anomalous sentences, albeit to differing degrees.

GENERAL DISCUSSION

The findings of these two pilot studies as well as the recent trends in psycholinguistic research and theory converge on the proposed redefinition of anomaly as interpretability. The finding that anomalous sentences, that is, sentences which violate linguistic rules, may or may not be interpretable points to an interaction between syntax and semantics in processing language. Recent work on the interpretation of metaphor within the framework of linguistic theory is also increasingly incorporating semantic considerations. For example, Lambert (1969) formulated a case grammar analysis of metaphor and anomaly, and Frentz (1974) devised and tested models for the interpretation of metaphor that were based on some of the tenets of generative semantics. Consistent with the view that interpretability may be more salient to language users than anomaly, Lambert contends that anomaly occurs when a sentence cannot be interpreted either literally or as a metaphor.

The findings of the two pilot studies that naive language users differ in their judgments of the interpretability of anomalous sentences and coincide in their ranking of the appropriateness of various contexts for the interpretability of anomalous sentences point to the role of strategies and context in the processing of language. The variation found in Experiment I and in the

Kypriotaki (1973) study may be related to task demands: both tasks required some creative effort on the part of the subjects. The agreement among subjects found in Experiment II and in Spencer's 1973 study may also be related to task demands: in both cases subjects were asked only to make judgments. Although individual and universal strategies are of importance in a psycholinguistic model of language, task-specific strategies may or may not relate to language structure and processing. Clark (1970) and Shannon (1973) suggest a relationship between strategies used in certain tasks and in normal processing. Clark contends that language users use their knowledge of language in determining the strategies of response on word association tasks. Shannon looked for and found strategies used by subjects in the forced interpretation of sentences violating agreement rules and contended that these were the same mechanisms used in the interpretation of nondeviant sentences.

It may be then that the interpretability of both difficult-to-process sentences and linguistically deviant sentences involves a general cognitive strategy of searching for meaning that is used in specific unnatural language tasks and also in normal language usage. Further support for this contention comes from Fillenbaum's 1970 study in which he asked subjects to paraphrase deviant sentences. Other subjects rated the paraphrases as more sensible than the original deviant expressions. Fillenbaum interprets his finding as indicating that subjects have an ability to impose interpretations on syntactically and/or semantically deviant utterances. Similarly, Hörmann (1971) contends that the interpretation of anomalous or metaphorical sentences should be viewed as a light that may eventually come on, depending on the situation, the speaker's intentions, and the hearer's expectations. The strategy that he describes for the interpretation of anomaly and metaphor is one of taking notice of a particular connection. Thus, meaning is not the existence of a connection, but the event of discovering it. He contrasts this view with that of the Katz and Fodor 1963 model, which he describes as having a sentence-stopping alarm bell for anomalous sentences.

In conclusion, the findings and discussion in this paper are recognized as tentative. Their intent is twofold: to advance the psycholinguistic investigation of metaphor; and, more generally, to provide some basic considerations for the further development of psycholinguistic theories of language. To these ends, it is suggested that the construct of anomaly be replaced by that of interpretability, that interpretability be considered a cognitive strategy of searching for meaning, and that the role of context be further investigated.

REFERENCES

Baker, W. J. and G. D. Prideaux (1973) Grammatical simplicity or performative efficiency? Paper presented at the meeting of the American Psychological Association, Montreal; August.

Bickerton, D. (1969) "Prolegoma to a linguistic theory of metaphor," *Foundations of Language* 5:34-52.

Blaubergs, M. S. (1973) Processing strategies in tests of the content and structure of word meanings. Paper presented at the meeting of the Southeastern Psychological Association, New Orleans: April.

_____ (1974) "Semantic anomaly from a psychological perspective." ERIC document ED 098 790.

Chomsky, N. (1957) *Syntactic Structures.* The Hague: Mouton.

Clark, H. H. (1970) "Word associations and linguistic theory," in J. Lyons (ed.), *New Horizons in Linguistics.* Hammondsworth, England: Penguin.

Ferris, D. (1970) "Grammatical vs. lexical validity of selectional subcategories," *Linguistics* 57:5-9.

Fillenbaum, S. (1970) "A note on the 'search after meaning': Sensibleness of paraphrases of well-formed and malformed expressions," *Psychonomic Science* 18:67-68.

Frentz, T. S. (1974) "Toward a resolution of the generative semantics/classical theory controversy: A psycholinguistic analysis of metaphor. *Quarterly Journal of Speech* 60:125-133.

Greene, J. (1972) *Psycholinguistics: Chomsky and Psychology.* New York: Viking Press, Penguin Books.

Hörmann, H. (1971) "Semantic anomaly, metaphor and humor (or do colorless green ideas really sleep furiously?)," *Folia Linguistica* 5: 310-330.

Hutson, B. A. (1973) How abstract is a young child's knowledge of syntax? Paper presented at the meeting of the American Psychological Association, Montreal: August.

Ingram, D. (1974) "Fronting in child phonology," *Journal of Child Language* 2:233-241.

Katz, J. J. and J. A. Fodor (1963) "The structure of a semantic theory," *Language* 39:170-210.

Kypriotaki, L. (1973) Is language rule-governed behavior? Paper presented at the tenth Southeastern Conference on Linguistics, Atlanta: November.

Lakoff, G. (1971) "On generative semantics," in D. D. Steinberg and L. A. Jakobvitz (eds.), *Semantics.* Cambridge: Cambridge University Press.

Lambert, D. (1969) The semantic syntax of metaphor: A case grammar analysis. Ph.D. dissertation, University of Michigan.

Matthews, R. J. (1971) "Concerning a 'linguistic theory' of metaphor," *Foundations of Language* 7:413–425.

Olson, D. R. (1970) "Language and thought: Aspects of a cognitive theory of semantics," *Psychological Review* 77:257–273.

Reddy, M. J. (1969) "A semantic approach to metaphor." *Papers from the Fifth Regional Meeting, Chicago Linguistics Society.* Chicago: University of Chicago Linguistic Society, pp. 240–251.

Schank, R. C. (1972) "Conceptual dependency: A theory of natural language understanding," *Cognitive Psychology* 3:552–631.

Shannon, B. (1973) "Interpretation of ungrammatical sentences," *Journal of Verbal Learning and Verbal Behavior* 12:389–400.

Spencer, N. J. (1973) "Differences between linguistics and nonlinguists in intuitions of grammaticality–acceptability," *Journal of Psycholinguistic Research,* 2:83–98.

Thomas, O. (1969) *Metaphor and Related Subjects.* New York: Random House.

6

On the acceptability of particles in sentences to which indirect object movement has applied

John M. Clifton
University of Wisconsin–Milwaukee
and
Indiana University

Greenbaum (1975:1) states that

> there is now a body of evidence demonstrating that the methods of elicitation [used by linguists] may affect judgments (e.g., Greenbaum 1973, Elliot *et al.* 1974, Greenbaum 1976).

In spite of this, even the most cursory review of recent literature by transformational generative linguists reveals that most data is obtained through informal questioning. It is clear, then, that if linguistics is to be considered a serious science, more emphasis must be put on closely controlled data collection techniques. In

Many thanks to Sidney Greenbaum, for whose class this experiment was conducted and who helped both with experimental design and analysis of the results; Andreas Koutsoudas, who suggested Emonds's study as a possible area of research and discussed the results with me; Ray Green, who allowed me to use the Spanish classes to conduct the experiment; V. Susarla, who helped with the statistics, and Carla Garnham, who helped with computer programming and statistics. Needless to say, any remaining errors are entirely my own.

particular, this means that acceptability judgments obtained through informal questioning should be further tested under more rigorous conditions. The experiment described in this paper represents an attempt to do just that with a group of sentences analyzed by Emonds (1972).

1

Edmonds (1972) is primarily interested in providing empirical evidence in support of the claim made by Emonds (1970) that the rule of Indirect Object Movement (IOM) must be a structure-preserving transformation. In addition, the analysis is interesting because it makes use of the ability to have two identical rules apply in different orders in different dialects. The first half of Emonds's paper is spent attempting to show that particles like *up* and *down*, as in (1) and (2) below, are actually intransitive prepositions.

(1) Susan looked the number *up*.
    The police tracked the murderer *down*.
(2) Susan looked *up* the number.
    The police tracked *down* the murderer.

If this is indeed the case, Emonds argues, then the particle should directly follow the direct object in deep structure and a rule of Particle Movement (PM), given as (3), is needed to derive sentences like (2) from their counterparts in (1).

(3) Particle Movement (optional)

$$X + V - \underset{[-\text{PRO}]}{NP} - [P]_{PP} - Y \Rightarrow 1\text{-}3\text{-}2\text{-}4,$$

where 1-2-3-4 is a VP
(A noun phrase and intransitive preposition which immediately follow a verb can be permuted as long as the verb and everything following it constitute a verb phrase.)

In the second half of the paper Emonds examines a number of sentences like those given in (4), (5), and (6).

(4) The secretary sent the stockholders out a schedule.
Some student paid the bank back his loan.
He has brought Dad down some cigars.
Bill fixed John up a drink.
(5) The secretary sent the stockholders a schedule out.
Some student paid the bank his loan back.
He has brought Dad some cigars down.
Bill fixed John a drink up.
(6) The secretary sent out the stockholders a schedule.
Some student paid back the bank his loan.
He has brought down Dad some cigars.
Bill fixed up John a drink.

Apparently on the basis of informal questioning,[1] Emonds claims sentences like those in (4), where the particle is positioned between the two noun phrases (BNP) are in general acceptable (A) for all speakers, while sentences like those in (5) where the particle is positioned sentence-final (SF) are in general unacceptable (U) for all speakers. He further claims that for one group of speakers (Dialect A), sentences like those in (6), where the particle is positioned post-Verb (PV) are acceptable, while for a second group (Dialect B), they are questionable (Q). For all other speakers (Dialect C), sentences which, like the first two, have an underlying *to* indirect object, are acceptable, while sentences which, like the last two, have an underlying *for* indirect object, are not. These results can be tabulated as in (7).

(7)

| | Position of particle | | | |
| | PV | | BNP | SF |
	to IO	*for* IO		
Dialect A	A	A	A	U
Dialect C	A	Q	A	U
Dialect B	Q	Q	A	U

Since IOM has applied in the sentences given in (4), (5) and (6), the final section of Emonds's paper consists of determining the correct formulation of the rule. There are at least three ways in which IOM might be formulated: (1) the indirect object could be moved to the left so as to precede the direct object; (2) the direct object could be moved to the right so as to follow the indirect object; or (3) the indirect object and the direct object could be interchanged. Emonds demonstrates that the first formulation is inadequate as it predicts that sentences like those in (5) should be acceptable since they can be derived simply by applying IOM. Furthermore, he demonstrates that the second formulation is inadequate as it predicts that sentences like those in (4) should be unacceptable since there is no way to get the particle BNP once IOM has applied. However, the third formulation correctly predicts both that sentences like those in (5) should be unacceptable since there is no way to permute the particle and the noun phrase following it, and that sentences like those in (4) should be acceptable since they result from the simple application of IOM to an underlying form in which the particle is positioned between the direct object and the indirect object. The dialectal variation regarding the acceptability of sentences like those in (6) is also predicted if (as in the third formulation) IOM is limited to structures in which the direct object immediately follows the verb and rule ordering is allowed.[2] Given this final formulation of IOM, sentences like those in (6) can be derived by applying PM after IOM. However, if PM is applied first, IOM will not be able to apply since the direct object will no longer follow the verb. Thus, Dialect A can be obtained by ordering IOM before PM, Dialect B can be obtained by ordering PM before IOM, and Dialect C can be obtained by splitting IOM into two distinct rules, one applying to *to* indirect objects and the other applying to *for* indirect objects. Then *to* IOM could be ordered from PM, which could in turn be ordered before *for* IOM. Thus, the final form of IOM is as in (8):

(8) Indirect Object Movement (optional)

$$X + V - NP - (P) - \left[_{PP} \left\{ \begin{matrix} \text{to} \\ \text{for} \end{matrix} \right\} - NP \right] - Y \Rightarrow 1\text{-}5\text{-}3\text{-}\emptyset\text{-}2\text{-}6$$
$$\quad\quad\quad [-\text{PRO}]$$

(A noun phrase immediately following a verb can be interchanged with a prepositional phrase containing a *to* or *for* preposition, with this preposition being deleted.)

As Emonds notes, this formulation of IOM is structure-preserving in accordance with Emonds (1970).

An examination of Emonds's analysis shows how crucial the acceptability judgments are. For example, it is crucial that particles not be acceptable in sentence-final position, since there is no way to move particles to the end of a sentence. It is also crucial that particles be acceptable between NPs. In spite of this, Emonds does acknowledge that there are exceptions to each of these generalizations; for example, *back* seems to be acceptable in sentence-final position. However, he offers no explanation for this, claiming simply that the exceptions are "unsystematic and quite limited in number" (1970:557). The purpose of this experiment, then, is to determine under carefully supervised conditions the acceptability of particles in the three possible positions.

2

A total of 169 students from eight first-semester Spanish classes at the University of Wisconsin–Milwaukee were used as subjects. About 67 percent of the subjects were female, about 78 percent were freshmen or sophomores, and about 79 percent had lived in Wisconsin for most of their life. None had ever participated in any type of language experiment before and only two had taken even an elementary linguistics course.

The 32 test sentences used in this experiment are listed in Table 1. Sentences (a), (b), and (c) in sets 1–6 are essentially those given in Emonds,[3] while those in sets 7 and 8 were added to test the hypothesis that the relative acceptability of the particle in different positions is to some extent a function of the particle itself, with *back* showing a higher acceptability in sentence-final position than other particles do. In each set, the position of the particle is post-Verb in the (a) sentence, between NPs in the (b) sentence, and sentence-final in the (c) sentence. In addition, sentence (d) is a passive formed on the indirect object. The (d) form was added to test the claim that subjects speaking Dialect C accept passives formed on *to* indirect objects but not passives formed on *for* indirect objects.

The subjects were divided into three groups by class section.

TABLE 1. Sentences used

---

(1) (a) The secretary sent out the stockholders a schedule.
     (b) The secretary sent the stockholders out a schedule.
     (c) The secretary sent the stockholders a schedule out.
     (d) The stockholders were sent out a schedule by the secretary.

(2) (a) Some student paid back the bank the loan.
     (b) Some student paid the bank back the loan.
     (c) Some student paid the bank the loan back.
     (d) The bank was paid back the loan by the student.

(3) (a) John read off Mary the figures.
     (b) John read Mary off the figures.
     (c) John read Mary the figures off.
     (d) Mary was read off the figures by John.

(4) (a) A clerk typed out John a permit.
     (b) A clerk typed John out a permit.
     (c) A clerk typed John a permit out.
     (d) John was typed out a permit by a clerk.

(5) (a) Bill fixed up John a drink.
     (b) Bill fixed John up a drink.
     (c) Bill fixed John a drink up.
     (d) John was fixed up a drink by Bill.

(6) (a) He brought down Dad some cigars.
     (b) He brought Dad down some cigars.
     (c) He brought Dad some cigars down.
     (d) Dad was brought down some cigars by him.

(7) (a) He gave back Sue the tapes.
     (b) He gave Sue back the tapes.
     (c) He gave Sue the tapes back.
     (d) Sue was given back the tapes by him.

(8) (a) The teacher handed back the students the papers.
     (b) The teacher handed the students back the papers.
     (c) The teacher handed the students the papers back.
     (d) The students were handed back the papers by the teacher.

The first two groups, composed of three sections each, had 61 and 62 subjects respectively, while the third group, composed of two sections, had 46 subjects. The test sentences were presented to the subjects in one of three modes: oral; written and timed; or written and untimed. Six randomized orders were used. All testing was conducted over a two-week period during the subjects' Spanish laboratory session so that tapes with the sentences or timings could be played over the subjects' headsets. During the first week Group 1 received the sentences orally, Group 2 received them written and were timed, and Group 3 received them written and were untimed. During the second week, 34 of the subjects from Group 1 were retested, receiving the sentences written and being timed, and 48 of the subjects from Group 2 were retested, receiving the sentences orally. As the distinctions between the three groups do not seem to have any effect on the acceptability judgments as far as Emonds's analysis is concerned, they will not receive any further attention here.[4]

The subjects were asked to indicate the acceptability of each sentence by circling the number on a six-point scale corresponding with their judgment (where 6 indicated "completely acceptable" and 1 indicated "completely unacceptable"). A six-point scale was used because on the one hand it could be easily reduced to a three-point scale (1 and 2 = U, 3 and 4 = Q, 5 and 6 = A) for use in testing Emonds's reported acceptability ratings, and on the other hand it provided somewhat finer distinctions than Emonds used in case this proved to be significant.

3

As part of the analysis of the acceptability judgments, both intrasubject and intersubject consistency were measured. *Intrasubject consistency* refers to the consistency of judgments made by one subject on different occasions, while *intersubject consistency* refers to the consistency of judgments made by different subjects. Intrasubject consistency was determined for the 82 subjects who judged the sentences twice by comparing their judgments when the sentences were presented in the oral mode with their judgments when the sentences were presented in a written mode. The correlations are given in Table 2. In general, these correlations are quite low, with only two over 0.600.[5]

When intrasubject consistency is this low, intersubject consistency can be expected to be low also—one would not expect one subject to vary in his responses on different occasions, but have different subjects respond the same way in general. This

TABLE 2. Correlations between oral and written modes

(1)	(a)	.253	(3)	(a)	.492	(5)	(a)	.423	(7)	(a)	.355
	(b)	.588		(b)	.510		(b)	.515		(b)	.611
	(c)	.515		(c)	.357		(c)	.432		(c)	.346
	(d)	.377		(d)	.433		(d)	.541		(d)	.354
(2)	(a)	.357	(4)	(a)	.174	(6)	(a)	.333	(8)	(a)	.399
	(b)	.273		(b)	.462		(b)	.265		(b)	.353
	(c)	.484		(c)	.451		(c)	.540		(c)	.479
	(d)	.261		(d)	.454		(d)	.290		(d)	.688

expectation is borne out when, for example, the mean acceptability scores and their standard deviations are examined. As can be seen from Table 3, the standard deviations range from 1.28 to 1.74 with an average of 1.56. When this is noted in light of the fact that mean scores themselves only range from 2.50 to 4.93 (out of a possible range of 1.0 to 6.0), it becomes clear that there is considerable variability between subjects. This variability can also be seen by examining the actual acceptability scores, as are given in Table 4. These scores can also be

TABLE 3. Mean acceptability scores
and standard deviations

		M	SD			M	SD
(1)	(a)	3.86	1.66	(5)	(a)	3.00	1.52
	(b)	3.79	1.58		(b)	3.05	1.58
	(c)	2.93	1.62		(c)	2.50	1.45
	(d)	4.92	1.38		(d)	2.50	1.48
(2)	(a)	3.15	1.55	(6)	(a)	3.31	1.66
	(b)	3.94	1.58		(b)	4.25	1.52
	(c)	3.38	1.68		(c)	3.64	1.68
	(d)	4.93	1.35		(d)	2.86	1.61
(3)	(a)	2.76	1.53	(7)	(a)	3.02	1.55
	(b)	2.86	1.55		(b)	4.20	1.51
	(c)	3.15	1.59		(c)	4.89	1.28
	(d)	2.90	1.60		(d)	3.90	1.60
(4)	(a)	4.06	1.66	(8)	(a)	3.25	1.64
	(b)	4.23	1.62		(b)	4.62	1.45
	(c)	3.03	1.59		(c)	4.08	1.62
	(d)	3.98	1.74		(d)	4.75	1.42

TABLE 4. Acceptability scores by sentence

		6-point scale						3-point scale		
		1	2	3	4	5	6	U (1 + 2)	Q (3 + 4)	A (5 + 6)
(1)	(a)	18	28	20	29	41	33	46	49	74
	(b)	14	29	31	26	40	28	43	57	68
	(c)	41	43	24	18	34	9	84	42	43
	(d)	5	10	11	24	37	82	15	35	119
(2)	(a)	32	32	32	38	21	14	64	70	35
	(b)	12	28	25	32	37	35	40	57	72
	(c)	31	27	32	27	29	23	58	59	52
	(d)	4	11	10	23	41	80	15	33	121
(3)	(a)	47	38	30	24	23	7	85	54	30
	(b)	40	42	31	25	20	11	82	56	31
	(c)	34	32	31	33	25	14	66	64	39
	(d)	45	35	25	31	22	11	80	56	33
(4)	(a)	17	18	26	29	35	44	35	55	79
	(b)	11	23	21	25	39	50	34	46	89
	(c)	37	34	35	28	20	15	71	63	35
	(d)	22	19	23	26	35	44	41	49	79
(5)	(a)	33	38	40	23	24	11	71	63	35
	(b)	34	38	29	36	14	17	72	65	31
	(c)	54	46	26	23	14	6	100	49	20
	(d)	59	34	32	26	10	8	93	58	18
(6)	(a)	28	39	24	29	28	21	67	53	49
	(b)	8	23	19	30	47	42	31	49	89
	(c)	25	26	25	29	37	27	51	54	64
	(d)	47	32	28	28	19	12	79	56	31
(7)	(a)	37	33	34	28	26	10	70	62	36
	(b)	8	15	39	25	36	45	23	64	81
	(c)	3	8	13	32	38	75	11	45	113
	(d)	14	26	27	34	32	36	40	61	68
(8)	(a)	29	38	30	26	26	20	67	56	46
	(b)	8	10	19	25	47	60	18	44	107
	(c)	13	24	25	24	42	41	37	49	83
	(d)	7	8	18	27	40	69	15	45	109

collpased, giving the Acceptable–Questionable–Unacceptable distinctions made by Emonds. In examining Table 4, it becomes evident that there is considerable disagreement as to the acceptability of the test sentences. For example, even though 121 subjects judged (2d) as acceptable, 15 (almost 10 percent) judged it unacceptable. Likewise, although 100 subjects judged (5c) unacceptable, 20 (over 10 percent) judged it acceptable.

Although the measures discussed above indicate there is much variability in acceptability judgments for the test sentences, this does not mean that the results are simply an undifferentiated mass of indecision. For example, there are definitely different degrees of acceptability, with sentences like (1d), (2d), and (3c) being more acceptable than sentences like (2a), which is more acceptable than sentences like (3a) and (5c). More definite patterning can be seen when we examine how the three positions of the particle are judged in relation to each other for each verb complex. Table 5 gives this information in terms of the Acceptable–Questionable–Unacceptable distinction made by Emonds. Given that there are three possible positions for the particle (PV, BNP, SF) and three possible acceptability judgments for each position (A, Q, U), there are twenty-seven possible combinations for each verb complex. These are listed on the left-hand side of the table with the number for each, according to verb complex, given after it. In each case, the first letter represents the judgment when the particle is in the PV position, the second letter represents the judgment when the particle is in the BNP position, and the third letter represents the judgment when the particle is in SF position. Similar types of information are given in Table 6, which gives the relative acceptability of the particle in the three positions. The letters a, b, c down the left-hand column represent the (a), (b) and (c) forms of each sentence (i.e., with the particle in the PV, BNP, and SF positions). The greater-than ($>$) sign indicates that the position to the left was judged more acceptable than the one to the right and the equals sign indicates both positions were judged equally acceptable. Tables 5 and 6 give somewhat different information. For example, Table 5 differentiates between judgments of 5-5-5 (AAA) and 3-3-3 (QQQ), whereas Table 6 classifies both as a = b = c. At the same time, Table 6

TABLE 5. Collapsed acceptability of triads

	1a–c	2a–c	3a–c	4a–c	5a–c	6a–c	7a–c	8a–c	Total
AAA*	20	15	9	22	6	22	22	28	144
AAQ	14	7	2	19	3	10	3	9	67
AAU	11	4	3	16	4	5	0	2	45
AQA	5	1	4	2	4	5	4	5	30
AQQ	4	1	7	9	5	2	4	0	32
AQU	8	2	1	5	5	0	0	0	21
AUA	2	1	0	0	2	1	3	2	11
AUQ	3	0	3	1	0	2	0	0	9
AUU	6	4	1	4	6	2	0	0	23
QAA	7	13	3	4	3	10	18	19	77
QAQ	3	14	5	13	3	11	11	14	74
QAU	6	2	1	5	3	5	0	0	22
QQA	2	6	6	1	2	7	14	6	44
QQQ	7	14	14	11	13	8	9	11	86
QQU	13	7	6	11	14	6	5	4	66
QUA	2	3	4	0	0	3	4	1	17
QUQ	2	4	8	1	4	0	1	0	20
QUU	7	7	8	9	20	3	0	1	55
UAA	1	11	5	2	1	8	18	16	62
UAQ	1	3	2	2	5	6	6	6	31
UAU	5	3	1	4	3	11	2	13	42
UQA	3	1	3	1	2	6	20	4	40
UQQ	4	12	9	4	9	5	7	6	56
UQU	11	13	7	3	11	11	1	8	65
UUA	1	1	5	1	1	2	9	2	22
UUQ	3	4	15	4	7	10	3	4	50
UUU	17	16	38	14	32	8	3	8	136

*The first letter in this sequence refers to the judgment of acceptability when the particle is in the post-verb position; next, when it occurs between NPs; and finally, when it is in sentence-final position.

differentiates between judgments of 3-4-3 (b > a = b) and 3-4-4 (b = c > a), whereas Table 5 classifies both as QQQ. Finally, to show the tendencies in Table 6 more clearly, the relative acceptabilities are given with indeterminacies merged. For example, half of the instances of a = b > c are added to a > b > c and the other half are added to b > a > c. Theoretically

TABLE 6. Relative acceptability within triads

	1a–c	2a–c	3a–c	4a–c	5a–c	6a–c	7a–c	8a–c
All possibilities							
a>b>c*	24	11	6	17	14	7	2	2
a=b>c	26	13	9	40	15	12	8	15
b>a>c	19	11	8	20	12	22	1	13
b>a=c	14	31	13	20	20	23	10	22
b>c>a	11	16	6	8	12	14	18	25
b=c>a	9	25	14	13	13	20	31	32
c>b>a	3	14	18	2	3	14	45	10
c>a=b	6	9	23	6	9	16	21	15
c>a>b	5	3	11	0	2	7	9	3
a=c>b	4	7	12	0	10	6	4	8
a>c>b	10	1	8	5	2	5	2	0
a>b=c	18	11	12	19	27	4	1	2
a=b=c	19	17	29	19	29	19	15	22
Indeterminacies merged							
a>b>c	46	23	16.5	46.5	35	15	6.5	10.5
b>a>c	39	33	19	50	29.5	39.5	10	31.5
b>c>a	22	44	19.5	24.5	28.5	35.5	38.5	52
c>b>a	10.5	31	36.5	11.5	14	32	71	33.5
c>a>b	10	11	28.5	3	11.5	18	21.5	14.5
a>c>b	21	10	20	14.5	20.5	10	4.5	5

*The letter a in this sequence refers to the type of sampling sentence in which the particle occurs in the post-verb position; b refers to occurrence between NPs; and c refers to occurrence in sentence-final position.

this gives an idea of what the results would have been had subjects been forced to rank the sentences with no "ties" allowed.

4

Analysis of the acceptability patterning reported in Tables 5 and 6 makes it clear that Emonds's analysis, in which the SF position is always unacceptable, the BNP position is always acceptable, and the PV position is either acceptable or questionable, is far too simplistic. If Emonds's analysis were correct, we would expect a preponderance of AAU or QAU ratings in Table 5 and a preponderance of b ⩾ a > c rankings in Table 6. Perhaps the easiest verb complexes to account for are *read off* (3) and *fix up* (5), in which the particles seem to be unacceptable in any position. One possible explanation for these complexes is that they are marked as not being able to undergo IOM.

The other sentences seem to indicate that the possible positions for the particle depend to some extent on the particle itself. For example, *send out* (1) and *type out* (4) are both acceptable if the particle is PV or BNP, but not if the particle is SF. These complexes, then, follow Emonds's reports. However, while *bring down* (6) has a strong preference for positioning the particle BNP, the SF position is slightly favored over the PV position. Finally, *give back* (7), *hand back* (8) and *pay back* (2) are all acceptable if the particle is BNP or SF, but not if the particle is PV, with *give back* definitely preferring the SF position over the BNP position, directly contradicting Emonds's analysis. It is clear, then, that Emonds's analysis is grossly insufficient.

One other thing which must be accounted for is why we find the amount of variability concerning the acceptability judgments that we do. A possible explanation takes into account that the test sentences used are for the most part the result of the interaction of at least two optional rules, Particle Movement and Indirect Object Movement. Furthermore, both rules are restricted in the number of instances in which they can apply when compared with, for example, Passive, Topicalization, or Raising. Thus, the number of instances in which both could apply would be very small, and this would be a source of potential confusion not unlike when a person encounters a seldom-used irregular verbal form.[6] It seems fairly clear from informal conversations with subjects that normally when a person is confronted with a sentence containing both an indirect object and a particle, IOM is not applied. In this way, the confusion associated with the interaction of the two rules is avoided. When a subject is forced to judge the acceptability of sentences in which the two rules have interacted, then, he is unsure and variability ensues. This points up a danger for the linguist gathering data through informal questioning when the constructions in question are seldom used. Here the possibility of molding the data to fit a particular model may be particularly strong since the initial reaction of the subject will probably be one of confusion and any number of nonlinguistic factors, such as the frequency of the particular verb complex or the overall "sound" of the sentence, could play a large role in determining the acceptability judgments elicited. In any case, linguists certainly need to be more careful in their data collection.

NOTES

1. At least this is what Emonds implies. He gives no specifics on this point.
2. Although Emonds does not note this fact, rule ordering is not crucial to his analysis, as long as we assume the three dialects could differ in the form of IOM. Such an analysis could use the following three forms of IOM.

(i) Indirect Object Movement (Dialect A)

$$X - NP - (P) - \left[_{PP} \left\{ \begin{array}{c} to \\ for \end{array} \right\} - NP \right] - Y \Rightarrow 4\text{-}2\text{-}\emptyset\text{-}1\text{-}5$$
$$\quad\quad [-PRO]$$

(ii) Indirect Object Movement (Dialect B)

$$X + V - NP - (P) - \left[_{PP} \left\{ \begin{array}{c} to \\ for \end{array} \right\} - NP \right] - Y \Rightarrow 1\text{-}5\text{-}3\text{-}\emptyset\text{-}2\text{-}6$$
$$\quad\quad\quad\quad [-PRO]$$

(iii) Indirect Object Movement (Dialect C)

(a) $X - NP - (P) - [_{PP} \ to - NP] - Y \Rightarrow 4\text{-}2\text{-}\emptyset\text{-}1\text{-}5$
    $\quad\quad [-PRO]$

(b) $X + V - NP - (P) - [_{PP} \ for - NP] - Y \Rightarrow 1\text{-}5\text{-}3\text{-}\emptyset\text{-}2\text{-}6$
    $\quad\quad\quad\quad [-PRO]$

Given form (i), the particle would be acceptable in the postverb position (PV) whichever order the Indirect Object Movement (IOM) and the Particle Movement (PM) transformations were applied in. Likewise, given (iii, a), the particle would be acceptable PV whichever order IOM and PM were applied in as long as the indirect object was a *to* indirect object as required by Dialect C. Although not much research has been done into the universal ordering principles for optional rules in syntax, it appears that either Minimal Application (Iverson, 1976) or Stifling (Hastings 1974) would predict that both (ii) and (iii, b) would apply before PM, thus preventing PM from applying. Thus, the particle would be questionable in all instances in which it is PV in dialect B, and if there was a *for* indirect object in Dialect C.

3. The only difference is that Emonds has "*his* loan" in sentences 2a–2c while I have "*the* loan," as this seems much more natural.

4. For more information concerning the difference between written and oral scores, see Clifton (1975).

5. It may be objected that any such correlation would obviously be low since there seems to be some difference in judgments when the sentences are presented orally as opposed to when they are presented written. However, as long as this difference is regular, a high correlation is possible. Therefore, the correlation of oral and written judgments and differences between oral and written judgments are in reality two separate issues.

6. This confusion could arise from different sources depending on what analysis of variation is accepted. If we assume with Emonds that dialects differ in terms of ordering, the ordering must be learned language-specifically and thus would be a source of confusion. On the other hand, if we assume that the dialect differences are due to a difference in the form of IOM, it is possible that a subject is unsure of whether it would apply to a new type of construction. In either instance, it is possible that surface structure constraints may have much to do with the acceptability of a sentence.

REFERENCES

Clifton, John M. (1975) On the acceptability of particles in sentences to which indirect object movement has applied. University of Wisconsin–Milwaukee. Manuscript.

Elliot, D., S. Legum and S. A. Thompson (1974) Considerations in the analysis of syntactic variation. SWRL Educational Research and Development, Los Alamitos, Calif. Mimeographed.

Emonds, J. (1970) Root and Structure-Preserving Transformations. Unpublished Ph.D. dissertation, M.I.T.

_____ (1972) "Evidence that indirect object movement is a structure-preserving rule," *Foundations of Language* 8:546–561.

Greenbaum, Sidney. (1973) "Informant elicitation of data on syntactic variation," *Lingua* 31:201–212.

_____ (1975) Experiments on judgments of syntactic acceptability and frequency—Report 1. University of Wisconsin–Milwaukee. Manuscript.

_____ (1976) "Contextual influence on acceptability judgments," *International Journal of Psycholinguistics.*

Hastings, Ashley J. (1974) Stifling. Indiana University Linguistics Club, Bloomington, Ind. Mimeographed.

Iverson, Gregory K. (1976) "A guide to sanguine relations," in A. Koutsoudas (ed.), *The Application and Ordering of Grammatical Rules.* The Hague: Mouton.

7

The linguist as experimenter

Sidney Greenbaum
University of Wisconsin–Milwaukee

The December 1975 meeting of the LSA featured a symposium on experimental linguistics. The symposium may be seen as signaling the emergence of a new linguistic subdiscipline, analogous to field linguistics and computational linguistics in that it is primarily characterized by methodology and research tools rather than by linguistic content or theory. Indeed, we could consider experimental linguistics to be a part of field linguistics. If we wish to distinguish between the two, we could find a difference that to some extent parallels the distinction between anthropology and sociology. Experimental linguistics generally requires more sophisticated informants; it is also more congenial for the experimental linguist to be a native speaker—or at least a fluent speaker—of the language under investigation.[1]

Experimentation concerned with language and requiring human subjects is by no means new. Within linguistics itself we have the institutionalized field of experimental phonetics. For its experimental techniques and research tools it has turned to other disciplines, the choice largely depending on the subdivisions within phonetics: to anatomy and physiology for articulatory phonetics, to physics for acoustic phonetics, and to psychology for auditory phonetics. The research generally has only marginal relevance for linguistic theory,[2] though it of course contributes to our knowledge of the processes that occur when we speak and understand speech. Those processes are also central concerns for psycholinguistic research, and, indeed, much of the experimentation in auditory perception has been conducted by psycholinguists.

Psycholinguistic research since about 1960 has been strongly influenced by transformational generative grammar. Psycholinguists were excited to hear of a linguistic theory that purported to account for the speaker's tacit knowledge of his language, a theory that was "concerned with discovering a mental reality underlying actual behavior" (Chomsky 1965:4). They were stimulated to devise experiments aimed at finding correspondences between the formal properties of the linguistic theory and the encoding–decoding processes that occur in actual speech communication, hoping that they would in that way obtain proof of the psychological reality of features of the linguistic model. The resulting research has frustrated expectations of isomorphism between the rules postulated for the linguistic model and the mental operations in the production and recognition of speech. But it has given impetus to new directions of research aimed at revealing the systems that underlie these operations, systems in which linguistic and psychological factors interact. At this stage it remains unclear what relationship will eventually be found to obtain between the psycholinguistic model of language behavior and the linguistic model (cf. Levelt 1974: chap. 3; Fodor et al. 1974:367–372). At any rate, there is no longer the simplistic view that psycholinguistics takes its subject matter from linguistics and is merely concerned with testing the psychological reality of the linguistic model.

We might consider the relationship between the two disciplines from the reverse point of view. What is the relevance of psycholinguistic research to linguistic theory? Despite the claim by some linguists that linguistics is a branch of psychology (e.g., Chomsky 1972:1), few linguists are prepared to surrender the autonomy of their discipline. It has been suggested that psycholinguistic evidence can be used to select between competing theories (Derwing 1973:304-322, Fromkin 1975, Fodor et al. 1974:512f.). But I doubt whether linguists will abandon a particular linguistic formulation on the basis of such evidence, though they might flaunt the evidence to discomfort an opponent. To start with, a linguist confronted by psycholinguistic evidence could claim that the linguistic model is not intended to be a performance model. After all, the failure to find evidence for the psychological reality of transformational rules (Fodor et al. 1974:368) has not induced transformational generative linguists to discontinue using transformational rules in their analyses or to feel insecure about their use. Furthermore, the linguist can insulate his theory completely by denying that it is intended to account for a speaker's knowledge of his language. For example, he can retain a mentalist viewpoint but claim that his theory accounts for the speaker's ability to make judgments about his language (Bever 1970:341-348, Stich 1974). Or he can adopt a nonmentalist viewpoint and claim that his theory is about language as a cultural or social institution (cf. Ringen 1975).

The goals of experimental linguistics are basically different from those of psycholinguistics, though inevitably some individuals have interests that overlap both fields. Research in experimental linguistics is directed toward supplying a controlled source of basic data for syntactic and semantic analysis, a source that is intended to supplement, and provide a check on, the two other sources of linguistic data: the linguist's introspection and corpuses. In transformational linguistics, primacy has generally been given to the linguist's own introspection, when he is a native speaker of the language. The usual practice has been that the linguist creates from introspection a corpus that he believes to be relevant to the area under analysis; acting as his own informant, he concurrently evaluates what he supplies in terms of such notions as 'acceptability' and 'ambiguity'. Of course, part of his corpus may derive from examples that have appeared in linguistic publications and he may check his reactions informally with colleagues and students. It is obviously convenient for a linguist to draw primarily on his own introspection: it requires much less time and effort than collecting a corpus and extracting the relevant data or conducting experiments and analyzing the results. But convenience should not be the sole criterion in research.

The objection against relying on a corpus is by now well known. A corpus is necessarily limited in size and scope, and therefore cannot include all that actually occurs in the language, let alone the potentialities of the language. Some features of the area under study are likely to be absent by chance. If the linguist wants to generalize about the language, he cannot restrict himself to what appears in a corpus. However, what is not sufficiently realized is that the same objection applies—usually with greater force—to the corpus derived from the linguist's introspection. The linguist inevitably fails to evoke a complete sample of what would be relevant to the area being studied. Linguistic journals contain many examples of revisions in analyses because (it is claimed) the original analyses failed to take account of relevant data.[3] I am not suggesting that linguists should refrain from using their introspection. I am merely saying that serious studies should not rely on introspection alone for corpus data.[4]

The linguist similarly does not have a privileged status when he evaluates his corpus in his capacity as a native speaker of the language. On the contrary, his evaluations are suspect, for two reasons: (1) he has been examining over a period of time a set of examples exhibiting close similarities and therefore his judgments will tend to become blurred (cf. Fraser 1971:178, Carden 1973a:5, fn. 5); and (2) he is inevitably prejudiced by his general theoretical position and by the specific hypotheses he is testing (Labov 1972b:198f.). Linguists frequently disagree over the evaluation of sentences that are presented as crucial to a linguistic argument. The disagreements may merely reflect biases induced by different theoretical positions.[5] When the linguist begins to feel unsure about his judgments or when he suspects that his theoretical bias is influencing his judgments, he should feel the need to elicit judgments from other speakers of the language.[6]

However, it is also possible that the disagreements reflect genuine differences in the language of the linguists or at least genuine differences in their intuitions about the language. It has of course long been known that there are differences in language that correspond with the regional or sociological backgrounds of the speakers. More recently, we have been alerted to variation that cannot be associated with the locality or status of the speakers. Carden has referred to language varieties of this type as "randomly distributed dialects," as distinct from regional and social dialects (Carden 1973b). He has claimed that "at least some randomly distributed dialects are defined by an informant response pattern involving a number of constructions" (Carden 1973b:27–28, fn. 12). Notice that the randomness lies in the absence of any nonlinguistic features that characterize the speakers; it is claimed that the responses themselves are related systematically. It has been argued that linguistic theory should account for language variation as manifested in regional, social, and random dialects, and furthermore that a unified-analysis methodology will provide evidence for selecting between competing analyses that favor different single dialects (Elliott et al. 1969; Carden 1973a, 1973b; Legum et al. 1974). Just as we might wish to examine phenomena in a range of languages in order to confirm hypotheses about linguistic universals, so might we wish to examine phenomena in a range of dialects in order to confirm hypotheses about the grammar of the specific language. At the very least, it might be argued that we need to examine phenomena from random dialects of speakers with the same regional and social background if the grammar is to be neutral between speaker and hearer. Clearly, the introspection of the linguist is inadequate for this purpose. We then have to collect from samples of speakers instances of the phenomena being investigated, or reactions to the phenomena, or both.[7]

As what I have just said implies, the data that can be elicited from informants fall into two broad classes: (1) behavioral data, representing language use; and (2) intuitional data, representing judgments, attitudes, and reports about use. In both cases the raw data require interpretation before they can be used in language description.

Elicited behavior provides information that is not so easily or conveniently available in observed natural behavior or in written texts: data on what occurs in the language, on relative frequencies of occurrence, and on differences in occurrence of frequency that correlate with linguistic or sociological variables. Furthermore, elicitation can give us information on potential use: what we might use if the opportunity arises or the occasion requires. For example, if someone had occasion to intensify *interested, alarmed,* and *appreciated,* could he use *very* for all three? Or even if he never uses the adverbs *utterly* and *indisputably,* could he know where to position them if required to do so? The artificiality of the test situation may well affect elicited behavior. However, the most spontaneous language—ordinary conversation—is the most difficult to record systematically without the intrusion of an observer (Labov 1972b:209f.).

Procedures for eliciting behavior provide data that are at various approximations to the natural use of language. They range from tape-recorded interviews—the closest to natural situations—to manipulations of isolated sentences. In between we have elicitation of open-ended responses to a given situation or to a previous utterance (Wolfram et al. 1975) and descriptions of action pictures (Legum 1975). Types of tests involving isolated sentences include operation tests, where subjects are asked to perform a grammatical task on a sentence. The task may be merely a distractor: for example, the subjects are required to replace *I* by *We* in *I regard him foolish,* where the issue is whether they feel *as* to be necessary. Or the task may introduce a putative deviance, as when they are required to turn into a question the sentence *He will probably stay late.* In both cases, the interest lies in the changes that are made to avoid the linguistic problem. Examples of changes in those two tests might be the insertion of *as* in the response *We regard him as foolish* and the restructuring of the sentence as *Is it probable that he will stay late?* in order to avoid *probably* in a question. In a third type of operation test the task may force a selection between two or more variants, as in the requirement to make the verb present in *None of the children answered the question.*[8] The tasks are more restricted in forced-choice completion tests (Quirk 1970, Kempson and Quirk 1971) and in word placement tests (Greenbaum 1976). In a forced-choice test a pair of sentences is presented, each containing a blank. The blanks are to be filled with two alternatives, each to be used once only. For example, one test requires that the sentences

(1) They _____ the bacon.
(2) They _____ the bacon reluctantly.

be completed by the insertions *munched* and *chewed*. Varying the contexts isolates the factors that influence choices. In a word placement test, a word (or perhaps a phrase) has to be inserted in a given sentence. The purpose of this test is usually to elicit the normal position of a linguistic item.[9] The open-ended completion test presents a fragment of a sentence and asks for the completion of the sentence (Greenbaum 1970; Greenbaum, 1974b). The results can be used to elicit information on frequencies of lexical or grammatical co-occurrences. Analysis of the data can also suggest lines of investigation for determining co-occurrence restrictions.

In most cases where behavior has been elicited, judgments or attitudes have also been elicited, and sometimes a battery of various tests of both types have been conducted as a check on reliability or on interpretation. Certain types of intuitional data also provide information that complements what can be obtained from behavioral data: in particular, reports of use and of relative frequency of use. These parallel closely what the linguist can extract from behavioral data, whether in a corpus or elicited: of course, perceived use and frequency may not correspond with actual use and frequency, but then the samples observed or elicited may not correspond with the totality of actual use and frequency, either. Evaluations of acceptability are somewhat tangential to behavioral data, since in principal they allow for a conflict between use and attitude. Other types of elicited judgments are even further removed from what can normally be extracted from behavioral data: judgments about meaning (synonymy, ambiguity, paraphrase, implication, etc.; cf. Bendix 1966, Leech 1970) and judgments about syntactic relatedness, for example, judgments on whether sentences belong to the same syntactic type and judgments on the cohesion between parts of a construction (for the latter, see Levelt 1974:27-63). It is by no means clear what types of judgments are appropriately elicited from informants and what types more properly should be made by the linguist. For example, are initial reactions about structural relations or appropriate classifications dependent wholly or partly on linguistic training, perhaps even if it is only the rudimentary grammar training at the precollege level? At all events, we should recognize that the evidence from intuitional data must pass through an interpretation filter before it can be incorporated into a linguistic description. The notions and terms used in experiments are primitive and are interpretable only in the light of a linguistic theory. For example, acceptability need not coincide with grammaticality as defined within a particular linguistic theory (cf. Langendoen et al. 1973, Langendoen and Bever 1973); ambiguity can be distinguished from vagueness (Binnick 1970; cf. Lütjen and Rudolph 1975); and the meaning of meaning is notoriously dependent upon a theory.

A series of judgments may be elicited to explore and relate different aspects of linguistic intuition or to check for reliability through two or more types of measurement. Thus, combinations of questions have been devised for assessing the extent to which subjects can report accurately on the use of forms in other dialects (Labov 1973). Several investigations of acceptability judgments have required subjects to rate sentences absolutely on an acceptability scale and also to rank sets of sentences for their relative acceptability, partly as a check on consistency but also because the two types of responses convey different though overlapping information (Greenbaum and Quirk 1970:107-110; Greenbaum 1974a; Mohan, 1977; Snow and Meijer, 1977). We also know that the evaluation of a sentence can be affected by contrast with another sentence to which it is juxtaposed (Greenbaum, 1977b; cf. Bever 1970 and Levelt 1974:22-26). Divergent reactions to isolated sentences are perhaps due in part to the differing ability of individuals to recollect a matching variant or to their recollection of differing variants. Judgments of syntactic frequency scale ratings of individual sentences have been compared with judgments of proportional frequency for the same sentences when presented in pairs (Greenbaum, work in progress). Scale judgments of frequency have also been compared with scale judgments of acceptability for the same sentences (Greenbaum 1975). In a study of the functions of adverbs, subjects were asked to judge the similarity of meaning of pairs of sentences and also to evaluate the acceptability of sentences related to the earlier pairs (Greenbaum and Quirk 1970:102-106; cf. Greenbaum 1969a: *passim*). The aim was to find out to what extent the function of an item changed when its position was changed. For example, the pair of sentences

(3) Really, the students work during the term.
(4) The students really work during the term.

was presented in a similarity test and the sentence

(5) Really the students really work during the term.

in an evaluation test.[10] It was thought that the unacceptability rating of the sentence with two instances of *really* would in part be determined by the extent to which the co-occurrence of the two instances was felt to be tautologous.[11] Batteries of semantic tests intended to elicit related information are used in Bendix (1966) and in Leech (1970).[12]

There are essentially two procedures for eliciting judgments: the questionnaire and the interview.[13] I include under questionnaires both written and oral forms; the interview is necessarily oral. It is common for the interview to be given to individuals and the questionnaires to groups, but the reverse is possible and has been practiced.[14] The basic difference is that the interview allows for interaction between the investigator and the subject. The advantage of that opportunity is that the investigator can explain more clearly what he is interested in and ask ancillary questions, while the subject can elaborate on his response. A questionnaire could permit and encourage further comments, as for example in Leech (1970), but it does not allow for interaction. The advantage of the questionnaire is that it is far more economical of time and can be more rigorously controlled to exclude distracting variables and to ensure uniformity in treatment of subjects. Furthermore, the impersonality of the questionnaire is more likely to prevent the intrusion of the investigator's bias. The most sensible approach would be to use the questionnaire for large sampling and the interview for more intensive probing. The interview could then provide material for subsequent questionnaires with larger groups of subjects.

I have earlier suggested that intuitional reports require interpretation. Our theoretical assumptions will determine what validity we ascribe to the various kinds of reports and what use we are prepared to make of them. Questions can also be raised as to the accuracy and reliability of intuitional reports (Ringen 1975:22 and fn. 30) and as to the variables in the experimental situation which can distort responses (Greenbaum 1973b). Here is an area where psycholinguists can directly aid linguistic research. There is an urgent need for research into the psychology of linguistic intuitions, as Bever has pointed out (Bever 1970:341-348). Because of their training and interests, psycholinguists are particularly qualified for that area.

Intuitional reports may be inaccurate because the subjects cannot accurately articulate their intuitions. For example, an acceptability report is not identical with an acceptability intuition, just as a report of use is not identical with actual use. As has been said elsewhere, "We may have strong beliefs about the forms we habitually use and we may also have strong views about the forms that ought to be used; these may be in harmony or in rueful conflict, but—needless to say—our beliefs about our own usage in no way necessarily correspond to the facts of our actual usage. Furthermore, we may tolerate usage in others that corresponds neither to the forms we believe we use ourselves nor to the forms that we believe are the most to be commended" (Greenbaum and Quirk 1970:2f., and cf. Greenbaum 1970:15f.). I should add that our reports about what others use may also be mistaken.

The distinctions I have made between intuitional reports and actual use are not intended as a rejection of intuitional evidence. It is common for people to say (perhaps correctly) that they would never use a given variant but have nevertheless heard others use it and themselves see nothing wrong with it. Is there any justification for refusing to give the variant some status within the description of their language? And while perceived norms may contrast with use, they may also influence use. We may take account of them in using the language—at least in our more careful speech and writing, when we have a greater opportunity to monitor our use of the language.[15] Furthermore, normative attitudes may be a factor in language change (cf. Labov 1972b:chaps. 1, 5).

There have been relatively few studies aimed at isolating and correlating these factors. Labov has devised tests on socially significant variants in pronunciation which distinguish between what subjects reported that they used and what they thought was correct; an Index of Linguistic Insecurity was calculated on the basis of the difference between the two choices (Labov

1972b:117f., 132f.). When one of the variants stigmatizes the use as uneducated or as belonging to a less prestigious group, the scope for self-deception certainly increases. Labov's Index is valid for what it is intended to measure, but the self-reports may be inaccurate as data for actual use, since they may be biased in favor of the prestigious variant. Labov also used subjective reaction tests based on the matched-guise technique developed by Lambert (Labov 1972b:143–158). These elicited the subjects' evaluation of the social significance of a variable. Both of those studies contrasted a very few stigmatized and prestige pronunciation variants.

We can measure the reliability of a test technique by repeating the experiment (cf. Carden 1975). From this point of view, how reliable are experiments eliciting linguistic judgments? There are four possibilities of replication: (1) we can repeat the experiment with different subjects from the same speech community; (2) we can repeat it identically with the same subjects after a lapse of time; (3) we can repeat it with the same subjects but using different though strictly comparable material; (4) we can use the same material with the same subjects but ask for different measurements, for example, rating and ranking judgments. The first type of replication poses the problem, What is the same speech community? We know that there are random dialects among speakers of the same regional and social background; but we do not know how many dialects there are, nor (of course) how they are distributed. Differences between two populations in the range of response patterns could be attributed to the relatively small size of the populations. The three other types of replication experiments test reliability through intra-subject consistency. The last of the three has limited value, because different measurements elicit different aspects of a subject's judgment. However, it can provide a gross test of consistency. For example, it would be inconsistent if a subject rated sentence A as fully acceptable and sentence B as dubious but subsequently ranked B as more acceptable than A. The remaining two types are more useful tests of reliability. Unfortunately, there have been few replication experiments and no longitudinal studies.

The few identical replication experiments have produced mixed results. The best results for acceptability evaluations of single sentences have been 90–95 percent consistencies for replication within a 30-minute interval (Greenbaum and Quirk 1970:43–48) and 87 percent for replication within a 30-day interval (Carden 1973b:7). However, consistencies have been poor for pattern responses in experiments where these have been sought (Carden 1975). Further research should reveal what types of sentences evoke more consistent results than others and also what types of subjects tend to be more consistent than others.

Replications of the third type should be built into experiments as a matter of course. In syntactic experiments we are interested in testing utterances as canonical examples representing a sentence type or exhibiting a particular syntactic feature. Inconsistent responses to lexical versions of what is supposedly the same construction may indicate unreliable subjects, but they also invite further analysis of the material to reveal unsuspected syntactic differences or the intrusion of irrelevant lexical differences. In three experiments on judgments of acceptability and frequency that I conducted recently, the material consisted of 50 pairs of sentences. The sentences within a pair had the same lexical content but differed syntactically. The second 25 pairs were lexically varied versions of the first 25 pairs. For example, the pair *Marvin saw Susan—Susan was seen by Marvin* recurred as *Bruce called Jane—Jane was called by Bruce.* The first two experiments required judgments for each sentence on a five-point scale. The third experiment required proportionate judgments of sentences within a pair. Consistency on responses in the two versions was measured in two ways: absolute consistency, when the subject marked the identical position for both versions; and near consistency, when the subject marked either the identical position or the next position on the scale. For the scale acceptability experiment, overall absolute consistency was 51.5 percent and overall near consistency was 79.9 percent; for the scale frequency experiment, the corresponding indices were 44.3 percent and 79.1 percent; and for the proportional frequency experiment they were 45.5 percent and 77.4 percent. Consistencies varied considerably from sentence to sentence. For example, in the scale acceptability experiment, absolute consistency for individual matched sentences ranged from 31.1 percent to 76.1 percent, while near consistency ranged from 69.2

percent to 94.2 percent. This varying degree of consistency requires further investigation into possible differences between the sentences. However, the results are reasonably good if we adopt the weaker measure of consistenty (cf. Greenbaum 1975).

Factors in the experimental conditions and the test design may confound the results of experiments to elicit intuitional or behavioral data. Subjects cannot .be expected to perform uniformly if the instructions or the terms in which judgments are to be made are vague; lack of explicitness in the wording of instructions can later make it difficult to interpret responses (Greenbaum and Quirk 1970:28–32). The setting of the experiment and the subject's relationship to the experimenter inevitably affect judgments. Anyone who has informally asked for judgments knows that informants are eager to please (or sometimes to vex) the questioner. The hoped-for response can be conveyed unintentionally by paralinguistic or kinetic means. Even in more formal experimentation, subjects are influenced by the setting in which the experiment is conducted. An experiment was conducted at University College London to test this variable (Greenbaum and Quirk 1970:50–58). A class of English literature students was without warning confronted by two white-coated persons unknown to them, who asked for their cooperation in an experiment. The class was divided in two, one half remaining with the white-coated figures for the experiment and the other half moving to another room where two linguists from the department, who were known to the students, conducted the experiment. After the experiment the students were asked to write down what they thought the purpose of the experiment was. Most of the group remaining with the white-coated persons thought it had a psychological purpose, while most of the others thought it had a linguistic purpose. The two groups correspondingly differed in some of their responses. It is better to let subjects know that the experiment is concerned with language rather than have them guess—and therefore react variously according to their guesses. Other variables in the presentation of material that are known to affect responses include the position of a sentence within a set of sentences (Greenbaum 1973b), the influence of a preceding sentence (Greenbaum, 1977b), and whether responses are timed or self-paced (Legum et al. 1974). To avoid sequence effects the material should be presented in several randomized orders. Since subjects vary in the speed of their reactions and we usually want initial reactions, it seems better not to time subjects but to ask them to respond as quickly as they can. We should expect that the medium of presentation will sometimes have an effect, since a stylistic difference may be relevant or the choice of intonation may affect interpretation. Some studies of interpretation and acceptability have therefore presented the material both visually and orally (Carden 1973a; Mohan 1977). One experiment has revealed that the medium in which responses are given can affect the results: differences have been noted according to whether judgments are given orally or in writing (Davy and Quirk 1969).

The choice of subjects is important. An initial decision is whether to use linguistically naive subjects. A recent study (Snow and Meijer, 1977) has shown that linguists differ in several respects from nonlinguists in their acceptability evaluations: linguists tended to reject more sentences, and (perhaps related to that), they tended to be more consistent in their judgments as measured over sets of sentences exhibiting the same syntactic feature but differing lexically. The linguists also showed greater agreement with one another. As the authors of the study say, the higher reliability of the linguists can be explained in more than one way. Perhaps they have trained themselves to ignore differences that are irrelevant to the feature being investigated, though the exclusions may well be relevant to others aspects of language. Or perhaps they have learned to allow their linguistic theory to influence their judgments on unclear cases. If the latter is correct, then care has to be taken in using the judgments in favor of the theory, and naive subjects are certainly preferable. Among naive subjects there are many differences that can affect responses. As would be expected, studies have shown that differences in age, level of education, occupation, and socioeconomic class correlate with differences in acceptability evaluations (Mittins et al. 1970; McDavid and O'Cain, 1977; Svartvik and Wright, 1977; and cf. Labov 1972b:chap. 2).

The initial selection of the material to be presented to subjects is crucial. In acceptability experiments, contextualization of the part in question may produce different responses (cf. Bolinger 1968 and van Dijk, 1977). A sentence may be judged odd in isolation but may be accepted when suitably contextualized. Or all that may be needed to change the response is contextualization within a longer sentence. For example, the passive of *turn to* was felt to be deviant in *The girl was turned to* but was accepted in *The Prime Minister was turned to for help by people suffering from the depression in the northeastern industrial areas* (Carvell and Svartvik 1969:18). A subject's reaction will depend on how easily he can imagine a linguistic or situational context for the sentences. The material can be biased stylistically. There may be an initial bias through the medium of presentation, visual or oral. But there are also differences in the formality of the language and in indications of a register setting, such as scientific discourse or literature.

Relatively little research has been done on the factors that enter into linguistic intuitions. The relationship between judgments of grammaticalness, meaningfulness, and familiarity has been investigated, though apparently these terms were not defined for the subjects (Danks and Glucksberg 1970). Grammaticalness and meaningfulness were found to be independent dimensions, but familiarity appeared to be some function of the other two factors and perhaps of other variables. Use of imagery has been shown to be a factor in acceptability judgments: high imagery (concrete) material will evoke higher acceptability ratings than low imagery (abstract) material (Levelt et al., 1977). Evidence has also been found for a personality variable in acceptability evaluations: the *yea*-saying factor, the tendency of some individuals to acquiesce (Mohan, 1977).

My survey of current research in experimental linguistics has posed a number of problems involved in elicitation experiments. That is not surprising. Research in this field is in its infancy and therefore much is still unknown. There is plenty of scope for refining existing techniques and for developing new approaches. We should be aware that factors affecting subjects in an experiment can equally affect the linguist in his study, when he consults his own intuitions, and we have seen additional reasons for possible distortions in his reports. The linguist can no longer rely solely on his introspection. All too often the data in linguistic books and articles are dubious, which in turn casts doubt on the analyses. Since analyses usually build on the results of previous analyses, the effect of one set of dubious data left unquestioned can have far-reaching repercussions that are not easily perceived. I look forward to the time when all linguists will naturally turn to elicitation to support crucial arguments and when all Departments of Linguistics will have courses in experimental linguistics.

NOTES

1. See Samarin (1967:202–204). Generally speaking, the conditions under which elicitation experiments take place will be more rigorously controlled and more subjects will be required.
2. See, however, Fromkin (1975:59–63).
3. Botha cites a number of examples (Botha 1973:232–234, 255–257). Of course, there may sometimes be disagreement over whether the data are relevant.
4. At the very least, linguists should consult the major reference grammars and descriptive specialized studies. I repeat what I have said elsewhere: "It is regrettable that there has been a conspicuous and unscholarly tendency in recent years for linguists working in English linguistics to neglect the masses of data about the English language that have been compiled by traditional grammarians. As a result, erroneous generalizations are made that lead to unfounded theoretical claims" (Greenbaum 1973a:2).
5. For examples of disagreement between linguists on sentences that are crucial to major theoretical issues, see Botha (1973:178–184).
6. Leech (1968:93) similarly argues for a course "in which the validity of introspective data, in a limited way, is acknowledged, but is held answerable, in the last resort, to evidence of a more objective kind."
7. Sociolinguists have ascribed greater validity to corpus collection for investigations of language variation—more specifically, to direct observations of vernacular speech (Labov 1972a, Labov 1972b:chap 8). If we are interested in language as an instrument of communication, then natural conversation is a primary object of study. And if differences between varieties are not absolute but rather are signaled by systematic differences in the frequencies with which particular variables are used, then the primary source for the frequency differences will be collections of utterances and texts. Even so, we cannot rely solely on the data from corpus collections, especially for syntactic and semantic investigations, because it is only for very common constructions that we can be confident of finding sufficient evidence. According to Labov, reports on frequency of use are unreliable, at least for variables that differ sharply in prestige, because "naive perception of our own and others' behavior is usually categorical" (Labov 1972b:226) and therefore we tend to report that a variable is used invariably.

8. For operation tests, see Quirk and Svartvik (1966) and Greenbaum and Quirk (1970). Langendoen uses a selection test to elicit tag questions (Langendoen 1970).
9. The word placement tests have also been used to elicit possible interpretations indirectly (Langendoen et al. 1973).
10. Attention was paid to intonational factors that might affect interpretation of the functions.
11. The acceptability reaction would in part be affected by a stylistic objection to the proximity of two items with the same form. Tests were devised for sentences with a number of other adverbs, e.g., *certainly, frankly, luckily, often.*
12. For a critique of the tests that Bendix uses and of his interpretation of them, see Ariel (1967).
13. On the issue of interview versus questionnaire, see Carden (1973a).
14. Carden has used group interviews (Carden 1973a:8), and I have given tests to subjects individually (Greenbaum 1974a:245, fn. 3).
15. There are several possibilities: (1) we might impose a stylistic constraint, for example, avoiding *like* as a conjunction in writing; (2) we might avoid a set of variants because of dissatisfaction with all the possibilities, as when we replace *data* as subject by, say, *information,* because on the one hand we know that the singular is condemned by some as uneducated and on the other hand we consider the use of the plural to be pedantic; (3) we might overcompensate for possible errors by extending the use of a form to contexts where the original objection does not apply, as in the hypercorrective use of *whom* as subject. See also Labov 1972b:chap. 3.

REFERENCES

Ariel, S. (1967) "Semantic tests," *Man* (n.s.) 2:535–550.

Bendix, E. H. (1966) *Componential Analysis of General Vocabulary.* Bloomington: Indiana University Press; The Hague, Mouton.

Bever, T. G. (1970) "The cognitive basis for linguistic structures," in J. R. Hayes (ed.), *Cognition and the Development of Language.* New York: John Wiley.

Binnick, R. I. (1970) "Ambiguity and vagueness," *Papers from the Sixth Regional Meeting, Chicago Linguistic Society,* pp. 147–153. Chicago: University of Chicago Linguistic Society.

Bolinger, D. (1968) "Judgments of grammaticality," *Lingua* 21:34–40.

Botha, R. P. (1973) *The Justification of Linguistic Hypotheses.* The Hague: Mouton.

Carden, G. (1973a) *English Quantifiers.* Tokyo: Taishukan.

_____ (1973b) "Dialect Variation and Abstract Syntax," in R. W. Shuy (ed.), *Some New Directions in Linguistics.* Washington, D.C.: Georgetown University Press.

_____ (1975) Syntactic and semantic data: Replication results. Yale University. Mimeographed.

Carvell, H. T. and J. Svartvik (1969) *Computational Experiments in Grammatical Classification.* The Hague: Mouton.

Chomsky, N. (1965) *Aspects of the Theory of Syntax.* Cambridge, Mass.: The M.I.T. Press.

_____ (1972) *Language and Mind,* enlarged ed. New York: Harcourt Brace Jovanovich.

Cohen, D. and J. R. Wirth (1975) *Testing Linguistic Hypotheses.* Washington, D.C.: Hemisphere Publishing Corporation.

Danks, J. H. and S. Glucksberg (1970) "Psychological scaling of linguistic properties," *Language and Speech* 13:118–138.

Davy, D. and R. Quirk (1969) "An acceptability experiment with spoken output," *Journal of Linguistics* 5:109–120.

Derwing, B. L. (1973) *Transformational Grammar as a Theory of Language Acquisition.* London: Cambridge University Press.

van Dijk, T. A. (1977) "Acceptability in context," in Greenbaum (1977a).

Elliott, D., S. Legum and S. A. Thompson (1969) "Syntactic variation as linguistic data," *Papers from the Fifth Regional Meeting, Chicago Linguistic Society,* ed. R. I. Binnick et al., pp. 52–59. Chicago: University of Chicago Linguistic Society.

Fodor, J. A., T. G. Bever and M. F. Garrett (1974) *The Psychology of Language.* New York: McGraw-Hill.

Fraser, B. (1971) "An analysis of 'even' in English," in C. J. Fillmore and D. T. Langendoen (eds.), *Studies in Linguistic Semantics,* pp. 150–178. New York: Holt, Rinehart and Winston.

Fromkin, V. A. (1975) "When does a test test a hypothesis, or, What counts as evidence?" in Cohen and Wirth (1975), pp. 43–64.

Greenbaum, S. (1969a) *Studies in English Adverbial Usage.* London: Longman; also Coral Gables, Fla.: University of Miami Press, 1970.

_____ (1969b) "The question of *But,*" *Folia Linguistica* 3:245–254.

_____ (1970) *Verb-Intensifier Collocations in English: An Experimental Approach.* The Hague: Mouton.

_____ (1973a) "Adverbial *-ing* participle constructions in English," *Anglia* 73:1–10.

_____ 1973b) "Informant elicitation of data on syntactic variation," *Lingua* 31:201–212.

_____ (1974a) "Problems in the negation of modals," *Moderna Språk* 68:244–255.

_____ (1974b) "Verb-intensifier collocations in American and British English," *American Speech* 49:79–89.

_____ (1975) Experiments on judgements of syntactic acceptability and frequency—Reports I, II. University of Wisconsin-Milwaukee. Mimeographed. (Revised version forthcoming in *Studia Linguistica.*)

_____ (1976) "Positional Norms of English Adverbs," *Studies in English Linguistics* 4:1–16.

_____ (ed.) (1977a) *Acceptability in Language*. The Hague: Mouton.

_____ (1977b) "Contextual influence on acceptability judgements," *International Journal of Psycholinguistics*.

_____ and R. Quirk (1970) *Elicitation Experiments in English: Linguistic Studies in Use and Attitude*. London: Longman; also Coral Gables, Fla.: University of Miami Press.

Kempson, R. M. and R. Quirk (1971) "Controlled activation of latent contrast," *Language* 47:548–572.

Labov, W. (1972a) "Some principles of linguistic methodology," *Language and Society* 1:97–120.

_____ (1972b) *Sociolinguistic Patterns*. Philadelphia: University of Pennsylvania Press.

_____ (1973) "Where do Grammars Stop?" in R. W. Shuy (ed.), *Report on the 23rd Annual Round Table Meeting on Languages and Linguistics*. Washington, D.C.: Georgetown University Press.

Langendoen, D. T. (1970) *Essentials of English Grammar*. New York: Holt, Rinehart and Winston.

_____ and T. G. Bever (1973) "Can a not unhappy person be called a not sad one?" in S. Anderson and P. Kiparsky (eds.), *A Festschrift for Morris Halle*, pp. 392–409. New York: Holt, Rinehart and Winston.

_____, N. Kalish-Landon and J. Dore (1973) "Dative questions: A study in the relation of acceptability to grammaticality of an English sentence type," *Cognition* 2:451–478.

Leech, G. N. (1968) "Some assumptions in the metatheory of linguistics," *Linguistics* 39:87–102.

_____ (1970) "On the theory and practice of semantic testing," *Lingua* 24:343–364.

Legum, S. E. (1975) Some child language and sociolinguistic constraints on linguistic metatheory. Paper given at LSA meeting, San Francisco.

_____, D. E. Elliott and S. A. Thompson (1974) Considerations in the analysis of syntactic variation. SWRL Educational Research and Development. Los Alamitos, Calif. Mimeographed.

Levelt, W. J. M. (1974) *Formal Grammars in Linguistics and Psycholinguistics*, vol. 3. The Hague: Mouton.

_____, J. A. W. M. Gent, A. F. Haans and A. J. A. Meijers (1977) "Grammaticality, paraphrase, and imagery," in Greenbaum (1977).

Lütjen, H. P. and K. Rudolph (1975) "Another note on *becoming*: A pilot study in ambiguity and vagueness," *Linguistiche Berichte* 40:1–25.

McDavid, R. I., Jr., and R. K. O'Cain (1977) "Prejudice and pride: Linguistic acceptability in South Carolina," in Greenbaum (1977a).

Mittins, W. H., M. Salu, M. Edminson and S. Coyle (1970) *Attitudes to English Usage*. London: Oxford University Press.

Mohan, B. A. (1977) "Acceptability testing and fuzzy grammar," in Greenbaum (1977a).

Quirk, R. (1970) "Aspect and variant inflexion in English verbs," *Language* 46:300–311.

_____ and J. Svartvik (1966) *Investigating Linguistic Acceptability.* The Hague: Mouton.

Ringen, J. D. (1975) "Linguistic facts: A study of the empirical scientific status of transformational generative grammars," in Cohen and Wirth (1975).

Samarin, W. J. (1967) *Field Linguistics.* New York: Holt, Rinehart and Winston.

Snow, C. and G. Meijer (1977) "On the secondary nature of syntactic intuitions," in Greenbaum (1977a).

Stich, S. P. (1975) "Competence and indeterminacy," in Cohen and Wirth (1975).

Svartvik, J. and D. Wright (1977) "The use of *ought* in teenage English," in Greenbaum (1977a).

Wolfram, W., R. Montes, P. Griffin and M. Wertz (1975) Extending a corpus: Language games for analyzing pragmatics. Paper given at LSA meeting, San Francisco.

8

On evaluating data concerning linguistic intuition

Jon D. Ringen
Indiana University at South Bend

INTRODUCTION

Noam Chomsky asserts that linguists have at their disposal an "enormous mass of unquestionable data concerning the linguistic intuition of the native speaker (often, himself)" (1965:20; see also 1961:225). Contemporary transformational generative linguists recommend the use of such data in *evaluating* transformational generative grammars and theories of language, and they repeatedly emphasize the importance of such data in the development of linguistic science. Indeed, Chomsky asserts that to neglect such data would be to "condemn the study of language to utter sterility" (1965:195; see also 1964:79).

To some critics, the practice of relying heavily on data concerning linguistic intuition has made transformational linguistics seem a scientific anomaly. According to these critics,

This work was supported in part by grant SOC 75-13423 from the National Science Foundation.

145

transformationalist methodology is scientifically suspect because data concerning linguistic intuition is subjective data, which is at best extremely unreliable and at worst putative data whose reliability cannot be assessed even in principle. Since the reliability of data must at least be in principle checkable, and since scientific data must be reliable data, if the critics are right, then transformational linguistics is indeed an anomaly.

There is a second facet of current linguistic practice which makes transformationalists' use of linguistic intuition seem to be a scientific anomaly. In fields like physics and chemistry, research training normally includes both considerable exposure to *methods* likely to produce reliable data and considerable training in the evaluation of the reliability and validity of data reported by others. At least two benefits accrue to fields in which such training is common. First, when conflicting data reports occur in the literature, there is little confusion about what procedures should be used to determine which of the conflicting reports is most reliable. Second, if the reported data bear on important substantive issues in the field, little time is lost in actually determining which of the conflicting reports is, in fact, most reliable.

These two aspects of normal practice in physics and chemistry seem to be absent from current linguistic practice. Whatever training contemporary transformationalists have had, the training has not induced many of them to attempt to assess the relative reliability of conflicting reports of linguistic intuition.[1] Yet linguists assert that data concerning linguistic intuition serve the same function and have essentially the same status as data in sciences like physics and chemistry.[2] In the face of such assertions, some explanation is needed for transformationalists' apparent failure to use or even to develop methods for assessing the reliability of data concerning linguistic intuition.

The explanation of this apparent failure and the inconclusiveness of discussions of the subjectivity of intuitive data turn out to be closely related. I submit that they both result from a fundamental lack of clarity about how (data concerning) linguistic intuition ought to be described and understood. In what follows, I will show how lack of clarity about the nature of intuitive data necessarily leads to confusion about whether, and if so, how, the reliability and validity of such data can be assessed. Clarification of *what linguistic intuitions are* is a first step in determining how the reliability of linguistic data can be assessed. What follows is an attempt to begin such clarification.

1. LINGUISTIC INTUITION, CLASSICAL PSYCHOPHYSICS, AND INTROSPECTIVE PSYCHOLOGY

As described by Chomsky (e.g., 1961:223; 1962:531; also Bach 1964:4), data concerning linguistic intuition are reports of native speaker (informant) judgments about properties of, or relations among, expression tokens (i.e., utterances or inscriptions). The data might include reports of (a) judgments that certain expression tokens are acceptable, grammatical, or ambiguous, (b) judgments that certain *sets* of expression tokens are synonymous or representative of some sentence type (or that they are not synonymous or are representative of different sentence types), and so on. Chomsky calls such data "introspective data" (1965:193–194) and claims that it is comparable to the reports of subjective judgments used as data in psychophysics (1961:225). Chomsky's remarks suggest that, on his view, either the data of introspective psychology or the data of psychophysics might serve as appropriate models for data concerning linguistic intuition. In what follows, I will consider whether Chomsky's view is defensible. That is, I will consider whether data concerning linguistic intuition is, in fact, fundamentally similar to data gathered in psychophysics or introspective psychology.

Traditionally, psychophysics and introspective psychology have both been "mentalistic" approaches to psychology. In both disciplines, verbal responses of experimental subjects have been treated as data concerning the subject's own mental states. Classical psychophysicists (such as G. Fechner) and classical introspective psychologists (such as W. Wundt and his student E. B. Titchener) seem to have thought that the mental states of concern to their disciplines were entities to which each person had access only in his own case. Further, Wundt and Titchener explicitly argue that this "privileged access"[3] of each person to his own mental states necessitates the use of introspective observation in gathering data about human mental processes. Wundt and Titchener explicitly set out to develop a methodology which would yield reliable introspective data.

It is now widely recognized that the Wundtian conception of introspective data is fundamentally incoherent. The difficulty is this: on Wundt's view, experimental subjects were reporting about the characteristics of logically private mental states, but, as discussions of Wittgenstein's (1953) "private language" argument make abundantly clear, putative "reports" about characteristics of private entities are *in principle* uncheckable. Hence, Wundt's introspective data could not count as data at all.

I think that the moral of this story is very clear. If linguistic intuitions are treated as logically private entities, assessment of the reliability of intuitive data is, in principle, impossible. If there is to be any hope of developing a principled methodology for assessing data concerning linguistic intuition, linguists must reject any view according to which linguistic intuitions are mental entities to which each speaker/informant has privileged access.[4]

From this negative conclusion, it *does not* follow that it is scientifically illegitimate to use intuitive linguistic data, nor does it follow that such data cannot properly be called introspective data or cannot properly be compared with data in psychophysics. The private-language argument simply puts constraints on what introspective data could legitimately be. Data must be checkable, putative reports of private entities are not checkable, and hence, introspective data cannot be about states to which each person has privileged access.

2. LINGUISTIC INTUITIONS AS DATA

Many critics of transformationalist methodology have asserted that the reliability of (at least certain) data concerning linguistic intuitions is *in principle* uncheckable (e.g., Labov 1972b: 106–107). If linguistic intuitions are treated as mental entities to which only the owner has access, then these critics are certainly right, and their criticisms locate a serious flaw in transformational methodology.

Transformationalists' lack of concern with this line of criticism suggests that either they are seriously confused about the nature of scientific data, or they really don't think data concerning linguistic intuition are scientific data, or they think the reliability of intuitive data is in principle checkable. Of these alternatives, the last is the most charitable, and hence in the absence of conclusive evidence to the contrary, I will assume that it constitutes the view that most linguists hold. It follows that linguists cannot treat linguistic intuitions as logically private entities and that one possible objection to transformationalist methodology can be raised concerning the scientific respectability of current linguistic practice. Even if the reliability of intuitive data are, in principle, checkable, appropriate procedures/methods for actually assessing their reliability must still be identified and described. And, of course, from assertions that assessment of linguistic data is possible, in principle, nothing whatsoever follows about what methods should actually be used.[5]

Current literature provides little assistance in determining what kinds of methods of assessment would be appropriate. Determining what kinds of methods of assessment would be appropriate requires some specification of the kind of evidence relevant to assessing the data in question. That in turn requires a relatively clear conception of the nature of the data to be assessed. I know of no systematic discussion of the nature of data concerning linguistic intuition,[6] but one of Chomsky's early suggestions provides a useful place to begin with such a discussion.

In his 1961 paper, "Some methodological remarks on generative grammar," Chomsky asserts that refusal to use data concerning linguistic intuition would

> eliminate linguistics as a discipline, just as surely as a refusal to consider what a subject senses or perceives would destroy psychophysics. (1961:225)

Chomsky asserts:

> In both cases, [i.e., linguistics and psychophysics] we are trying (though in very different ways) to find a basis for intuitive judgments. In both cases, furthermore, the difficulty of obtaining reliable and relevant reports is quite apparent. (1961:225)

This passage suggests that the difficulties to be expected in assessing intuitive linguistic data are like those encountered by psychophysicists in assessing the subjective judgments of their experimental subjects. It also suggests that reports of subjective responses in psychophysics can serve as a useful model for data concerning linguistic intuition. In the remainder of this paper, I want to explore those suggestions.

3. LINGUISTICS AND PSYCHOPHYSICS: SOME SIMILARITIES

Psychophysicists employ a wide variety of experimental methods, and it would be impossible to adequately discuss even a representative sample of these methods here. However, such experimental methods share a number of fundamental features which can be easily described.[7]

A simple psychophysical experiment may involve only two participants: an experimenter (E) and an experimental subject (S). In a typical psychophysical experiment, E presents S with a stimulus (or stimulus situation) whose variations can be described by physical dimensions. The precise physical dimensions of the stimuli to be presented by E are measured and recorded. S is instructed to make some response to the stimuli presented. E presents the stimuli, S responds, and E records the response made by S.

An experiment may involve only a single object or it may involve a large number of subjects. The stimuli presented may be more or less complex, the only restriction being that the magnitude of the stimuli be measurable along some physical dimension. The subject's response may or may not be verbal. I want to focus on a case where a verbal response is made by S.

In one psychophysical experiment, E presents S with two metal objects whose weights have been carefully measured and recorded. One weight is placed in S's left hand and the other in his right hand. S is instructed to report whether he judges the two objects to be equal in weight, or, if he judges the objects to be of unequal weight, to report which of the two objects he judges to be heavier. A record of S's response could be presented as follows:

I. S_1 said, "I judge the weight in my left hand to be heavier."

Such a record constitutes part of the data gathered in psycho-physical experiments. I assume this is the kind of data which Chomsky had in mind when he first suggested a parallel between linguists' use of linguistic intuition and psychophysicists' use of subjective judgments about physical magnitudes. Thus, a careful linguist might record something like the following:

II. I(nformant)$_1$ said, "I judge T [a specific expression token] to be ambiguous."

So construed, the data of psychophysics and that concerning linguistic intuition exhibit at least two similarities. First, they are records of responses to stimuli presented. In psychophysics, they are records of S's responses to measured physical stimuli presented by E. In linguistics they are records of informant responses to expression tokens presented by the linguist. In addition, both kinds of data take the same form. They are records of sentences uttered by an informant (or experimental subject), and the subject in the sentence uttered is a first-person pronoun. Thus, the data consist of records of "first-person sentences" uttered by the informant or experimental subject in question.

There are a number of quite different questions that can be asked about the reliability and validity of psychophysical data of the sort I have illustrated. Reflecting on which, if any, of these questions can appropriately be asked about data concerning linguistic intuition sheds considerable light on how linguistic data and psychophysical data differ.

4. THE RELIABILITY OF LINGUISTIC AND PSYCHOPHYSICAL DATA: SOME QUESTIONS

The most obvious (and probably the least interesting) question which can be asked about the reliability of psychophysical data concerns the trustworthiness of E's record of S's response. Simply put, the question is:

(1) Did S make the response/utter the sentence which E recorded?

This question and similar questions about the trustworthiness of an investigator's records are of obvious relevance in both linguistics and psychophysics. Data *should* consist of reports of phenomena which actually occurred. Methods for assessing this kind of reliability necessarily involve assessing an investigator's integrity and perceptiveness, but they also require assessing possible effects of (unconscious) experimenter bias (cf. Rosenthal 1963). Labov describes a simple procedure for minimizing the effect of experimenter bias when he draws "the painfully obvious conclusion" that "linguists cannot continue to produce data and theory at the same time" (Labov 1972a:199). It is something of a mystery why this conclusion has been so seldom reflected in current linguistic practice.

At least two further questions can be asked about the reliability of the kind of psychophysical data exemplified in I. The questions can be stated as follows:

(2) Does S's utterance correctly describe the judgment S actually made? (Or, more generally, is S's response a reliable indicator of what his judgment actually was?)
(3) Is S's judgment correct? (Or, more generally, how accurate is S's judgment?)

Both of these questions are, in fact, asked about psychophysical data, and if psychophysical data are, in fact, records of *judgments* reported by experimental subjects, it must be the case that both questions can be appropriately asked. The reasons that the questions must be appropriate are quite straightforward: (a) it is a conceptual truth that *judgments* are actions whose correctness can (at least in principle) be objectively assessed, and (b) it is also a conceptual truth that *reports* are statements whose veracity (truth or falsity) can (at least in principle) be objectively ascertained. Reflection on how psychophysicists might check the veracity and correctness of an experimental subject's reports suggests two quite different models for data concerning linguistic intuition, and it raises serious questions about whether responses of linguistic informants can legitimately be treated as expressions of intuitive *judgments*.

As I have described psychophysical data, the response of an experimental subject is a type of first-person report. It is the subject's report of a judgment he made. At the very least, assessing the *veracity* of such a report requires determining whether the subject was lying or whether he misspoke in describing his judgment. Assessing these characteristics of a subject's actions is (at least in principle) unproblematic, and we make such assessments quite frequently. The specific details of how such assessments could be made are irrelevant to my present purpose. I want only to make a simple conceptual point. The conceptual point is this: if one is interested in the veracity of an utterance, one needs to know more than whether the utterance occurred or not. In addition, one needs to know *at least* whether the utterance was carefully and sincerely made (i.e., made so as to avoid misspeaking or lying). Thus, questions (1) and (2) are importantly different. They reflect one difference between treating a person's utterance simply as a verbal response and treating it as a report.

Some philosophical psychologists have recently argued that assessing the veracity of a certain class of first-person reports requires *only* determining whether they were carefully and sincerely made by a competent language user. The class of reports in question consists of a person's reports about (at least some) of his own mental states. Sensations (like pain) and after-images constitute paradigm cases of the kinds of mental states in question. It is argued that people have "final epistemic authority"[8] with respect to reports of such mental states of their own. The view that a person has final epistemic authority about certain of his own mental states is simply the view that the sincere, careful, first-person reports of a competent language user constitute the weightiest evidence another person can have about certain states of the speaker's mind. A person's reports of (for example) his own pains *can* be shown by others to be false or mistaken. The speaker can be shown to be lying, to have misspoken, or to be incompetent in using parts of the language (or, perhaps, even to be deceiving himself). Since there are objective ways of determining these things, speakers do not have "privileged access" to their mental states, and first-person reports about which a speaker has final epistemic authority are not subject to the charge that their veracity is in principle uncheckable. Nevertheless, for those mental states/reports about which people are said to have final epistemic authority, once it is determined that a first-person report was made sincerely, by a competent language user, there is no other evidence strong enough to show the speaker's assertion to be false.[9]

There are two reasons for noting this feature of first-person reports about sensations and afterimages. First, a person's utterances about his own sensations (and afterimages) can be treated as reports, and hence assessing data concerning such reports involves more than assessing data concerning mere (verbal) behavioral responses. To assess the latter kind of data only question (1) needs to be addressed. Assessing the former kind of data requires addressing both question (1) and question (2).

The difference between reports and mere verbal responses points to some questions concerning the assessment of intuitive linguistic data, and this is the second reason for displaying the difference. We can ask at least two rather fundamental questions:

(4) Are informant responses appropriately treated simply as utterances whose veracity need not be assessed, or should such responses be treated as some kind of report?

(5) If informant responses can be appropriately treated as a kind of first-person report, then should they be treated simply as reports about mental states like sensations and afterimages or should they be treated as reports of judgments?

Mentalistic linguists are, I think, committed to treating an informant's responses as reports of his own mental states, but it has never been made clear what kind of mental states are involved. Frequently (see p. 147 above), data concerning linguistic intuition are described as reports of informant *judgments*. But judgments are quite different from afterimages or sensations. It makes no sense to discuss the *correctness* of an afterimage or sensation, but a mental state cannot be a judgment unless its correctness can be assessed. We can ask whether linguistic intuitions are more appropriately compared with judgments or with mental states like sensations.

If linguistic intuitions are appropriately compared with sensations, then assessing the reliability of data concerning linguistic intuition requires addressing both questions (1) and (2). But question (3) could not even be raised about such data. On the other hand, if linguistic intuitions are judgments, then linguistic intuitions must be the kinds of mental states about which question (3) can be raised. Answering question (3) requires some procedure of assessment which is independent of the report of the person whose judgment is being assessed. Even if one does have final epistemic authority about *what his own judgments are,* he has no such status with respect to whether his judgments are correct. If a linguistic informant can be said to be reporting a *judgment,* then it must be (in principle) possible to specify objective procedures/criteria in light of which the *correctness* of the judgment can be assessed. The model provided by psychophysics clearly illustrates what is at issue here.

A primary aim of psychophysical investigations is to discover and precisely describe the relationships which obtain between the objectively determinable physical dimensions of stimuli and "subjective" judgments/estimates of the magnitudes of those dimensions. Thus, psychophysical methodology is essentially concerned with actually *measuring* disparaties between judgments reported by experimental subjects and the objective/ physical states of affairs about which judgments are made. In a psychophysical experiment, not only is the subject asked to judge whether the weight in his right hand is heavier than that in his left, but the weights are weighed to determine which of the two is, in fact, heavier. The availability and use of such weighing procedures indicate that psychophysical data *can* legitimately be described as reports of judgments. I will now argue that this fact about psychophysics raises a serious problem for Chomsky's comparison of psychophysics and linguistics.

5. LINGUISTIC INTUITION IN PRACTICE: BEHAVIORAL RESPONSES, IDIOSYNCRATIC MENTAL STATES, OR LINGUISTIC JUDGMENTS?

The basic problem with Chomsky's comparison is that it is not clear whether responses of linguistic informants can be legitimately treated as any kind of judgment at all. This is because it is not at all clear how the *correctness* of linguistic judgments could be assessed. That is, even if an informant's response qualifies as a first-person *report,* it is not clear that it qualifies as a report of a *judgment.* It can so qualify only if assessing its correctness is (in principle) possible. Specifying how the correctness of an informant judgment should be assessed would require specifying a linguistic analogue to the scales, meter sticks, or light meters that can be used in assessing the correctness of the subjective judgments of the psychophysicists' experimental subjects. That is, it requires specifying some independent procedure, other than an informant's sincere, careful self-report, which will serve as a criterion for the correctness or incorrectness of any judgments which that informant might report. Linguists have not explicitly discussed such criteria, and in the case of putative judgments of linguistic informants, I am rather at a loss to imagine what such a criterion of correctness could be. But, for the purposes at hand, my lack of imagination is irrelevant. I am, again, simply making a conceptual point: before informant responses can count as reports of judgments, some criterion for distinguishing correct from incorrect judgments must be specifiable. This is true regardless of whether assessments of correctness are actually performed. Such a criterion is specifiable for judgments reported in psychophysical experiments. I suggest that it is at least open to question whether such criteria are specifiable for the responses of linguistic informants, and hence it is open to question whether informant responses are judgments at all. If they are not, then there is a fundamental respect in which Chomsky's analogy between linguistic data and psychophysical data breaks down. In particular, responses of subjects in psychophysical experiments are reports of judgments, but responses of linguistic informants, even if reports of mental states, are *not* reports of judgments. If this is correct, then it is simply inappropriate to attempt to assess the correctness of the "intuitions" reported by linguistic informants. If this negative conclusion is correct, then a model for introspective linguistic data still remains to be identified. Of the four models of linguistic data considered here,[10] only that provided by first-person reports of sensations remains unquestioned. It is worth considering the viability of this model.

As noted above (see p. 153), the reliability of such data is, in principle, checkable, and hence this model of linguistic data is not subject to the criticisms which can be made of the model provided by classical introspective psychology. Furthermore, linguists' use of the "my idiolect–your idiolect" gambit and their frequent assertions that they are constructing grammars of idiolects mesh nicely with this model: the veracity of reports of sensations is not called into question by the fact that reports of different people conflict, and intersubject agreement in the kind of sensation reported gives no evidence that the *sensation* was correct. Similar things can be said about reports of intuitions about idiolects. I suggest that the model provided by first-person reports of sensations *does* provide an appropriate model for interpreting what is in fact done in current linguistic practice.[11]

SUMMARY

What I have said so far makes it possible (a) to clearly describe some alternative models for data concerning linguistic intuition and (b) to raise a number of clearly formulated questions about the nature of such data and about methods appropriate for assessing their reliability and validity. In particular, we can ask whether data concerning linguistic intuition are most appropriately treated (a) simply as records of an informant's behavioral (e.g., verbal) responses, or (b) as records of verbal responses constituting first-person reports of mental states about which the informant has final epistemic authority, or (c) as records of first-person reports of the informant's linguistic judgments.

Which of these three models is most appropriate for data concerning linguistic intuitions depends on which, if any, of the questions (1), (2), (3) (see p. 152) can appropriately be asked about such data.[12]

What I have provided here are some suggestions about which questions can appropriately be asked. A fuller discussion would require a systematic examination of which, if any, of the three questions could possibly be addressed by specific methods currently used by linguists in gathering linguistic data. I hope to have said enough to indicate why such an examination is worth carrying out. It will serve the purpose of clarifying *why* specific methodologies are (or are not) appropriate for assessing "introspective" linguistic data of the sort transformationalists claim they need. I hope what I have said will suggest ways in which experimental linguists[13] and theoretical linguists can together begin seriously considering that problem.

NOTES

1. See Botha (1973:174–250) for discussion.
2. For discussion see Bach (1964:4) and Chomsky (1961:223–225, 1964:79).
3. As I am using the term here, a person (P) can be described as having privileged access to a specific mental state if and only if P is the only person who can know (even in principle) of the presence and characteristics of that state. I will use the term "logically private entity" to refer to states to which a person has privileged access. Mischel (1970) argues that Wundt and Titchener were committed to the view that people have privileged access to (at least some) of their own mental states.

   William Alston (1971) clearly distinguishes a variety of senses in which people have been said to have privileged access to their own mental states. The variety of privileged access described above is not one of those described in Alston's paper.
4. The case for the uncheckability of the "data" of classical introspective psychology is developed in Mischel (1970). The implications of this argument for the methodology of transformational generative linguistics are discussed in Ringen (1975). Savage (1970) discusses evidence that Fechner and the contemporary psychophysicist S. S. Stevens treat responses of experimental subjects as reports about subjective magnitudes to which only the subject has access.
5. Indeed, such assurances do not even begin to suggest *why* data concerning linguistic intuition are even relevant (much less why they are of fundamental importance) for linguistic research. One might ask (rather irrelevantly in the context of this paper), Why *must* linguists rely on intuition *as data* at all?
6. Bever (1970) and Chomsky (1965) do strike a distinction between judgments of acceptability and judgments of grammaticality. Botha (1973) discusses the relevance of this distinction to the problem of assessing the reliability of intuitive data. However, the questions I am raising here are not systematically discussed by any of these writers. The questions I am raising bear equally on the assessment of intuitive data concerning acceptability and that concerning grammaticality.
7. The following description is based on Fechner (1860), Savage (1970), and Underwood (1949).

8. For discussion of "final epistemic authority," see Morick (1970: ix–xvii).

9. Some philosophers (e.g., Morick 1970:ix–xvii) have argued that people have final epistemic authority about all of their own mental states. Controversies about the defensibility of this claim are irrelevant to the purposes of this paper. For my purposes, it is enough that pains and afterimages constitute clear cases of mental states about which people do have final epistemic authority.

10. The four models of data are: (1) verbal responses, (2) first-person reports of sensations, (3) first-person reports of judgments, and (4) first-person reports of logically private mental states (i.e., "data" of the sort sought by classical introspective psychologists).

11. However, there is at least one reason for questioning whether heavy reliance on such data in the task of constructing grammars for idiolects is appropriate in a scientific study of natural language. Languages and even dialects are quite obviously social phenomena, and social phenomena are by definition interpersonal and intersubjective. Grammars and data which exhibit no sensitivity to this fact would seem to be inadequate in principle for accomplishing the aim of a scientific study of language.

12. It is worth noting that analogues to these questions can be used in reflecting about how nonverbal data concerning linguistic intuition should be construed.

13. See Greenbaum and Quirk (1970) for a discussion of various sorts of elicitation experiments.

REFERENCES

Alston, W. (1971) "Varieties of privileged access," *American Philosophical Quarterly* 8:223–241.

Bach, E. (1964) *An Introduction to Transformational Grammars.* New York: Holt, Rinehart and Winston.

Bever, T. (1970) "The cognitive basis of linguistic structures," in J. Hayes (ed.), *Cognition and the Development of Language.* New York: John Wiley.

Botha, R. (1973) *The Justification of Linguistic Hypotheses.* The Hague: Mouton.

Chomsky, N. (1961) "Some methodological remarks on generative grammar," *Word* 17(no. 2):219–239.

—— (1962) "Explanatory models in linguistics," in E. Nagel, P. Suppes, and A. Tarski (eds.), *Logic, Methodology, and Philosophy of Science.* Stanford, Calif.: Stanford University Press.

—— (1964) "Current issues in linguistic theory," in J. Fodor and J. Katz (eds.), *The Structure of Language.* Englewood Cliffs, N.J.: Prentice-Hall.

—— (1965) *Aspects of the Theory of Syntax.* Cambridge, Mass.: M.I.T. Press.

Fechner, G. (1860) *Elements of Psychophysics*, vol. I, translated by Helmut E. Adler. New York: Holt, Rinehart and Winston, 1966.

Greenbaum, S. and R. Quirk (1970) *Elicitation Experiments in English: Linguistic Studies in Use and Attitude*. London: Longman; also Coral Gables, Fla.: University of Miami Press.

Jones, O. R. (ed.) (1971) *The Private Language Argument*. London: Macmillan.

Labov, W. (1972a) *Sociolinguistic Patterns*. Philadelphia: University of Pennsylvania Press.

———— (1972b) "Some principles of linguistic methodology," *Language in Society* 1:97–120.

Mischel, T. (1970) "Wundt and the conceptual foundations of psychology," *Philosophy and Phenomenological Research* 31:1–26.

Morick, H. (ed.) (1970) *Introduction to the Philosophy of Mind*. Glenview, Ill.: Scott, Foresman.

Ringen, J. (1975) Linguistic intuition and introspective 'observation'. Paper read at the Winter Meeting of the Linguistic Society of America, San Francisco.

Rosenthal, R. (1963) "On the social psychology of the psychological experiment: The experimenter's hypothesis as an unintended determinant of experimental results," *American Scientist* 51:268–283.

Samarin, W. (1967) *Field Linguistics*. New York: Holt, Rinehart and Winston.

Saunders, J. T. and D. F. Henze (1967) *The Private Language Problem*. New York: Random House.

Savage, C. W. (1970) *The Measurement of Sensation*. Berkeley: University of California Press.

Titchener, E. (1896) *An Outline of Psychology*. New York: Macmillan.

Underwood, B. (1949) *Experimental Psychology*. New York: Appleton-Century-Crofts.

Wittgenstein, L. (1953) *Philosophical Investigations*. London: Blackwell.

Wundt, W. (1904) *Principles of Physiological Psychology*, vol. I., translated from the fifth German edition, 1902, by E. B. Titchener. New York: Macmillan.

III

LANGUAGE TYPOLOGIES

9
Typological regularities in postnominal relative clauses

Bruce T. Downing
University of Minnesota

1. INTRODUCTION

Recent progress in the description of relativization processes in a wide variety of languages, principally within the descriptive framework provided by the theory of generative grammar, has made it possible to begin seriously to address questions concerning a structural typology of relative clauses. The present paper is concerned with discovering generalizations concerning the internal structure of postnominal relative clauses as a structural type. In the process an attempt will be made to show how

Some of the material in this paper is drawn from an earlier paper entitled "Toward a Typology of Adjective Clauses," which I presented at the forty-eighth annual meeting of the Linguistic Society of America, San Diego, December 28–30, 1973.

I am indebted to secondary sources for most of the data and much of the analysis of particular languages presented here; these sources are acknowledged in the appropriate places in the text. For their assistance in providing additional data and in some cases discussing analyses with me, I would like to thank Şeyda Balkan, Anatoly Liberman, Helena Pereyra, and Kenneth Truitner. None of them bear any responsibility for the accuracy or interpretation of the data as presented here.

typological facts of this kind can be expressed by means of syntactic rules having the status of principles of universal grammar.

There are a number of typological questions we can ask with regard to relative clause formation across languages. The obvious typology of relative clauses divides them into classes on the basis of their position with respect to the head or modified nominal. Since clauses adjoined directly to the head noun may either precede or follow it, there are two principal positional types, which we may call *prenominal* and *postnominal*. To the extent that languages do not allow unreduced, finite restrictive clauses in both positions, languages as well as relative clauses can be classified on this basis.[1] A third positional type, in which a "correlative" relative clause is preposed or postposed to the entire clause containing the modified nominal, I have discussed from a typological point of view elsewhere (Downing 1974); this type will be ignored for present purposes.

It has been noted by Greenberg (1966), and by many others since, that the division of languages into prenominal relative and postnominal relative types corresponds *in general* to a division into the word-order types OV (in which the verb normally follows other predicate elements such as objects) and VO (in which the verb precedes such elements), respectively. In other words, most SOV languages have the order Rel Clause + Nominal (or else have relative clauses that are not embedded at all), while SVO and VSO and VOS languages have the order Nominal + Rel Clause.

A typology is most interesting, of course, when it is found that some logically possible types do not occur (as for example the nonoccurrence of *OSV and *OVS among the logically possible word-order types), or when absolute correlations are found between the properties on which the typology is based and other linguistic or nonlinguistic features (for example, Greenberg's Universal 16: "In languages with dominant order VSO, an inflected auxiliary always precedes the main verb" (Greenberg 1966:85)). The relative-clause-order typology is by these standards not particularly interesting, since of the two logically possible orderings both are found, and the rather strong correlation with word-order types described above nevertheless fails in both directions. Chinese, for example, is a surface SVO language with prenominal relative clauses, and Persian is an SOV language with postnominal relatives.

In order to try to save the generalization concerning word-order correlations in a form strong enough to be predictive (e.g., "If verbs precede their objects, then relative clauses follow their heads, and vice versa"), two courses are open (apart from correcting the recalcitrant languages). The usual approach has been simply to label those languages for which the correlation holds as "regular" and those for which it does not as "transitional" (cf. Lehmann 1973:49, fn. 1), so that the correlation can be said to hold (by definition) for the regular languages. The other possibility would be to attempt to identify some property or properties of nonregular languages like Chinese and Persian which may be said to allow or to require the regular word-order correlation to be violated. It is conceivable that no such properties will be found. But this approach at least leaves open the possibility that an exceptionless generalization will be found.

Apart from the problem of explaining the exceptionality of languages like Chinese and Persian (and explaining the regular word-order correlation found in other languages), there are a number of other typological questions about relative clauses which have not yet received fully satisfactory answers. In most cases these questions remain at the level of determining the observable facts of relative clause structure across languages. Here are some that seem worth pursuing:

- Is there an interesting typology concerning the internal structure of relative clauses?
- Is there a correlation between internal clause structure and the prenominal or postnominal position of the clause?
- Is there a correlation between basic word-order type (SOV, SVO, VSO, VOS) and the internal structure of relative clauses? Do postnominal clauses have the same internal properties regardless of word order, or do postnominal clauses in SVO and VSO languages, for example, differ in characteristic ways? Are relativization patterns in SOV languages mirror images of the patterns found in VSO or VOS languages?
- Can strong correlations be found between the structure of relative clauses and other properties of the language in question, such as the degree of case marking, general con-

straints on deletion, freeness of word order, cliticization of pronouns, etc.?

Answers to some of these questions will be suggested in the course of this paper; the others must await further research.

As Gerald Sanders points out (p. 259, this volume), a language typology is a means of bringing out generalizations in the data in a form that makes clear the kinds of rules and constraints required in the theory of grammar and the grammars of particular languages, which principles may be explicable in turn by reference to psychological mechanisms. Grammatical rules and possible explanations for the universal characteristics of postnominal relative clauses will be considered below. But first let us look at some basic facts of relative clause structure.

There are a number of characteristic properties of postnominal relative clauses which apparently are never found in prenominal clauses:

A. Only postnominal relative clauses may contain an obligatorily initial relative particle or nominal that is not generally present in that position in the corresponding unmarked simple sentence. This initial element may be (a) a distinctive relative particle; (b) a complementizer of more general distribution; (c) a pronoun that agrees with its antecedent (the head noun) in case, number, etc.;[2] or (d) a noun phrase or prepositional phrase containing the *relative nominal* (i.e., the nominal of the subordinate clause that is coreferential with the head) in a pronominal form. This marker may be obligatory in at least some types of relative clauses in a given language.

B. If an initial relative pronoun is used, it may be identical in form with the interrogative pronoun; in any case it is a *strong* form, not a clitic or a nondemonstrative personal pronoun.

C. The original relative nominal may be deleted or may be retained in a weak pronominal form, independently of whether a pronominal copy appears in initial position.

In the case of prenominal relative clauses, there are also some distinct properties:

D. In prenominal relative clauses there is never an obligatory clause-initial marker. (There may or may not be a clause-*final* marker.)

E. There is no obligatory movement of the relativized nominal (or a pronominal copy of it) to either the beginning or the end of a prenominal relative clause.

F. In prenominal relative clauses there is no pronominal form of the relative nominal distinct from forms used in other nonrelative and noninterrogative functions. That is, if the relative nominal is retained, it is retained in a weak pronominal form; it does not have an interrogative or special relative form.

2. SOV LANGUAGES WITH PRENOMINAL RELATIVE CLAUSES

For purposes of comparison with the postnominal clause types to be discussed below and to illustrate the principles listed above, we may briefly consider the basic facts of relativization in two SOV languages, Japanese and Turkish.

2.1 Japanese

In Japanese (data from McCawley 1972) there is usually no specific relativization of the embedded clauses other than deletion of the relative nominal;[3] in some cases (e.g., in the possessive), this nominal is retained, in pronoun form (cf. McCawley 1972:205). When the relative clause contains a copula, however, the copula takes a special dependent form.

Sentence (1a) is a simple transitive sentence of Japanese, which is embedded as a relative clause, with the object deleted, in (1b). (Square brackets will be used in all examples to indicate the boundaries of the relative clause.)

(1) a. Yamada-san ga   sa'ru   o   ka'tte   iru
       Mr. Yamada NOM   monkey ACC   keep-PTCP be-PRES
       'Mr. Yamada keeps a monkey'
    b. [Yamada-san ga   ka'tte   iru]   sa'ru
       Mr. Yamada   NOM   keep-PTCP be-PRES monkey
       'the monkey that Mr. Yamada keeps'

2.2 Turkish

In Turkish there are two different relativization processes, the choice depending on whether or not the relative nominal is the subject of its clause. In both cases the relative nominal is deleted and the verb takes a nondefinite (participial) form.[4]

(2) a. Adam   kadın-a   yüzüğ-ü   sat-tı
         man   woman-to   ring-the sell-PAST
         'The man sold the woman the ring'
     b. [adam-ın yüzüğ-ü   sat-tığ-ı]   kadın
         man's   ring-the selling-POSS'D woman
         'the woman that the man sold the ring [to]'
     c. [kadın-a   yüzüğ-ü   sat-an] adam
         woman-to   ring-the selling man
         'the man that sold the woman the ring'

Sentence (2a) is a simple transitive sentence which is embedded with indirect object relativization in (2b) and with subject relativization in (2c). In both of these languages the coreferential nominal is generally deleted, there is no reordering of sentence elements, and there is no distinctive clause-initial or clause-final marker of relativization except for the participial affixes of Turkish.

These examples seem to be representative of relativization processes in SOV languages other than those employing the "correlative" relative construction.

3. SVO LANGUAGES WITH POSTNOMINAL RELATIVE CLAUSES

Let us now consider some representative SVO languages with regular, postposed relative clauses. We can distinguish three types: (a) languages with initial relative markers but no relative pronouns; (b) languages with initial relative pronouns; (c) languages with both relative particles and relative pronouns, combined or as alternatives.

3.1. The Complementizing Type

In a number of SVO languages all postnominal relative clauses
are identical to the corresponding simple sentences except that
(a) they are introduced by a more or less distinctive nonpro-
nominal particle, serving as a connective or complementizer, and
(b) the relative nominal is either omitted (in certain positions)
or appears as a simple pronoun in its normal sentence position.
In addition, there may be some minor modifications that apply
in subordinate clauses more generally. Among languages of this
type are Bahasa Malaysia (Omar 1973, Frommer 1974), Akan
and Hausa (Schachter 1973), Modern Standard Hebrew (Hayon
1969), Vietnamese (Payne 1974), and Colloquial Egyptian
Arabic (Keenan 1974). To illustrate this type, data will be given
for selected languages from this group.

3.1.1. Bahasa Malaysia. Bahasa Malaysia (data from Keenan 1972, Omar 1973, Frommer 1974) is a regular SVO
language with postnominal relative clauses. The relative clause is
introduced by the invariant marker *yang,* and the coreferential
nominal is deleted unless it is oblique. Definite determiners
follow the relative clause. Sentence (3b) shows relativization of
the subject of a clause identical in underlying form with the
simple sentence (3a).

(3) a. Guru   mem-baca buku
       teacher ACT-read book
       'The teacher is reading a book'
    b. guru   [yang mem-baca buku] itu
       teacher REL   ACT-read book   the
       'the teacher who is reading a book'

One notable fact about Malay is that there is no relativization
on surface direct objects; when the object is relativized the
clause takes a passive (as in (4) below) or pseudo-passive form.
When the relative nominal is the object of a preposition it is not
deleted—see sentence (5).

(4) buku [yang sudah di-baca   oleh Ali] itu
    book REL have   PAS-read by   Ali   the
    'the book that Ali has read'

(5) guru   [yang Ali   mem-beri buku kepada-nya] itu
    teacher REL   Ali   ACT-give book to   him the
    'the teacher to whom Ali gave a book'

In addition to these types, there are relative clauses on locative and temporal heads which are introduced by the general words for place and time instead of *yang*. Thus (6a) occurs alongside the less acceptable (6b). It is not clear whether these words are to be analyzed as complementizers or as preposed relative adverbs, although the latter analysis would perhaps explain the deletion of the whole prepositional phrase (rather than just the coreferential nominal) when *tempat* is used.

(6) a. bilik [tempat dia   tidur] itu
       room *place* he   sleep the
       'the room where he sleeps'
    b. bilik [yang dia   tidur didalam-nya] itu
       room REL he   sleep inside-it   the
       'the room that he sleeps in'

An alternative process of relativization in the speech of "English-educated" Malaysians will be noted below.

3.1.2. Akan. In Akan (data from Schachter 1973), a Niger-Congo language of Ghana, the coreferential nominal in the clause is retained in pronominal form, the only change being the addition of the clause-initial particle *áà,* as shown in the examples in (7). The tone changes indicated in the examples result from a phonological process that applies in relatives as well as certain other subordinate clauses.

(7) a. mìhúù àbòfrá.
       I-saw   child
       'I saw a child'
    b. mìhúù nò.
       I-saw   him
       'I saw him'
    c. àbòfrá [áà   mìhúù nó]
       child   REL I-saw   him
       'a child that I saw'

3.1.3. Hausa. The postnominal relative clauses in Hausa (data from Schachter 1973), an Afro-Asiatic language of Nigeria, are generally marked by an invariant initial particle *da.* The coreferential nominal is deleted from some positions but not others: deletion is obligatory for direct objects, but optional for indirect objects, while subjects are retained as pronouns. In the examples in (8) tones have been omitted.

(8) a. sun gaya wa   yaron.
        they told IOM the-child
        'They told the child'

    b. yaron   [da suka gaya {masa}]
                                   {wa }

        the-child REL they told (him
        'the child that they told'

The form *suka* in place of *sun* 'they' is the result of a process that assigns special forms to pronouns and some aspectual markers in certain types of subordinate clauses. The Indirect Object Marker *wa* is incorporated into the pronoun *masa* in the first version of (8b); in the second the pronoun is omitted.

3.1.4. Vietnamese. As a final example of an SVO language with no relative pronoun, we may choose Vietnamese (data from Payne 1974 and Kenneth Truitner). The initial particle *má* has a variety of uses as a connective; in relative clauses it may be omitted under some conditions, but, like English *that,* must be retained when no subject follows. The relative nominal is regularly omitted, as in (9) and (10).

(9)   nhá   [tôi   ở]
      house   I   be-located
      'the house I live in'
(10) quyển sách [mà   anh   nói hôm nọ]
      DET   book PRT   gentleman talk day other
      'the book that you (polite) talked about the other day'

In (9) *nhá* 'house' is omitted from the relative clause and there is no complementizer. In (10) the direct object is omitted, but the complementizer is retained. There is no evidence for a fronting rule for relativization in Vietnamese; questions likewise are formed with indefinite pronouns in normal word order.

3.2 The Pronoun–Fronting Type

A relatively small number of SVO languages apparently use only the second of the common relativization processes found in postnominal relative clauses. In these languages the relative NP assumes a special relative form (sometimes but not always identical with the interrogative pronoun) and is placed in clause-initial position. If it is the object of a preposition, the entire prepositional phrase is often moved; frequently more extensive Pied-Piping (Ross 1967) is permitted or required. Although the original nominal is usually deleted when the relative pronoun is placed at the front of its clause, in some languages a weak pronominal form of this nominal may be retained (cf. Perlmutter and Orešnik 1973, Keenan 1974). Languages of the pronoun-fronting type are Umbundu (Wald 1970), Rumanian (Keenan 1974), Classical Greek (Adams 1972), Hindi (Masica 1972), Slovenian (Perlmutter and Orešnik 1973), Bulgarian (Morgan 1972:68), and perhaps some dialects of Arabic. Relativization in Umbundu, Rumanian, and Classical Greek will be briefly described for illustration.

3.2.1. Umbundu. Umbundu (data from Wald 1970) is a Bantu language spoken in Angola. The postnominal relative clause in Umbundu is introduced by a proform of the relative nominal which is the regular inflected demonstrative pronoun. This is illustrated in (11).

(11) ulume   [una   ndamõla hela]   wayongola okulya
     man   that(one) I-saw   yesterday   wanted   to eat
     'The man whom I saw yesterday wanted to eat'

As in other Bantu languages (cf. Givón 1969) where the demonstrative follows the noun it modifies, it is not possible in Umbundu to have two consecutive occurrences in *una;* the one form may serve the function of both determiner of the head noun and relative pronoun. However, it is not possible to consider *una* to be merely a determiner, for the following reasons.

Umbundu has a question-word fronting rule; question words are distinct from relative pronouns. It is a general rule in

Umbundu, applying in questions and elsewhere, that movement of an NP triggers a vowel change in which /o/ becomes /a/ in subject pronouns. Wald argues that the appearance of this vowel change in relative clauses is therefore evidence of a movement rule in relativization, rather than mere deletion of the relative NP. Since *una* appears even when a proform of the relative NP is retained, as in relativized genitives, the process must involve copying, as has been argued for a number of other languages. Sentence (12) illustrates relativization on a possessive modifier of an object in Umbundu; *una* 'that' refers to *olusi* 'his'.

(12) ulume [una ufeko alya olusi lwahē] wasanjuka
      man   that girl   ate his fish   happy
      'The man whose fish the girl ate is happy'

When the subject of a clause is relativized in Umbundu the marker *w-* attaches to the verb, so that such a clause may be minimally different from a construction with an object relative; cf. (13), in which the subject is relativized, with (14), where *una* represents the relativized object.

(13) ulume [una ʍamol̄a]   walya
      man   that PRT-he-saw ate
      'The man who saw (something) ate'
(14) ulume [una amol̄a] walya
      man   that he-saw ate
      'The man whom he saw ate'

3.2.2. Rumanian. According to Keenan (1974) the initial relative pronoun in Rumanian has distinct forms for subject, object, indirect object, and genitive cases, distinguishing different functions of the relative nominal in its clause. At the same time, an unstressed resumptive pronoun is retained in its original position within the clause, as illustrated in the object relativization in (15) and the indirect object relativization in (16) (data from Keenan 1974).

(15) barbatul [pe   care femeia l-   a lovit]
      the-man whom the woman him hit
      'the man whom the woman hit'

(16)   femeia   [careia   John   i-   a dat   cartea]
        the-woman to-whom   John   to-her   gave   the-book
        'the woman to whom John gave the book'

3.2.3. Classical Greek. Classical Greek (data from Adams
1972) was an SVO language with postnominal clauses introduced
by the relative pronouns *hós* (usually restrictive) or *ho/t-*
(usually nonrestrictive). Thus, definite relatives were constructed
very much as with the WH-pronouns in modern English, as
shown in (17) and (18).

(17)   autós   estin   he   stratēgós   [hòn   ezētoûmen]
        he   is   the   general   whom   we-sought
        'He is the general whom we sought'
(18)   labòn   toùs   hippéas   [hoi   êsan   autôi]
        taking   the   cavalry   which   are   to-him
        'taking the cavalry which are his'

Adams thinks that indefinite relatives in Classical Greek are
formed by moving the indefinite pronoun *tis* from the head
position into the relative clause by a clitic rule and attaching it
to the stressed relative pronoun, as shown in (19).

(19) a. *makários   tǐs [hós   ousían   kaì   noûn   ékei] $\Longrightarrow$
     b.   makários   [hós-tis   ousían   kaì   noûn   ékei]
          'Happy [is] whoever possesses property and sense'

3.3. Languages Utilizing Both Complementizers
and Relative Pronouns

Probably the majority of SVO languages with postnominal
relative clauses use some combination of the relativization
processes already illustrated. In fact, I do not think much
importance can be attached to the dichotomy I have made,
apart from the fact that two distinct processes exist. For one
thing, further investigation will almost certainly show that both
processes are possible in some of the languages already mentioned; it has been reported by Keenan and elsewhere, for
example, that "English-educated" speakers of Malay regularly
form relative clauses using forms of the interrogative pronoun in

initial position instead of the particle *yang*. Givón (1973) reports a similar development in colloquial Hebrew, where the interrogative pronoun *mi-* or *ma-* is combined with the traditional relative particle *še-* to form a relative marker *mše-*. It appears that both processes are available generally to SVO languages and either may be favored at any given time. A glance at the history of English reveals a series of changes, from the use of the demonstrative *sē* and the particle *ðe,* alternatively or in the combination *sē ðe* in Old English, to Early Modern English *hwich ðat,* etc., to the modern-day choice between the WH-pronouns and the invariant particle *that* or zero relative (cf. Downing 1973, Geoghegan 1975).

Among other SVO languages that exhibit both relative pronouns and relative particles are Tunisian Arabic (Craig 1971) and most of the modern European languages, including Albanian, Danish, Russian, French, and Spanish. In most cases there is a stylistic difference when a choice is involved; in most cases also, some positions can be relativized on with only one or the other of these two processes. Illustrations will be given for Tunisian, Russian, Albanian, and Danish.

3.3.1. Tunisian Arabic. In Tunisian Arabic (basically SVO with subject deletion possible; data from Craig 1971) the relative clause follows its head, preceded, when the antecedent is definite, by the invariant *illi.* The relative clause itself has exactly the form of a simple unembedded sentence, with the limitation that the coreferential NP must have pronominal form. When it is the subject, it may also be omitted, but under just the conditions that permit subject pronouns to be omitted in any clause. Sentences (20) and (21) illustrate relativization on subject and object respectively.

(20)	il	ra.žil	[illi	(huwwa)	mša.	li-il	blad]
	the	man	REL	he	went	to the	town
	'the man who went to town'						
(21)	il	tawla.t	[illi	ža.b-	hum]		
	the	tables	REL	brought-	them		
		f. pl.			f. pl.		
	'the tables that he brought'						

Objects may also be omitted optionally, according to Craig, under fairly complex conditions, for example, when there is no antecedent:

(22)   ana   šuf-t   [illi   Naži.b   ša.f-(u)]
       I   saw   REL   Nažiib   saw-him
       'I saw who Nažiib saw'

There is also a process of relativization with the question-word *wi.n* 'where', as in (23).

(23)   il   dar   [fi-wi.n   t-uskun]
       the   house in-where   you-live
       'the house that you live in'

As is generally the case when interrogative pronouns are used, clauses with *wi.n* do not have resumptive pronouns.

The restrictions on deletion of coreferential terms in Tunisian relative clauses are shown by Craig to follow from general constraints on reduction which also constrain equi-NP deletion and coordination reduction (cf. also Sanders and Tai 1972).

3.3.2. Russian. It is common knowledge that Russian is a highly inflected language with rather free word order. It appears nevertheless that SVO is the unmarked surface order and relative clauses follow their heads. There are two distinct processes of relativization in Russian (data from Loop 1974 and Anatoly Liberman).

The first, which is used almost exclusively in more formal Russian, employs an initial relative pronoun *kotorij-*, which also serves as the question word meaning 'which'. (It incidentally is cognate with English *whether,* originally 'which of two'.) This process is used for relativization of subjects, objects, indirect objects, and genitives. Sentence (24) shows object relativization.

(24) Vot čelovek, kotorovo ja v'id'el včera
     'Here's the fellow whom I saw yesterday'

The second type uses, instead of the relative pronoun, the invariant clause-initial particle *čto,* with deletion of the coreferential NP. This type is acceptable only in informal styles, and only when the relative nominal is the (inanimate) subject of its clause. An example is (25):

(25) dom, čto stoit u-dorogi
      house that stands at-road
      'the house that stands near the road'

Only *čto* can be used when the relative clause modifies a whole clause rather than a particular nominal. *Čto* has two other uses in Russian; it serves as the inanimate question-word 'what' and the clausal complementizer 'that'. Although traditional Russian grammar treats relative *čto* as a pronoun in its relative use, optionally replacing *kotorij* under restrictive conditions, it is more plausible to consider it, like English relative *that,* as an instance of the complementizer.

3.3.3. Albanian. Another SVO language with both types of relativization is Albanian (data from Morgan 1972). Albanian has two series of interrogative words, both of which furnish relative pronouns. Of the *k-* series only *ku* 'where' and *kur* 'when', which have no inflected forms, are used. The *cil-* stem, translated 'who/which', is used for the other cases. Each form is inflected for gender, number, and case with the definite determiner and preceded by the adjective particle, which also precedes all adjectival and genitive forms. When the relative nominal is the object of a preposition, as in (26), the preposition is carried along to the front of the clause.

(26) Qyteti [në të cilin banonte tër jetën]
      city-the in PRT which (she) lived all life-the
      'the city in which she lived all her life'

The second process requires the introductory particle *që* (the general complementizer) with deletion rather than pronominalization of the relative nominal. Since prepositions cannot be stranded, this process cannot be used to relativize on the object of a preposition. Relativization on a direct object is illustrated in (27).

(27)   revizioni   [që   kam   shkruarë   më 1921]
        revision-the   REL   (I) have   written   in 1921
        'the revision that I wrote in 1921'

3.3.4. Danish. Relative clauses in Danish (data from Sadock 1972) are usually formed with the particle *som,* which also means 'as'. In the spoken language, however, it is very common to delete *som.* Like English *that* and Vietnamese *má, som* cannot be deleted if the relative nominal is the subject:

(28) Den mand [som skrev den bog] er min bror.
      'The man that wrote the book is my brother'

In more literary style, *som* may be replaced by *der* (apparently a pronoun) but only when it is the subject that is relativized. This of course does not imply a movement rule, since the subject will already be in initial position. Sadock notes that the second of two conjoined clauses must begin with *som* rather than *der,* as shown in (29).

(29) den   mand   (som)   vi   snakkede   om   og $\begin{Bmatrix} som \\ *der \end{Bmatrix}$ spiller
     blokfløjte
     'the man that we talked about and that plays the recorder'

3.3.5. English, Spanish, French. It should be obvious that the relative particle *that* in English has just the properties of the relative complementizers in the languages discussed here, while the relatives of interrogative form (*who, which, whose, where,* etc.) are very similar in their uses to the relative pronouns of other SVO languages. It can be argued similarly that Spanish *que* is a relative particle distinct from the inflected pronouns (*a*) *quien, el cual,* etc. A weaker case can be made for such a dichotomy in French, where *que* (identical in form to the general complementizer) is used exclusively in object relativization while only the clearly pronominal forms *qui, dont,* (*au*)*quel, où,* etc. are used elsewhere. Perlmutter (1972), however, calls attention to the use of *que* in sentences such as (30a), occurring alongside the regular (30b).

(30) a. l'homme [que tu as dit qui lui a parlé]
          'the man that you said spoke to him'
      b. l'homme [à qui tu as dit qu'il a parlé]
          'the man to whom you said that he spoke'

According to Perlmutter, the *qui* in (30a) is a contraction of *que*
il, although it is not felt to be so by native speakers I have
asked. In any case *que* appears in (30a) as a complementizer
even though it is the subject that is relativized.

3.4. Summary

This completes our survey of postnominal relativization in
SVO languages. A broad sample of languages has been examined
to test the claim that these languages constitute a rather uniform
type with respect to relativization processes. Three central
processes have been identified: (a) copying of the relative
nominal (or a NP or PP containing it) as a relative pronoun at
the beginning of the clause, with the relative nominal taking a
strong pronominal form; (b) insertion of a relative particle
(complementizer) at the beginning of the clause; (c) deletion of
the (original) relative nominal. If not deleted, the relative
nominal invariably has an anaphoric form. As Table 1 shows, all
possible combinations of these three processes are found, with
the exceptions to be noted.

TABLE 1. Co-occurrence of relativization processes in SVO languages

Language	Initial NP containing relative pronoun	Initial relative particle (complementizer)	Retention of subject or object relative NP
1. –	No	No	No
2. –	No	No	Yes
3. Hausa	No	Yes	No
4. Akan	No	Yes	Yes
5. Umbundu	Yes	No	No
6. Rumanian	Yes	No	Yes
7. Colloquial Hebrew; English	Yes	Yes	No
8. –	Yes	Yes	Yes

The absence of languages in categories 1 and 2 in the table, that is, languages in which there is never an initial relative marker or pronoun in postnominal relative clauses, suggests the possibility of strengthening the generalization A above, as follows:

A'. In every language with postnominal relative clauses, at least some of these clauses will have a clause-initial relative marker.

Schwartz (1971) cites Dyirbal as an exception to this generalization, however; I have not verified this. Allowance must be made in any case for this initial marker to be optional or absent under certain conditions. We have seen in fact evidence for the same principle governing omission of the relative particle in three languages, Danish, English, and Vietnamese: the initial particle can be omitted provided that the subject of the relative clause precedes the verb in surface structure.

Category 7 of Table 1 has two subtypes: those like Colloquial Hebrew and Old and Middle English, which allow the relative pronoun and the complementizer to occur together, and those like Russian and Modern English, which allow either one or the other. (Modern Hebrew retains object relatives optionally, but only when the interrogative pronoun is not used.) Category 8 as a type is not excluded in principle, but seems unlikely because of its redundancy. Both the Hebrew and Rumanian types (categories 6 and 7) are relatively rare, apparently for the same reason.

The last column in Table 1 refers to the omissibility of relativized subjects and/or objects only. The Accessibility Hierarchy proposed by Keenan and Comrie (1972) predicts that for each language, some range of positions in a universal ordering will be relativizable, with subjects being the universally relativizable category. It is also predicted that each process of relativization will apply to a contiguous range of positions on this hierarchy, and that if deletion of the relative nominal (without copying) is allowed at all, the range of deletable nominals will include the subject, i.e., the subject is both more generally relativizable and more readily deletable. So far as I can determine, the languages considered here function in accord with Keenan and Comrie's predictions of relative accessibility to relativization.[5]

4. UNIVERSAL RULES FOR RELATIVIZATION IN SVO LANGUAGES WITH POSTNOMINAL RELATIVE CLAUSES

The processes we have observed imply for the *grammar* of relativization a limited set of universal syntactic rules available at least to all SVO languages with postnominal relative clauses. Each universal rule performs an elementary transformational operation.

First of all, the fact that the relative nominal always has an anaphoric form follows from a universal principle of left-to-right pronominalization into subordinate clauses, which is not specifically a relativization process. The first relativization rule is accordingly the process of assigning a strong pronominal form (e.g., +WH or +DEM) to the relative nominal, to which a fronting rule will apply to place it at the beginning of its clause. This strong form is frequently, but not invariably, identical to the interrogative pronouns.

In the languages I have investigated, it is regularly, but not quite universally, the case that initial relative pronouns are found only if there is a question-word fronting rule for questions as well. Thus it is plausible at least that the *second* univeral relativization rule, relative pronoun fronting, is only a special case of the fronting rule that applies in questions (cf. Schwartz 1971), which likewise must be stated so as to apply only leftward and only in SVO languages (cf. Bach 1971). Sanders and Tai (1972) have hypothesized that the universal rule is instead the copying rule that applies also in topicalization or left-dislocation of main clause nominals. According to their hypothesis, relativization will be parallel to topicalization (with the original nominal deleted) in languages like English, and parallel to left-dislocation (with the original NP retained in pronominal form) in languages in which the Immediate Dominance condition (which prohibits deletion from certain positions) holds.

I have not been able to test this hypothesis in the full range of languages discussed here, but it does appear that the facts presented by Keenan in various publications documenting the Accessibility Hierarchy would call into question any such clear-cut dichotomy. On the other hand, considerable evidence has been amassed from a variety of languages for a close inter-relationship between topicalization processes and relativization (cf. Schachter 1973).

The third universal relativization process is the deletion of the weak (original) relative nominal, under conditions that vary from language to language, as noted above. A final rule inserts the relative complementizer. In most languages it cannot be included if there is a relative pronoun; in some it is optional if the head nominal is followed by the subject of the relative clause.

To summarize, the postnominal relative clause in SVO languages can be described as resulting from the application of some combination of the universal rules listed below:

(General) Pronominalization

I. Strong (e.g., WH-) Pronoun Substitution
II. Copying (obligatory; leaves weak pronoun behind)
III. Deletion of Weak Pronoun
IV. Relative Complementizer Insertion

These rules may be independently selected for each language with the exception that Rule II operates only on the output of Rule I (only specially marked pronouns can be fronted), and, in any language, if Rule I applies Rule II must apply. Similarly, assuming that initial relative markers (pronouns or particles) are found in postnominal clauses in all SVO languages, we may state a second universal condition: in SVO languages at least, Rule IV must apply if Rule II does not. (An exception will be noted below.)

The principles of relativization in individual languages of the appropriate type may be described as a particular selection from among these universal rules, along with a specification of language-particular rules (the "housekeeping rules" of Bach 1971), as illustrated below for Hausa, Akan, Umbundu, Rumanian, and English. (The statements in parentheses describe rule applications that follow from universal conditions.)

Hausa

I. (and therefore II) does not apply.
III. Deletion: obligatory for direct objects; optional for indirect objects; subject pronouns remain.
IV. Insert *da*. (Must apply.)

Housekeeping: Substitution of special subordinate clause pronoun forms.

Akan

I.   (and therefore II) and III do not apply.
IV. Insert *áà*. (Must apply.)
Housekeeping: Tone change rule for subordinate clauses.

Umbundu

I.   Substitute demonstrative pronoun for relative nominal.
II. (Must apply.)
III. Delete weak pronoun if subject or object; retain genitive, etc.
IV. Does not apply.
Housekeeping: If subject pronoun is deleted, attach *w-* to verb.

Rumanian

I.   Applies in all cases.
II. (Must apply.)
III. Does not apply.
IV. Does not apply.

English

I.   Optionally substitute appropriate WH-proform; obligatory on prenominal possessives and most adverbials and in appositive relative clauses.
II. (Must apply.) Pied-Piping, obligatory under some conditions.
III. Obligatory.
IV. Insert *that* if Rule II does not apply; optional if subject follows; otherwise obligatory.

5. VX LANGUAGES WITH POSTNOMINAL RELATIVE CLAUSES

To return now to some questions asked at the outset, we are interested in determining to what extent the processes observed in SVO languages apply also in verb-initial (VX) languages with postnominal relative clauses, and what the differences if any are. Let us again examine some instances.

5.1. Zapotec

Valley Zapotec, spoken in Mexico (data from Rosenbaum 1971), is a VSO language, in which, however, focused or emphasized constituents and question words always precede the verb. The relative clause in sentence (31) could be generated by the application of the Deletion and Complementizer rules (III and IV), if *ni* is taken as a subordinating particle.

(31)   rumbeʔ abel la   gunaʔ   [ni   been   ĭumI]
        knows   Abel the woman   REL   made   baskets
        'Abel knows the woman who made baskets'

However, the fact that the plural marker accompanies *ni* in sentences like (32) suggests that *ni* is a pronoun rather than a particle.

(32)   rumbeʔ xwain de bado [de ni   badeed abel mulE]
        knows Juan PL child PL REL gave   Abel money
        'Juan knows the children to whom Abel gave money'

This in turn, along with other arguments presented by Rosenbaum (1971) that a single movement rule is involved in both question and relative clause formation, suggests the derivation of both sentences by Rules I, II, and III:

I.   Substitution of the relative form (PL)*ni* for the relative nominal.
II. (Must apply.)
III. Obligatory (except in some "inaccessible" positions).
IV. Does not apply.

Thus we find that Zapotec, a VSO language, uses a relativization process found in SVO languages, by allowing a violation of verb-initial order in the relative clause. We must look elsewhere to find how relatives are formed when strict verb-initial order is maintained. A good example is Jacaltec, as described by Colette Craig.

5.2. Jacaltec

Jacaltec, a VSO language spoken in Guatemala (and unrelated to Zapotec; data from Craig 1973) has rigid verb-initial order, ergative case marking, and postnominal relative clauses. In Jacaltec the verb is inflected for both subject and object. Relative clauses in Jacaltec employ neither a relative pronoun nor a relative particle. (The language has complementizers that are used elsewhere, but neither they nor the articles are used in forming relatives.)

In relativizing on a subject or object in Jacaltec the relative nominal is deleted and the corresponding clitic is deleted from the verb. In addition, if it is a transitive subject that is deleted, the intransitivizing suffix *-n(i)* (which serves a variety of uses in the formation of complex sentences) is added to the verb. Relativization on an intransitive subject is shown in (33), on a transitive subject in (34).

(33)   xwil   naj   winaj   [x'apni ewi]
        I-saw   the   man   came   yesterday
        'I saw the man who came yesterday'
(34)   xwil   naj   winaj   [xwatx'e-*n* hun   tu']
        I-saw   the   man   made-INT   one   that
        'I saw the man who made that'

In relativizing on a possessor NP, the pronoun itself is deleted, but there is no verbal clitic to delete; other oblique cases are relativized by optional deletion of the object of a preposition without the deletion of the personal clitic attached to the preposition. Without adducing all of the details, we can see that relativization here involves only Rule III, deletion of the relative nominal, plus a system of "verb-coding" (Keenan's term)—adding or deleting a verb or preposition affix that indicates the role of the relative nominal—which helps to disambiguate the structure of the clause. Keenan (1972) has described another verb-initial language, Malagasy, a VOS language employing a system of verb-coding of a rather different sort and no relative pronouns or particle; I will not attempt a summary here.

5.3. Old Irish

Another interesting example is Old Irish, described by Ruth and W. P. Lehmann (1975) as a VSO language with a "poorly developed" postnominal relative. There was normally no relative marker (as in sentence (35)), although some person forms were preceded by the particle *no*.

(35)   bruden   [ro.boī   i   nHērinn]
        hostels   it-was   in   Erin
        'hostels which were in Erin'

The verb which begins the relative clause is unaltered in form, so that the construction is like Japanese except for the reversal of the position of the verb.

However, Old Irish did have special relative verb forms that were used in some persons in the present tense, as in (36), where *gaibes* is the third-singular relative absolute of *gaibid*.

(36)   is   oinfer   [gaibes   buaid]
      is   one-man   takes   prize
      'It is one man who takes the prize'

We may now state the following tentative conclusions, which receive confirmation from the few examples of VX languages here considered, regarding the internal structure of postnominal relative clauses as a type.

G. A language which has VX structure in main clauses may utilize the relativization processes described above for SVO languages in forming postnominal relative clauses, giving a relative structure Head + Rel + V + X, where Rel is a relative particle or pronoun.

H. If a language has strict verb-initial relative clause structure, relativization in postnominal relative clauses will involve inflectional changes on the (clause-initial) verb with weak pronominalization or deletion of the relative nominal.

Thus, we find that postnominal relative clauses do not constitute a uniform type; rather, the choice of relativization processes depends not only on the position of the clause with respect to its head but also on word-order properties of the language. With regard to relativization processes, postnominal relatives in strict VX language are more similar to prenominal relative clauses than to postnominal relatives in SVO languages.

6. RELATIVIZATION AND PERCEPTUAL PROCESSING

We turn now to the question of how the use of different relativization processes in SVO and VSO languages may be explained.

A number of papers dealing with the perceptual processing of relative clauses have pointed out that in an SVO language, if a relative clause on the subject were to begin with a verb, the resulting sequence S[V would be subject to misinterpretation as a simple predication, SV... Avoidance of this consequence is presumably the reason why English allows *the man I saw* without a marker but does not allow *that* to be omitted from *the man that saw me* (cf. Bever and Langendoen 1972); the result would sound like the sentence *The man saw me.* In strict verb-initial languages this perceptual problem does not arise: since the main verb precedes all other sentence elements, any verb that follows must be subordinate. The main function of verb marking in relative clauses of VX languages, therefore, would be to indicate the *type* of subordination and the role of the relative nominal within its clause.

It follows from these considerations that either a marker or a nominal phrase is required before the verb for perceptual disambiguation in SVO languages, but that verb marking alone is sufficient for relativization in VX languages. In XV (verb-final) languages, an initial relative clause may be taken as a main clause unless either there is deletion of the relative nominal (under circumstances in which it would not be omitted otherwise) or else the verb at the end of the clause is marked as being subordinate. Neither of these conditions seems to be met consistently in Japanese, but at least one or the other is generally found in Turkish relative clauses.

These perceptual considerations provide a basis of explanation for the following generalizations:

I. In SVO languages the first element of a postnominal relative clause must be a complementizer, a relative pronoun, or the subject of the relative clause.
J. There are no relative pronouns (i.e., no strong pronouns moved to initial or final position) in prenominal relative clauses, nor in postnominal relative clasues in strict verb-initial languages.

7. RELATIVIZATION IN IRREGULAR SOV AND SVO LANGUAGES

It remains to ask what form relativization takes in two languages with inconsistent word-order characteristics, Persian (SOV with postnominal relatives) and Chinese (SVO with pre-nominal relatives).

7.1. Persian

We have seen that in SVO languages with postnominal relative clauses the requirement (I, above) of a preverbal element in relative clauses prevents the formation of structurally ambiguous SV sequences. When postnominal relatives occur in a SOV language, the same problem may arise, but only with intransitive subordinate clauses, i.e., only in the sequence S [X V] Y V where X is null and the subject of the relative clause is deleted under relativization. The likelihood of perceptual ambiguity is thus less than in "regular" SVO/Nom Rel languages. A more general perceptual problem in such languages is simply to recognize the boundaries of the subordinate clause, that is, to determine whether elements following a given main clause nominal are part of a subordinate clause. For both purposes an introductory marker is needed.

Persian (data from Tabaian 1975) provides such a marker in the form of the relative particle *ke* (distinct from interrogative *ki* 'who'). Subject and object relative nominals are deleted, but a pronoun is retained in oblique cases (see example (37)). In addition, the head noun takes a special suffix, -*i*, further marking the clause boundary.

(37)   (an)   märd-i   [ke   ketab-ra   be-*u*   dad-i]
       the   man-REL   THAT   book-OBJ   to-him   gave-you
       'the man to whom you gave the book'

When the direct object is relativized, a further boundary marker may be introduced: the specific direct object marker, which is preposed and attached to the relative particle *ke*, as in (38).

(38)   (an)   märd-i   [(ra)-ke   did-i]
       the   man-REL   OBJ-THAT   saw-you
       'the man whom you saw'

Thus Persian uses all of the relativization processes associated with SVO languages.

If postnominal clauses are thus easily disambiguated in SOV languages, why are they so rarely found? The reason suggested by Kuno (1974) is that this order maximizes the possibility of center embedding. To get around the problem of center embedding, Persian uses both extraposition and a correlative construction; the marking of the head noun with the REL suffix presumably aids in identifying the antecedent when the clause has been removed from its head. As a general rule we should expect that surface marking will be maximized where extraposition or other movement rules are utilized to avoid center embedding.

7.2. Chinese

The final case to be examined is Mandarin Chinese (data from Hou 1974). Should we expect a language that has prenominal relatives but SVO word order to use a relativization process of the SVO/Nom Rel type or of the SOV/Rel Nom type, as illustrated by Japanese and Turkish (see sections 2.1 and 2.2 above)?

The processing problem in this case is the same as in other cases of prenominal relatives; it must be possible to tell whether an initial clause is a relative clause or a main clause. This determination will be facilitated if the relative nominal is omitted; but if oblique cases are deleted, the function of the relative nominal within its clause may be obscured. There is no possibility of misconstruing the relative verb as a predicate with the head nominal as subject, since it will always either precede the subject or follow the verb of the main clause. A complementizer can be expected, however, positioned at the end of the clause, before the head, where it will prevent the problem of conjunction juxtaposition in multiple embeddings pointed out by Kuno (1974). Since the verb will not always be final, we should expect a nonverbal marker.

This is essentially what we do find in Chinese. Sentences (39), (40), and (41) illustrate relativization on the subject (deleted), object (optionally deleted), and the object of a preposition (retained), respectively. The clause-final complementizing particle is *de*.

(39) [dale   wo   de]   neige   ren laile
     hit   me   REL   that   man came
     'The man that hit me came'
(40) [wo   dale   (ta)   de]   neige   ren   laile
     I   hit   him   REL   that   man came
     'The man that I hit came'
(41) [wo gen ta   nian   zhungwen de]   neige ren laile
     I   with him   studied Chinese REL   that man came
     'The man with whom I studied Chinese came'

This brief examination of two typologically irregular languages suggests that the general typological differences in relativization between languages with prenominal as opposed to postnominal clauses are observed in these languages as well. The data examined in this paper suggest the generalization that the subordinate status of the verb of a relative clause will be marked on the verb only if the verb is consistently adjacent to the head nominal, and thus only in postnominal clauses in VX languages and prenominal clauses in XV languages. Accordingly, we would not expect verb marking for relativization in either Chinese (with the order [(S) V (O)] Nom) or Persian (with Nom [(S) (O) V]. In languages in which the verb of the relative clause is not required to immediately precede or follow the head nominal, we expect a relative particle, between the head and the clause proper, as found in Chinese and in Persian. We have seen that relative pronouns occur only in postnominal relative clauses in which the verb is not initial. The occurrence of a clause-initial object clitic in Persian shows that the use of relative pronouns may not be limited to SVO languages but can perhaps be expected in any language that has the relative structure Nom [S X]. The word order of the main clause in Persian affects relativization only to the extent that it provides a reason for the use of extraposition of relative clauses.

8. CONCLUSION

The aim of this paper has been to investigate universal characteristics of relative clause marking through an examination of postnominal relative clauses in a number of languages of SVO and VSO word-order types and through comparison with relativization in prenominal clauses and in languages of SOV word order. This investigation has led to the formulation of a number of generalizations concerning the internal structure of relative clauses, stated as implications based on word-order types and relative clause position. In addition, it has been shown that the variations in the internal structure of relative clauses in postnominal clauses in SVO languages can be described as resulting from the selection by each language from among a limited set of universal relativization rules, the choice of which is partly determined by other typological properties of the particular language.

NOTES

1. Andrews (1975) lists five languages having both prenominal and postnominal relative clauses: Classical Tibetan, Hottentot, Quechua, Papago, and Turkish. But not all of these have finite clauses in both positions.
2. Relative clauses introduced by a pronoun appositive to the head nominal, taking the case marking appropriate to the function of that nominal in the matrix clause, are found in Old English and a number of other languages. This kind of case marking is especially common in

headless and reduced relative clauses. Relative markers of this type will be ignored in the remainder of this paper since they are not found in full relative constructions in any of the languages chosen for illustration.

3. Andrews (1975) claims that deletion of the relative nominal in Japanese follows from general principles affecting anaphora in Japanese.

4. There is also a postnominal relative clause in Turkish, similar to the Persian relative construction discussed below, from which it was borrowed. Its use is largely restricted to formal styles.

5. One exception will be noted below: in Hausa relativized objects are deleted but subjects are not.

REFERENCES

Adams, Douglas Q. (1972) "Relative clauses in Ancient Greek," in P. M. Peranteau, J. N. Levi and G. C. Phares (eds.) (1972), pp. 9–22.

Andrews, Avery (1975) The grammar of relative clauses. M.I.T. Unpublished manuscript.

Bach, Emmon (1971) "Questions," *Linguistic Inquiry* 2:153–166.

Bever, T. G. and D. T. Langendoen (1972) "The interaction of speech perception and grammatical structure in the evolution of language," in Robert P. Stockwell and Ronald K. S. Macauley (eds.), *Linguistic Change and Generative Theory*, pp. 32–95.

Craig, Colette G. (1971) Notes on the formation of complex sentences in Tunisian Arabic, with emphasis on the relative clause. Harvard University. Unpublished paper.

_____ (1973) General characteristics of Jacaltec relative clauses. Unpublished draft of a chapter of Harvard University Ph.D. dissertation.

Downing, Bruce T. (1973) Relative *that* as particle: A reexamination of English relativization. Paper presented at the California Linguistic Association Summer Conference, Santa Cruz, July.

_____ (1974) "Correlative relative clauses in universal grammar," *Minnesota Working Papers in Linguistics and Philosophy of Language* 2:1–17.

Frommer, Paul R. (1974) Some notes on relativization in Bahasa Malaysia. University of Southern California, Los Angeles. Unpublished paper.

Geoghegan, Sheila Graves (1975) "Relative clauses in Old, Middle, and New English," *Working Papers in Linguistics* no. 18:30–71. Columbus, Ohio: Department of Linguistics, The Ohio State University.

Givón, Talmy (1969) Studies in ChiBemba and Bantu Grammar. Ph.D. dissertation. UCLA.

_____ (1973) Some trends in Spoken Hebrew relativization. Department of Linguistics, UCLA. Unpublished paper.

Greenberg, Joseph (1966) "Some universals of grammar with particular reference to the order of meaningful elements," in J. H. Greenberg (ed.), *Universals of Language*, pp. 73–113. Cambridge, Mass.: The M.I.T. Press.

Hayon, Yehiel (1969) *Relativization in Hebrew: A Transformational Approach.* Ph.D. dissertation, University of Texas. Ann Arbor, Mich.: University Microfilms.

Hou, John Y. (1974) Relative clause formation in Chinese. University of Southern California, Los Angeles. Unpublished paper.

Keenan, Edward L. (1972) "Relative clause formation in Malagasy (and some related and some not so related languages)," in P. M. Peranteau, J. N. Levi and G. C. Phares (eds.) (1972), pp. 169–189.

——— (1974) "The logical status of deep structures (logical constraints on syntactic processes)," in Luigi Heilmann (ed.), *Proceedings of the Eleventh International Congress of Linguists,* pp. 477–490. Bologna: Societa editrice il Mulino.

——— and Bernard Comrie (1972) Noun phrase accessibility and universal grammar. Paper presented at the Annual Meeting of the Linguistic Society of America, Atlanta, December.

Kuno, Susumo (1974) "The position of relative clauses and conjunctions," *Linguistic Inquiry* 5:117–136.

Lehmann, Winfred P. (1973) "A structural principle of language and its implications," *Language* 49:47–66.

Lehmann, R. P. and W. P. Lehmann (1975) *An Introduction to Old Irish,* New York: Modern Language Association.

Loop, Terry (1974) Russian relative clauses. University of Southern California, Los Angeles. Unpublished paper.

Masica, Colin (1972) "Relative clauses in South Asia," in P. M. Peranteau, J. N. Levi and G. C. Phares (eds.) (1972), pp. 198–204.

McCawley, James (1972) "Japanese relative clauses," in P. M. Peranteau, J. N. Levi, and G. C. Phares (eds.) (1972), pp. 205–214.

Morgan, J. L. (1972) "Some aspects of relative clauses in English and Albanian," in P. M. Peranteau, J. N. Levi and G. C. Phares (eds.) (1972), pp. 63–72.

Omar, Asmah Haji (1973) "Noun phrases in Malay," *Language Sciences* 26:12–17.

Payne, John (1974) Vietnamese—typological check. Cambridge University. Mimeographed.

Peranteau, Paul M., Judith N. Levi and Gloria C. Phares (eds.) (1972) *The Chicago Which Hunt: Papers from the Relative Clause Festival.* Chicago: The Chicago Linguistic Society.

Perlmutter, David M. (1972) "Evidence for shadow pronouns in French relativization," in P. M. Peranteau, J. N. Levi and G. C. Phares (eds.) (1972), pp. 73–105.

——— and Janez Orešnik (1973) "Language-particular rules and explanation in syntax," in Stephen R. Anderson and Paul Kiparsky (eds.), *A Festschrift for Morris Halle,* pp. 419–459. New York: Holt, Rinehart and Winston.

Rosenbaum, Harvey (1971) "Constraints in Zapotec questions and relative clauses," in *On the Theory of Transformational Grammar* (Report to NSF GS-2468). Austin: Department of Linguistics, University of Texas.

Ross, John Robert (1967) Constraints on variables in syntax. Ph.D. thesis, M.I.T.; available from the Indiana University Linguistics Club.

Sadock, Jerrold (1972) "A conspiracy in Danish relative clause formation," in P. M. Peranteau, J. N. Levi and G. C. Phares (eds.) (1972), pp. 59–62.

Sanders, Gerald A. (1977) "A functional typology of elliptical coordinations," in Fred R. Eckman (ed.), *Current Themes in Linguistics*, pp. 241–270. Washington, D.C.: Hemisphere Publishing Corporation.

―――― and James H.-Y. Tai (1972) "Immediate dominance and identity deletion," *Foundations of Language* 8:161–198.

Schachter, Paul (1973) "Focus and relativization," *Language* 49:19–46.

Schwartz, Arthur (1971) "General aspects of relative clause formation," *Working Papers on Language Universals*, vol. 6, pp. 139–171. Stanford, Calif.: Committee on Linguistics, Stanford University.

Tabaian, Hessam (1975) "Conjunction, relativization, and complementation in Persian," *Colorado Research in Linguistics* 5:1–182.

Wald, Benji (1970) "Relativization in Umbundu," *Studies in African Linguistics* 1:131–156.

10

On the explanation of some typological facts about raising

Fred R. Eckman
University of Wisconsin–Milwaukee

1

The purpose of this paper is to propose an explanation for some facts concerning the process of raising in a number of languages. Throughout most of the work on generative grammar, this process has been assumed to account for the relationship of the (a) and (b) sentences in (1)-(3).

(1) a. John$_i$ believes that he$_i$ is rich.
    b. John believes himself to be rich.
(2) a. It seems that you are rich.
    a'. It is certain that you will win.

I would like to express my gratitude to Gerald Sanders for taking the time to discuss this topic with me at length and for his many suggestions. Thanks also to Dan Dinnsen, Edith Moravcsik, and Linda Schwartz for their helpful comments and criticisms. I would also like to express my appreciation to my informants: S. Abu Absi (Lebanese arabic); A. Acikgenc (Turkish); M. Eid (Egyptian arabic); M. Forner (German); M. Friedman (Hebrew); J. Klim (Polish); A. Koutsoudas (Greek); M. Meyers (French); E. Moravcsik (Hungarian); and R. Topalian (Armenian).

(2) b. You seem to be rich.
    b'. You are certain to win.
(3) a. It is easy to like you.
    a'. It is fun to tease you.
    b. You are easy to like.
    b'. You are fun to tease.

In each of these examples, the (b) sentences are assumed to be derived from the structure underlying the (a) sentences by a rule which optionally raises an NP out of the embedded clause into the matrix sentence. In order to be able to refer more easily to the sentence types in (1)-(3), let us call the raising operation involved in the derivation of (1b) as subject-to-object, or S-O raising; that involved in the derivation of (2b) and (2b') as subject-to-subject, or S-S raising; and that involved in deriving (3b) and (3b') as object-to-subject, or O-S raising.

If one can generalize from the sample of languages in Table A1 in the Appendix, then it is apparently true that all languages have grammatical sentences of the (a) type in (1)-(3). However, there are a number of languages in which some or all of the corresponding (b)-type sentences are ungrammatical; and moreover, there appears to be an implicational relation regarding the occurrence of these sentence types. Specifically, there are languages like Armenian, Egyptian Arabic, Hebrew, Lebanese Arabic, and Turkish in which sentences like (1b) are grammatical but sentences like (2b) and (3b) are ungrammatical. In addition, there are languages like Hungarian, Modern Greek, and Polish in which both (1b) and (2b) are grammatical but sentences like (3b) are ungrammatical. Finally, languages like English, French, and German have all the (b)-type sentences in (1)-(3). The data for all of these languages are given in Table A1.

From these data, we can see that it is apparently the case that if a language has S-O raising, it may or may not have the other two types of raising. If, on the other hand, a language has S-S raising, it will have S-O raising, but it may lack the third type, O-S raising. However, if a language has O-S raising, it will have the other two raising processes. In other words, it is apparently true that there are no languages in which sentences like (3b) are grammatical while sentences like (1b) or (2b) are ungrammatical; nor is it possible for a language to have grammatical sentences

like (2b) and lack grammatical sentences like (1b). These facts
are summarized in (4).

(4)

S-O	S-S	O-S	Examples
Yes	No	No	Armenian, Egyptian, Hebrew, Lebanese, Turkish
Yes	Yes	No	Hungarian, Modern Greek, Polish
Yes	Yes	Yes	English, French, German
No	No	No	None
No	Yes	Yes	None
No	No	Yes	None
No	Yes	No	None
Yes	No	Yes	None

For a theory of language to explain these facts, it must be the
case that these facts follow as a necessary consequence of that
theory's characterization of the process of raising. That is, these
facts can be explained if it necessarily follows from the derivation of the sentences in (1)–(3) that any language which has O-S
raising necessarily has S-S raising and that any language which
has S-S raising has S-O raising.

2

We shall begin our characterization of raising with the analysis
of the sentences in (1). The first assumption which we shall
make is that any language which has sentences like (1b),
necessarily has a rule of Raising, which moves a subject NP out
of any complement clause into the next higher sentence. Given
this, the first question which we have to face is why it should
be that if a language has raising at all, it necessarily has
sentences like (1b), but not necessarily those like (2b) or (3b).
This particular fact can be explained in part by invoking a
principle formulated by Perlmutter and Postal (in preparation),
called the Relational Succession Law, which can be stated
roughly as in (5).

(5) Relational Succession Law
Any argument raised out of a complement sentence, S, assumes the same grammatical relation as S.

For example, in sentences like (1a) the complement sentence, *that he is rich,* functions as the grammatical object of the verb, *believes.* Consequently, when the pronoun *he* is raised out of that complement sentence, *he* becomes the object of *believes.* In sentences like (2b), (2b'), (3b), and (3b'), however, it is assumed that at some point in the derivation the complement sentence is the subject of the matrix verb. Therefore, any NP raised out of the complements in the (a)-type sentences in (2) and (3) becomes the superficial subject of the matrix sentence.

The Relational Succession Law makes it unnecessary to state any constraints on the position into which an NP can be raised. Rather, the position that the raised element will assume follows from the grammatical function of the complement sentence. Given this, the fact that all languages which have any raising at all necessarily have sentences like (1b) can be explained by the fact that all languages have object complement sentences. Therefore, if the grammar of a language contains the rule of Raising, then since all languages have object complements, such a language will necessarily have raising into object position.

The Relational Succession Law can also be used to explain why some languages which have sentences like (1b) may lack sentences like the (b) type in (2). To see this, let us make the assumption that the same rule of Raising applies to derive all of the (b)-type sentences in (1)-(3). That is, this rule of Raising is assumed to raise NP's out of both subject and object complements. Given this assumption along with the Relational Succession Law, the fact that some languages may lack sentences like (2b) and (2b') can be explained if it is the case that the languages in which sentences like these are ungrammatical are just those languages which do not have subject complement sentences. This would mean that the complement clauses in the structures underlying (2a) and (2a') can never assume the grammatical relation of subject. This being the case, Raising could not apply because the Relational Succession Law would make no prediction regarding the grammatical function into which the NP would be raised. One consequence of this hypothesis is that in all languages in which sentences like (2b) and (2b′) are grammatical, it should also be the case that sentences like those in (6) are also ungrammatical.

(6) a. That you will win is certain.
    b. That Mary is rich bothers John.

As can be seen from the data in Table A2, this hypothesis is borne out. Hungarian, Modern Greek, and Polish, which have S-S raising, also have grammatical sentences with subject complements. On the other hand, Armenian, Egyptian and Lebanese Arabic, Hebrew, and Turkish, which do not have S-S raising, do not have grammatical sentences with subject complements. Thus, this analysis not only explains why all languages which have S-S raising also have S-O Raising, but in addition it can correlate the grammaticality of sentences like (2b) and (2b′) in a language with the grammaticality of those like (6).

There is one important point regarding sentences like (6) which should be made. When referring to either subject or object sentential complements, a distinction is being drawn between sentences like (1a) and (6), on the one hand, and those like (7), on the other, where the complement clause has a superficial nominal head.

(7) a. John believes the fact that he is rich.
    b. The fact that Mary is rich bothers John.

Since Raising applies only to clauses without heads, and not to clauses with heads, the correlation which is predicted by the Relational Succession Law is that a language which has grammatical sentences like (1b) and (6) should also have grammatical sentences like (2b).

Moreover, if we make the assumption that Raising is a universal rule, the only languages which would exhibit no raising at all would be only those languages in which all complement clauses, both subject and object, have superficial nominal heads. Thus, in a language where there is no raising whatever, it should be the case that sentences like those in (7) are grammatical, but sentences like (1a) and (6) are ungrammatical. The facts collected so far indicate that all languages have sentences like (1a), and therefore, if Raising is a universal rule, all languages should have sentences like (1b).

To recapitulate briefly, we have proposed that the facts regarding the distribution of sentence types (1) and (2) in natural languages can be explained by assuming a rule of Raising, which moves an NP from either a subject or object complement sentence into the next higher clause, and by incorporating the Relational Succession Law into the theory of grammar. Since all languages have object complements, a language which has the rule of Raising will have sentences like (1b). Since some languages do not have subject complements, such languages will lack sentences like (2b). Since there are no languages which have subject complements without also having object complements, there can be no language which has sentences like (2b) but lacks sentences like (1b).

3

Turning now to the characterization of the sentences in (3), let us focus our attention on the following facts: (1) all languages which have sentence types like (3b) have those like (2b); (2) some languages which have S-S raising lack O-S raising; and (3) the process of raising involved in the derivation of sentences like (3b) raises the object of the complement clause rather than the subject of the complement clause, which in these sentence types cannot be raised:

(8) a.   It is fun for Mary to tease John.
    b.   *Mary is fun to tease John.

Thus, any theory of raising must be able to explain the following:

(9) a.   A language which has O-S raising also has S-S raising.
    b.   A language which has S-S raising may lack O-S raising.
    c.   The only NP which is raisable in the structure underlying (3a) is the object of the complement clause and not the subject.

To begin with (9a), the fact that all languages which have grammatical sentences like (3b) also have sentences like (2b) can be explained if we assume that sentences like (3b) are derived by raising an NP out of a subject complement. Given this, then the Relational Succession Law predicts that the raised element will become the superficial subject of the next higher clause. Therefore, in order to have sentences like (3b), a language must have both a rule of Raising and subject complements. But if a language has these two things, then it will necessarily have sentences like (2b). Consequently, the implicational relationship between O-S raising and S-S raising is explained.

To explain the two facts listed in (9b) and (9c), let us propose, following Kimball (1971), that sentences like (8a) are derivable from the two underlying representations shown in (10).

(10) a. [$_S$is fun for someone [$_S$Mary tease John$_S$]$_S$]
     b. [$_S$is fun for Mary [$_S$Mary tease John$_S$]$_S$]

This makes the claim that sentences like (8a) are ambiguous, and are paraphrasable by the sentences in (11).

(11) a. Mary's teasing John is fun for someone.
     b. For her$_i$ to tease John is fun for Mary$_i$.

Now, given an underlying representation like (10b), it is clear that to derive a sentence like (8a), the subject of the complement clause must be deleted, producing a structure like (12).

(12) [$_S$is fun for Mary [$_S$tease John$_S$]$_S$]

If Raising is now applied to this structure, it is clear that it is the object of the complement clause which must be raised. Putting aside, for the moment, the question of what guarantees that Raising applies only to structures like (12) and not those like (10a), we are making the claim that the sentences in (13) are synonymous with (11b) and contrast semantically with (11a). Although the semantic judgments are somewhat fine, the facts seem to bear out this claim.

(13) a. John is fun for Mary to tease.
      b. John is fun to tease, for Mary.
      c. For Mary, John is fun to tease.
      d. For Mary, it is fun to tease John.

Given the assumption that O-S raising takes place only with respect to structures like (12), in which the subordinate subject has been deleted, it is clear that in order for a language to have sentences like (3b), it must be able to move the object of this subordinate clause into subject position. If the grammar of a language contained a constraint which prevented objects from being moved into subject position, then such a language would necessarily lack sentences like (3b). To test this hypothesis, we must be able to find other consequences of such a constraint.

A possible correlation that one might expect if a language could not move an object into subject position to derive sentences like (3b) is that such a language would also lack passive sentences like (14).

(14) The door was closed by the boy.

Inspection of the data in Table A1 shows that Hungarian, Modern Greek, and Polish have both S-O and S-S raising but do not have O-S raising. As is seen from the data in Table A3, none of these languages has passive sentences like (14). However, Table A3 shows that French and German, which have O-S raising, also have passive sentences.

Thus, this analysis of O-S raising can explain why it is that some languages which have S-S raising lack O-S raising by assuming that these languages obey a language-specific constraint which prevents objects from being moved into subject position. The assumption of this constraint makes it possible to correlate the absence of sentences like (3b) in a language with the absence of passive sentences and to correlate the presence of sentences like (3b) with the presence of passive sentences.

Given this characterization of O-S raising, let us now reconsider the structures in (10) to determine why it is that Raising cannot apply to (10a). Recall that our explanation for why the object is raised in structures like (10b) is that the subject of the subordinate clause is obligatorily deleted under identity with the higher dative NP. In structures like (10a), however, deletion cannot apply to the subject of the subordinate clause since the condition of identity is not met. The question which arises, therefore, is why the subject of the complement clause cannot be raised. As is seen from the sentence in (15), if the subordinate subject in (10a) is raised, an ungrammatical sentence results.

(15) *Mary is fun (for someone) to tease John.

To explain this fact, let us consider the type of clauses in which the subject can be raised. A reconsideration of the sentences in (1) and (2) reveals that for each of the (b)-type sentences where a subject has been raised, there is a corresponding, synonymous sentence in which the NP which has been raised in the (b) sentences is the subject of a subordinate clause with a finite verb. The hypothesis which one could propose, therefore, is that subjects are raisable only out of finite clauses and not out of clauses which are nonfinite. Given this, the fact that the subject of the subordinate clause in (10a) cannot be raised is due to the fact that this clause must take a *for . . . to* complementizer, as shown by the sentences in (16), making this clause nonfinite.

(16) A. a. For Mary to tease John is fun.
        b. It is fun for Mary to tease John.
     B. a. For Mary to tease John is fun for everyone.
        b. It is fun for everyone for Mary to tease John.

If this hypothesis is correct, then it should not be possible to raise a subject out of any nonfinite clause, regardless of the type of raising that is taking place. Thus, for example, given the sentences in (17) where it is clear that *for* must be a complementizer and not a dative marker, we see that if the subject of the complement clause is raised, an ungrammatical sentence results.

(17) A. a. I intended for the boy to stay after class.
        b. *I intended the boy to stay after class.
     B. a. I loathe for that girl to sing dixie.
        b. *I loathe that girl to sing dixie.

The restriction that subjects cannot be raised out of nonfinite complement clauses seems to be just a special case of a more general constraint which prevents any movement of subjects out of these clauses. Consequently, as can be seen from the sentences in (18), the subordinate subjects in the (a) sentences in (17) cannot be questioned or relativized.

(18) A. a. *Who did I intend to stay after class.
     b. *The boy whom I intended to stay after class is my brother.
  B. a. *Who do I loathe to sing dixie.
     b. *The girl whom I loathe to sing dixie is my sister.

Therefore, the fact that the subject of the subordinate clause in structures like (10a) cannot be raised is a consequence of the constraint which accounts for the ungrammaticality of the sentences in (17Ab), (17Bb) and (18).

To sum up the characterization of O-S raising, we have proposed that the facts listed in (9) can be explained by assuming (1) that O-S raising involves raising an NP from a subject complement; (2) that the grammars of languages which have S-S raising but lack O-S raising contains a nonuniversal constraint which prevents an object from being moved into subject position; and (3) a universal constraint which prevents raising a subject NP from a nonfinite clause.

There is one important consequence of this analysis which should be pointed out. Assuming that it is the verb of the clause into which an NP is raised that governs whether raising can take place, under the present analysis, it is not necessary to mark these verbs as to the type of raising which can occur. Rather, all that is necessary is that the verb be marked as one which allows an NP in a subordinate clause to be raised. Whether the raisable element is the subject or object, and whether it is raised into subject or object position follow from other independently motivated principles of grammar.

Thus, for example, given a predicate like *is a cinch,* it is clear from the sentences in (19) that either S-S or O-S raising is possible.

(19) a. It is a cinch that you will win the election.
   b. You are a cinch to win the election.
   c. It is a cinch for someone to operate this machine.
   d. This machine is a cinch for someone to operate.

Given that the structure in (20a) underlies the sentences in (19a and b), and that (20b) underlies (19c and d), it is only necessary to specify in the lexical entry of *is a cinch* that this predicate allows a subordinate NP to be raised.

(20) a. [$_S$is a cinch [$_S$you will win the election$_S$]$_S$]
   b. [$_S$is a cinch for someone [$_S$someone operate this machine$_S$]$_S$]

The fact that any raised NP will become the superficial subject follows from the Relational Succession Law. Moreover, the fact that the subject of the complement in (20a) is raisable, whereas the subject of the complement in (20b) is not raisable, is due to the fact that the complement clause is finite in (20a) but not finite in (20b). Finally, since the subject of the complement in (20b) must be obligatorily deleted, producing (21), it follows that if Raising applies to this structure, only the object of the subordinate clause can be raised.

(21) [$_S$is a cinch for someone [$_S$to operate this machine$_S$]$_S$]

To conclude, we have proposed an explanation for the implicational relation between O-S, S-S, and S-O raising. To explain these facts, we have made the following assumptions: (1) a rule of Raising which raises an NP out of a complement clause; (2) the Relational Succession Law; (3) a nonuniversal constraint which prohibits the raising of an underlying object into superficial subject position; and (4) a universal constraint which prohibits raising a subject out of a nonfinite clause. The facts in question can be explained, given these assumptions along with the following facts: (1) all languages have object complements, and (2) some, but not all languages, have subject complements.

APPENDIX

TABLE A1. Raising data

Armenian

S-O raising

ǰane	gentatre	te	ink	harust	e
John	believes	that	he	rich	is

'John believes that he is rich'

ǰane	inkzinke	harust	elalun	gentatre
John	himself	rich	to be	believes

'John believes himself to be rich'

S-S raising

vesdah	e	te	tun	bidi	šahis
sure	is	that	you	will	win

'It is sure that you will win'

*tun	vesdah	es	šahil		
you	sure	are	to	win	

'You are sure to win'

O-S raising

türin	e	kez	sirel
easy	is	you	to like

'It is easy to like you'

*tun	türin	es	sirel
you	easy	are	to like

'You are easy to like'

Egyptian Arabic

S-O raising

John	faakir	inn-u	ɣani
	believes	that he	rich

'John believes that he is rich'

John	faakir	nafsu	ɣani
	believes	himself	rich

'John believes himself to be rich'

S-S raising

yi-zhar	inn-ak	ɣani
seems	that you	rich

'It seems that you are rich'

*inta	bitizhar	ɣani
you	seem	rich

'You seem to be rich'

Egyptian Arabic

O-S raising

    sahl   çalayya   ʔabsitak
    easy   for me   I please you
    'It is easy for me to please you'

    *inta   sahl   çalayya   ʔabsitak
    you   easy   for me   I please you
    'You are easy for me to please'

French

S-O raising

    Jean croît qu'il est riche
    'John believes that he is rich'

    Jean se croît riche
    'John believes himself to be rich'

S-S raising

    Il semble que vous êtes riches
    'It seems that you are rich'

    Vous semblez riches
    'You seem to be rich'

O-S raising

    Il est difficile de voir Jean
    'It is difficult to see John'

    Jean est difficile à voir
    'John is difficult to see'

German

S-O raising

    John glaubt dass er reich ist
    'John believes that he is rich'

    John glaubt sich reich (zu sein)
    'John believes himself to be rich'

S-S raising

    Es scheint mir dass Sie reich sind
    'It seems that you are rich'

    Sie scheinen reich zu sein
    'You seem to be rich'

German

O-S raising

> Es ist leicht John zu befriedigen
> 'It is easy to please John'

> John ist leicht zu befriedigen
> 'John is easy to please'

Hebrew

S-O raising

John	mahamin	she-hu	ashir
	believes	that he	rich

'John believes that he is rich'

John	mahamin	atzmo	liyot	ashir
	believes	himself	to be	rich

'John believes himself to be rich'

S-S raising

ze	nire	she-ata	ashir
It	seems	that you	rich

'It seems that you are rich'

*Ata	nire	liyot	ashir
You	seem	to be	rich

'You seem to be rich'

O-S raising

Ze	kal	lesapek	otcha
it	easy	please	you

'It is easy to please you.'

*Ata	kal	lesapek
you	easy	please

'You are easy to please.'

Hungarian

S-O raising

János	azt	hiszi	hogy	ö	gazdag
John	that	thinks	that	he	rich

'John thinks that he is rich'

János	gazdagnak	hiszi	magát
John	rich (*dat.*) thinks		himself

'John thinks himself to be rich'

TABLE A1. (continued) Raising data

Hungarian

S-S raising

Úgy	látszik	hogy	János	szereti	Máriát
so	seems	that	John	likes	

'It seems that John likes Mary'

János	szeretni	látszik	Máriát	
John	to like	seems	Mary	

'John seems to like Mary'

*te	könnyű	vagy	Máriának	szeretni
you	easy	are	Mary (dat.)	to like

'You are easy for Mary to like'

Lebanese Arabic

S-O raising

John	bifakkir	ʔinnu	gani	
	thinks	that he	rich	

'John thinks that he is rich'

John	bifakkir	haalu	gani	
	thinks	himself	rich	

'John thinks himself to be rich'

S-S raising

byizhar	ʔinnak	bithib Mary	
appears	that you	like	

'It appears that you like Mary'

*bitizhar (ʔinnak)	bithib Mary	
you appear	like	

'You appear to like Mary'

O-S raising

saçb	ʔinnu Mary	tudrub John	
hard	that	hit	

'It is hard for Mary to hit John'

*John	saçb (ʔinnu) Mary	tudrub	
	hard	hit	

'John is hard for Mary to hit'

Modern Greek

S-O raising

perimeno	oti	o	janis	tha to kerdisi
I expect	that	(nom.)	John	will it win

'I expect that John will win it'

Modern Greek

S-S raising

perimeno	ton		jani		na to kerdisi
I expect	(*acc.*)		John		to it win

'I expect John to win it'

fenete	oti	ise	plusios
seems	that	you are	rich

'It seems that you are rich'

fenese	na	ise	plusios
you seem to		you are	rich

'You seem to be rich'

O-S raising

ine	diskolo	na	efxaiistais	ton	jani
is	easy	to	please	(*acc.*)	John

'It is easy to please John'

*o	janis	ine	diskolo	na	efxaiistais
(*nom.*)	John	is	easy	to	please

'John is easy to please'

Polish

S-O raising

Jan	wiezy	że	jest	bogotym
John	believes	that	he is	rich

'John believes that he is rich'

Jan	uwaza	się za	bogotego
John	believes	self as	rich

'John believes himself to be rich'

S-S raising

Wydaje	się	że	jesteś	bogotym
seems	self	that	you are	rich

'It seems that you are rich'

Wydajesz się		bogotym
you seem self		rich

'You seem to be rich'

O-S raising

jest	latwo	cię	zadowolić
is	easy	you	please

'It is easy to please you'

*jesteś	latwy	do	zadowolenia
you are	easy	to	please

'You are easy to please'

TABLE A1. (*continued*) Raising data

Turkish

S-O raising

John	inanir	ki		kendisi	zengin	dir
	believes	that		he	rich	is

'John believes that he is rich'

John	kendinin	zengin		olduğuna	inanir
	himself	rich		to be	believes

'John believes himself to be rich'

S-S raising

emin dir ki		sen		kazanačaksin
certain is that		you		will win

'It is certain that you will win'

*kazanmak eminsin
to win   you are certain
'You are certain to win'

O-S raising

seni	memnun	etmek		kolay	dir
you	to	please		easy	is

'It is easy to please you'

*memnum etmeye   kolaysin
to   please   you are easy
'You are easy to please'

TABLE A2. Subject complement data

Armenian

genere	ǰanin	te		merin	harust	e
bothers	John	that		Mary	rich	is

'It bothers John that Mary is rich'

*te	merin	harust	e		genere	ǰanin
that	Mary	rich	is		bothers	John

'That Mary is rich bothers John'

Egyptian Arabic

ʔakud	inn-ak	ħa-ti-ksab
certain	that you	will win

'It is certain that you will win'

TABLE A2. *(Continued)* Subject complement data

Egyptian Arabic

*inn-ak	ḥa-ti-ksab	ʔakud
that you	will win	certain
'That you will win is certain		

French

C'est embêtant que Marie est riche
'It is annoying that Mary is rich'

Que Marie est riche est embêtant
'That Mary is rich is annoying'

German

Es gefällt Johann nicht dass Mary reich ist
'It does not please John that Mary is rich'

Dass Mary reich ist gefällt Johann nicht
'That Mary is rich does not please John'

Hebrew

ze	margiz et	John	she Mary	ashira
it	bothers	John	that Mary	rich
'It bothers John that Mary is rich'				

*She Mary	ashira	margiz et	John
That Mary	rich	bothers	John
'That Mary is rich bothers John'			

Hungarian

(az) bántja	Jánost	hogy	Mari	beteg
it bothers	John (*acc.*)	that	Mary	sick
'It bothers John that Mary is sick'				

hogy	Mari	beteg	(az) bántja Jánost
that	Mary	sick	it bothers John (*acc.*)
'That Mary is sick bothers John'			

Lebanese Arabic

byiz	izni	ʔinnu	John	gani
bothers	me	that	John	rich
'It bothers me that John is rich'				

TABLE A2. (*continued*) Subject complement data

Lebanese Arabic

*ʔinnu	John	gani	byiz	izni
that	John	rich	bothers	me

'That John is rich bothers me'

Modern Greek

me	enoxli	oti	o	janis	ine	plusios
me	bothers	that	(*nom.*)	John	is	rich

'It bothers me that John is rich'

oti	o	janis	ine	plusios	me	enoxli
that	(*nom.*)	John	is	rich	me	bothers

'That John is rich bothers me'

Polish

Drazni	Janka	źe	Marysia	jest	bogota
bothers	John	that	Mary	is	rich

'It bothers John that Mary is rich'

Że	Marysia	jest	bogota	drazni	Janka
'That	Mary	is	rich	bothers	John'

Turkish

Johni	rahatsiz eden	Marynin	zenginliği	dir
John	it bothers	that Mary	rich	is

'It bothers John that Mary is rich'

*Ki	Mary	zengin	dir	Johni	rahatsig eder
that		rich	is	John	bothers

'That Mary is rich bothers John'

TABLE A3. Passive data

French

La porte a été fermé par le garçon
'That door was closed by the boy'

German

Die Tur wird von dem Jungen geschlossen
'The door was closed by the boy'

TABLE A3. (*continued*) Passive data

Hungarian						
*az	ajtó	be volt	csukva	a	fiú	által
the	door	was	closed	the	boy	by
'The door was closed by the boy'						

Modern Greek					
*o	stratiotis	lavoθike	apo	ton	jani
(*nom.*)	soldier was	wounded	by	(*acc.*)	John
'The soldier was wounded by John'					

Polish				
?Pies	byl	uderzony	przez	chtopca
dog	was	hit	by	boy
'The dog was hit by the boy'				

REFERENCES

Kimball, John (1971) "Super Equi-NP Deletion as Dative Deletion," *Papers from the Seventh Regional Meeting, Chicago Linguistics Society.* Chicago: Chicago Linguistics Society.

Perlmutter, David, and Paul Postal (In preparation) *Relational Grammar.*

Postal, Paul (1974) *On Raising.* Cambridge, Mass.: The M.I.T. Press.

11

On aspiration and
deaspiration processes

Kathleen Houlihan
University of Minnesota

1

Aspiration and deaspiration rules of various types are found in many different languages. However, not all of the logically possible types of such rules are found to occur. The standard theory of generative phonology (Chomsky and Halle 1968) does not provide a means of distinguishing between the types of aspiration and deaspiration rules which do occur and those which do not. This paper considers the types of languages in which aspirated and unaspirated stops are found, the types of aspiration and deaspiration rules in these languages, and possible explanations of why these kinds of rules, and not others, are found in natural languages.

The present discussion is limited to a consideration of aspiration in voiceless stops. I will not refer to aspirated fricatives,

I am grateful to Daniel A. Dinnsen, Catherine O. Ringen, and Charlotte Webb for their valuable comments and suggestions on an earlier version of this paper.

since they seem to be less common than aspirated stops, although the generalizations made here should also apply to aspiration in fricatives. I will also not discuss the so-called "voiced aspirates," which are considered by Ladefoged (1971) to be murmured rather than aspirated. However, "voiced aspirates" do seem to pattern phonologically in the same ways as do the voiceless aspirated stops.

Aspirated stops have been characterized by Lisker and Abramson (1964) as those in which there is a lag in voice onset time (VOT) after the release of closure and before the voicing begins for the following segment. Ladefoged (1971) calls this lag a period of voicelessness. Unaspirated stops are those in which the release of closure is followed almost immediately by the beginning of voicing. In final position of a word or utterance, aspirated stops would seem to be those in which the release is followed by a noisy period of relatively high intensity and duration, while unaspirated stops are those which are either unreleased or in which the release is followed by noise of relatively low intensity and duration.

These definitions characterize stops which are postaspirated, that is, those in which aspiration follows the stop closure. I also would like to consider preaspirated stops, such as those found in Tarascan, Lapp, and Icelandic, in which aspiration, defined as a period of voicelessness, precedes the stop closure. Later discussion of aspirated stops is intended to refer to both preaspirated and postaspirated stops.

2

There appear to be five types of languages with respect to the distribution of aspirated and unaspirated stops.

Type I. Languages with one series of voiceless stops, which are always unaspirated (e.g., Spanish, French, Finnish, etc.).

Type II. Languages with one series of voiceless stops, which are sometimes aspirated and sometimes unaspirated (e.g., English, Swahili, German, etc.). In these languages, stops are aspirated word-initially and syllable-initially in medial stressed syllables. In German, stops may also occasionally be aspirated in medial unstressed syllables. Examples are given in (1):

(1) English: [pʰ]*ass*, [pʰ]*arade, a*[pʰ]*art* (Moulton 1962)
Swahili:[1] [tʰ]*ando* 'swarm', *mwi*[tʰ]*uni* 'in the forest',
una [tʰ]*aka*[tʰ]*aka* 'you are dirty' (Polomé 1967)
German: [tʰ]*ag* 'day', [tʰ]*ablett* 'tablet',
A[tʰ]*om* 'atom' (Moulton 1962)

Type III. Languages with two series of voiceless stops, one of
which is lax and the other tense. The lax series is always
unaspirated and the tense series is sometimes aspirated (e.g.,
Cypriot Greek, Tarascan, Lapp, etc.). In Cypriot Greek, the
tense stops, called "geminate" by Newton (1972), are short and
aspirated in absolute initial position, long and aspirated word-
initially after a vowel in a preceding word, short and unaspirated
word-initially after a consonant in a preceding word, and long
and aspirated word-medially after a vowel. They do not occur
word-medially after a consonant or word-finally. Examples are
given in (2):

(2) [pʰefto] 'I fall', [appʰaros] 'horse' (Newton 1972)

In Tarascan, tense voiceless stops (C′) are aspirated word-
initially, but aspiration is optional when following a consonant
in a preceding word. They are preaspirated medially after vowels
and unaspirated medially after consonants. Examples are given in
(3):

(3) [kʰéri] from /k'éri/ 'big'
[šɑnkʰéri] or [šɑnkéri] from /šani k'éri/ 'very big'
[imɑkʰɑmɑ́kuhti] from /imá k'amákut'i/ 'he/she/it/they fin-
ished it'
[pʰíntɑni] from /p'ínt'ani/ 'to remove from the fire'
(Foster 1969, 1971)

Type IV. Languages with two series of voiceless stops, one of
which is always unaspirated and the other sometimes aspirated
and sometimes unaspirated; there are no additional differences in
length or tenseness (e.g., Sanskrit, some dialects of Hindi). In
Sanskrit, the second series of voiceless stops is aspirated in all
positions except syllable-final. Examples are given in (4):

(4) [ǰit] versus [ǰitas] versus [ǰitsu] 'conquering', nom. sg.,
    nom. pl., loc. pl.
    [mat] versus [mathas] versus [matsu] 'destroying', nom.
    sg., nom. pl., loc. pl. (Whitney 1889)

In some dialects of Hindi, the second series of voiceless stops
is aspirated in all positions except word-final, and in others it is
aspirated in all positions except syllable-final.

Type V. Languages with two series of voiceless stops, one of
which is always unaspirated and the other always aspirated (e.g.,
standard Hindi, Thai, Cantonese). In standard Hindi, the second
series of voiceless stops is aspirated in all positions, as is shown
in (5):

(5) [rəkha] versus [rəkhkər] versus [rəkh] 'to put', past part.,
    ger., fam. imp.
    [mətha] versus [məthkər] versus [məth] 'to churn', past
    part., ger., fam. imp.

In Thai and Cantonese, the second series of voiceless stops is
always aspirated, but it only occurs word-initially (Noss 1964,
Chao 1947).

3

These five types of languages can be distinguished from each
other by the types of aspiration or deaspiration rules, or the
lack of such rules, required in an analysis of their aspirated and
unaspirated stops.

3.1.1. In Type I languages, there are no alternations among
voiceless stops involving aspiration. These languages, then, have
neither aspiration nor deaspiration rules.

3.1.2. In Type II languages, voiceless stops are either aspirated
or unaspirated in predictable phonological environments, and
need not be distinguished on the basis of aspiration in underlying representations. The standard analysis of these languages
posits voiceless unaspirated stops as basic and derives the

aspirated stops by an aspiration rule which applies word-initially and also syllable-initially in stressed syllables. Using "$" to represent a syllable boundary (Vennemann 1972), the rule could be formulated as in (6):

$$
(6) \quad \begin{bmatrix} -\text{sonorant} \\ -\text{continuant} \\ -\text{voice} \end{bmatrix} \rightarrow [+\text{aspirated}] \; / \begin{Bmatrix} \#\underline{\quad} \\ \$\underline{\quad} \; [+\text{stress}] \end{Bmatrix}
$$

The alternative analysis would posit aspirated stops as basic and derive the unaspirated stops by a rule which deaspirates stops word-medially in unstressed syllables, such as the one given in (7):

$$
(7) \quad [+\text{aspirated}] \rightarrow [-\text{aspirated}] \; /[+\text{segment}] \; \$\underline{\quad} \; [-\text{stress}]
$$

Objections to this second analysis are primarily on the grounds of phonological universals. It is a commonly held view that all languages have voiceless unaspirated stops. Jakobson and Halle (1971) consider the voiceless labial stop [p] to be the "optimal" consonant and the one acquired first in child language acquisition in all languages. If this claim is a universal of language and all languages do have voiceless unaspirated stops, and if this universal is true of both phonetic and phonemic levels of representation, then Type II languages, under the second analysis, would constitute the only violations of this universal, in that their inventory of underlying segments would contain voiced stops and voiceless aspirated stops, but no voiceless unaspirated ones.[2] If we consider this absence of underlying voiceless unaspirated stops as sufficient grounds for rejecting the second analysis, then Type II languages must be analyzed as having voiceless unaspirated stops as basic and a rule of aspiration similar to the one given in (6) above.

3.1.3. In Type III languages, where tense stops are aspirated in some environments and unaspirated in others, aspiration is predictable from tenseness but not vice versa. The simplest analysis, then, is one which posits tense unaspirated stops as basic and derives the tense aspirated ones by an aspiration rule. The alternatives are either (1) to posit tense aspirated stops and a deaspiration rule; or (2) to posit lax aspirated stops and two rules, one tensing all aspirated stops and the other deaspirating certain aspirated stops. The first alternative requires positing a more complex (or more marked) type of segment as basic, and the second requires two rules instead of one. On the basis of simplicity, then, these languages must be analyzed as having a rule which aspirates certain of the basic tense unaspirated stops.

This is the analysis proposed by Friedrich (1971) for Tarascan, one of the Type III languages. He claims that speakers are aware of the tenseness of the second series of voiceless stops, but not of the aspiration, and that the stops are always tense but not always aspirated. He argues that aspiration is secondary and that tenseness is the primary characteristic of the stops in question. I will conclude here, then, that aspirated stops in Type III languages are derived from underlying tense unaspirated stops by an aspiration rule.

Stops are aspirated in Cypriot Greek at the beginning of an utterance and at the beginning of a word-initial or a word-medial syllable when preceded by a vowel. The rule is given in (8), where "/" represents a phrase boundary:

$$(8) \quad \begin{bmatrix} -\text{sonorant} \\ -\text{continuant} \\ +\text{tense} \end{bmatrix} \rightarrow [+\text{aspirated}] \; / \left\{ \begin{matrix} / \\ V \left\{ \begin{matrix} \$ \\ \# \end{matrix} \right\} \end{matrix} \right\} \underline{\qquad}$$

In Tarascan stops are aspirated at the beginning of an utterance and at the beginning of word-initial and word-medial syllables when preceded by a vowel. Aspiration is optional at the beginning of a word when there is a preceding consonant. Using standard notational conventions, this situation must be stated as two rules, the first of which is obligatory and the second of which is optional. These are given in (9):

$$(9) \; a. \quad \begin{bmatrix} -\text{sonorant} \\ -\text{continuant} \\ +\text{tense} \end{bmatrix} \rightarrow [+\text{aspirated}] / \left\{ V \left\{ \begin{matrix} \$ \\ \# \end{matrix} \right\} \right\} \underline{\qquad} \text{OBLIGATORY}$$

$$b. \quad \begin{bmatrix} -\text{sonorant} \\ -\text{continuant} \\ +\text{tense} \end{bmatrix} \rightarrow [+\text{aspirated}] \; /C\#\underline{\qquad} \text{OPTIONAL}$$

3.1.4. In Type IV languages, aspirated stops contrast with unaspirated stops only in the feature of aspiration and, therefore, must be analyzed as underlying aspirated stops. However, these stops are unaspirated in certain positions, namely, word-finally in some dialects of Hindi and syllable-finally in Sanskrit. Rules of deaspiration must be posited for these languages, a rule like the one given in (10) for certain dialects of Hindi and like the one given in (11) for Sanskrit:

(10) [+aspirated] → [−aspirated] /____ #

(11) [+aspirated] → [−aspirated] /____ $\left\{ \begin{matrix} \$ \\ \# \end{matrix} \right\}$

3.1.5. In Type V languages, aspirated stops contrast with unaspirated stops only in the feature of aspiration, and, as in Type IV languages, the aspirated stops must be analyzed as underlying aspirated stops. However, there are no alterations between aspirated and unaspirated stops, and therefore no aspiration or deaspiration rules need be posited for these languages.

4

From the above analyses, we can make the following generalizations about aspiration and deaspiration rules:

(12) a. Aspiration rules apply syllable-initially and word-initially.

b. Deaspiration rules apply syllable-finally and word-finally.

c. Aspiration rules that apply under certain conditions syllable-initially in word-medial syllables also apply under at least all the same conditions syllable-initially in word-initial syllables, but not necessarily vice versa.

d. Deaspiration rules that apply syllable-finally in word-medial syllables also apply syllable-finally in word-final syllables, but not necessarily vice versa.[3]

It appears that there are no rules of the following types:

(13) a. Aspiration rules that apply syllable-finally or word-finally.[4]

b. Deaspiration rules that apply syllable-initially or word-initially.

c. Aspiration rules that apply under certain conditions syllable-initially in word-medial syllables but do not apply under all the same conditions syllable-initially in word-initial syllables.[5]

d. Deaspiration rules that apply syllable-finally in word-medial syllables but do not apply syllable-finally in word-final syllables.

The standard theory of generative phonology does not provide any basis for distinguishing the types of rules in (12) from the nonoccurring types in (13). In the remainder of this paper, I will consider alternative theories which may provide a principled basis for excluding rules of the types given in (13) as possible rules in natural languages, while allowing rules of the type given in (12). I first consider two theories proposed in the literature which disallow rules like (13a) and (13b), and then I propose a theory of historical change which will disallow rules like (13c) and (13d).

5

Within the standard theory of generative phonology, no constraints are placed on the environments in which particular types of rules can apply. Aspiration rules are as expected syllable-finally and word-finally as they are syllable-initially and word-initially. Deaspiration rules are as expected syllable-initially and word-initially as they are syllable-finally and word-finally. However, there appear to be no languages, for example, that are similar to English but in which voiceless stops are aspirated at the ends of either stressed or unstressed syllables in word-medial position and at the ends of all syllables in word-final position. Nor do there appear to be any languages, for example, that are similar to Sanskrit but in which aspirated voiceless stops are deaspirated at the beginnings of all syllables, both word-initially and word-medially. The standard theory would allow for the possibility of such languages. Two recent theories of phonology which do impose constraints on the types of rules that can apply in various positions would, however, disallow languages like the hypothetical, nonoccurring ones just mentioned.

5.1.1. The first of these theories is the Simplex-Feature Hypothesis proposed by Sanders (1974). Within this theory, all segments are characterized by the presence or absence of unary or simplex features, rather than by positive or negative values of binary or complex features, as in the "standard" theory. Further, all phonological rules are either insertions or deletions of either features or segments. If aspirated stops are characterized by the presence of a feature ASPIRATION and unaspirated stops are characterized by the absence of this feature, as Sanders suggests, then aspiration rules are insertion rules and deaspiration rules are deletion rules. There is a general constraint in this theory that only insertion rules, and not deletion rules, apply word-initially, and only deletion rules, and not insertion rules, apply word-finally. As Sanders notes, this constraint will correctly restrict aspiration rules to applying only in word-initial position and deaspiration rules to applying only in word-final position. If the constraint is extended to restrict insertions and deletions at syllable boundaries as well as at word boundaries, it will correctly allow rules of the types in (12a) and (12b), while disallowing rules of the types in (13a) and (13b). Rules like (12a) are allowed on the same grounds as all insertion rules in initial position are allowed, and rules like (12b) are allowed on the same grounds as all deletion rules in final position are allowed. Rules like (13a) are disallowed on the same grounds that all insertion rules in final position are disallowed, and rules like (13b) are disallowed on the same grounds that all deletion rules in initial position are disallowed.

5.1.2. Another theory which imposes constraints on the environments in which rules can apply is the theory of Natural Generative Phonology, proposed by Vennemann (1971 and 1972) and Hooper (1974). Within this theory, feature-changing rules are either "strengthening" rules or "weakening" rules, as determined by reference to a hierarchy of segmental strength. Rules which change segments from a weaker to a stronger position on the strength hierarchy are strengthening rules, and rules which change segments from a stronger to a weaker position on the hierarchy are weakening rules. Hooper claims that rules which apply syllable-initially are strengthening rules and those which apply syllable-finally are weakening rules. Since word-initial position is usually also syllable-initial position and word-final position is usually also syllable-final position, strengthening but not weakening rules should apply word-initially and weakening but not strengthening rules should apply word-finally. If aspirated stops are stronger than unaspirated stops on the strength hierarchy, as is suggested by Hooper, then aspiration rules are strengthening rules and their occurrence only syllable-initially and word-initially follows from this theory. Similarly, deaspiration rules would be weakening rules, and their occurrence syllable-finally and word-finally would also follow from this theory.

In this particular case of aspiration and deaspiration rules, the two theories considered here, the Simplex-Feature Hypothesis and the theory of Natural Generative Phonology, make exactly the same claims about the positions in which aspiration and deaspiration rules will apply, and there is no basis for choice between them. Thus, to the extent that either theory is supported by empirical evidence, either is sufficient to explain the positions in which aspiration and deaspiration rules apply, stated as (12a) and (12b) above.

6

While the types of rules that occur and do not occur, given in (12a) and (12b), and (13a) and (13b), respectively, can be accurately characterized by either the Simplex-Feature Hypothesis or the theory of Natural Generative Phonology, the occurring types of rules in (12c) and (12d) remain to be distinguished from the nonoccurring types in (13c) and (13d). The generalization in (12c) is that aspiration rules that apply in word-medial syllables also apply word-initially under at least all the same conditions, but not necessarily vice versa. For example, stops are aspirated in English in medial stressed syllables, and they are also aspirated word-initially in unstressed as well as stressed syllables. However, the fact that aspiration applies word-initially in unstressed syllables does not imply that it also applies word-medially in unstressed syllables. In Cypriot Greek and Tarascan, stops are aspirated both word-medially and word-initially, unless they are preceded by a consonant. In addition, in Tarascan word-initial stops are aspirated optionally even if they are preceded by a consonant. Thus, we see that aspiration rules apply word-initially in an environment that is at least as general as, and is usually more general than, the environment in which they apply syllable-initially in word-medial syllables.

The generalization in (12d) is that deaspiration rules that apply syllable-finally in word-medial syllables also apply word-finally, but not necessarily vice versa. Thus, if a deaspiration rule applies syllable-finally in word-medial syllables, as in Sanskrit, it will also apply word-finally. However, a deaspiration rule may apply word-finally without also applying syllable-finally in word-medial syllables, as in some dialects of Hindi.

Aspiration and deaspiration rules, then, are equally or less restricted in word-marginal positions than they are in word-medial positions. As noted in (13c), there appear to be no languages in which, for example, stops are aspirated syllable-initially only in medial syllables or in which stops are aspirated syllable-initially in all medial syllables but word-initially only if the syllable is stressed. Similarly, as noted in (13d), there appear to be no languages, for example, in which stops are deaspirated syllable-finally only in medial syllables or in which stops are deaspirated syllable-finally in all medial syllables but word-finally only if the syllable is unstressed. Again, there is no reason within the standard theory why this should be the case. The standard theory does not even recognize syllable boundaries, much less propose any constraints on the generality of rules conditioned by syllable boundaries with respect to those conditioned by word boundaries.

6.1.1. A partial explanation for the equal generality of application of aspiration rules at word boundaries as at syllable boundaries can be found by considering the hierarchical arrangement of boundaries.

McCawley (1968) and Harms (1968) discuss a hierarchy of syntactically and morphologically determined boundaries, with morpheme boundary being the lowest boundary on the hierarchy, phrase boundary the highest, and word boundary, as well as any language-specific intermediate boundaries, between the two. They both note that a rule which applies in the presence of any given boundary also applies in the presence of any higher boundary in the hierarchy. Thus, a rule which applies at a morpheme boundary also applies at a word boundary and a rule which applies at a word boundary also applies at a phrase boundary. If syllable boundary is added to such a hierarchy, as the lowest boundary, then the fact that rules like aspiration and deaspiration rules which apply at syllable boundaries word-medially also apply at word boundaries would follow from such a hierarchical system. It would further follow that rules which apply at word boundaries also apply at phrase boundaries, which appears to be the case as well.

This hierarchy of boundaries will satisfactorily explain the facts with respect to deaspiration rules, but it alone is not sufficient to explain those concerning aspiration rules. In the case of deaspiration, the syllable or word boundary is the only conditioning environment, at least in the languages under consideration here. If the syllable boundary is recognized in phonological theory, the deaspiration rule for Sanskrit can be simply stated as in (14):

(14) [+aspirated] → [−aspirated] /___ $

Given the hierarchy of boundaries proposed by McCawley and by Harms, the rule in (14) will apply not only before syllable boundaries but also before word and phrase boundaries.

In the case of the aspiration rules discussed above, however, the situation is not quite as simple. The hierarchy of boundaries will explain the fact that aspiration in English applies word-initially in stressed syllables, because it applies syllable-initially in stressed syllables in word-medial position. The aspiration rule for English cannot be simplified to refer only to syllable boundaries, however, since aspiration in word-initial position applies more generally than it does word-medially. The rule must still mention the word boundary, as in the rule given in (6), in order to account for the aspiration in word-initial unstressed syllables. In other words, the hierarchy of boundaries alone does not explain the fact that aspiration in English, and other Type II languages, applies more generally word-initially than it does word-medially, although it does predict that such rules will not apply less generally word-initially than they do word-medially.

In Type III languages, such as Tarascan and Cypriot Greek, in order for the hierarchy of boundaries to insure that aspiration rules will apply at least as generally word-initially as they do word-medially, we must assume not only that a rule applying *at* a lower boundary also applies at all higher boundaries but also that a rule, such as aspiration, which is conditioned by an environment *across* a syllable boundary will also apply when conditioned by that same environment across a word boundary. Feature-changing nonprosodic rules like aspiration are usually considered to be "word-level" rules that do not automatically apply across word boundaries. For example, a rule that assimilates a nasal consonant to the place of articulation of a following consonant may apply across a syllable boundary within a word in some language, but we would not expect that such a rule would automatically also apply across a word boundary, unless the word boundary were specifically mentioned in the structural description of the rule. Thus, for rules like nasal assimilation, we would not want to claim that the presence of a lower boundary, such as a syllable or morpheme boundary, between a segment undergoing a change and a segment conditioning a change necessarily implies the presence of all higher boundaries in the same position. However, if we distinguish assimilatory rules, like nasal assimilation, from nonassimilatory feature-changing rules, like aspiration and deaspiration, we could claim that the occurrence of a syllable boundary in the structural description of a nonassimilatory rule implies the occurrence of all higher boundaries in the same position. Given this revision, the relevant part of the aspiration rules in Tarascan and Cypriot Greek, where stops are aspirated syllable-initially and word-initially unless preceded by a consonant, could be stated as in (15):

(15) $\begin{bmatrix} C \\ +tense \end{bmatrix} \rightarrow [+\text{aspirated}] \ /V \ \$\underline{}$

The fact that aspiration rules usually apply more generally, rather than just equally generally, in word-initial position would, however, still remain unexplained.

6.1.2. In order to explain the greater generality, as well as the equal generality, of the application of aspiration and deaspiration rules at word boundaries compared to syllable boundaries, I suggest we consider the historical development of such rules. We have seen examples above of these rules, or subrules of these rules, applying at word boundaries but not at syllable boundaries. However, we have seen no examples of the rules applying at syllable boundaries but not at word boundaries. It seems reasonable to assume that aspiration and deaspiration rules originally applied only at the largest phonological boundaries, perhaps utterance or phrase boundaries, and later spread to word boundaries and finally to syllable boundaries. If these kinds of rules can never apply at syllable boundaries unless they have previously applied only at word boundaries, the equal generality of application at word boundaries can be explained. We should note again that the situation appears to be the opposite for assimilation rules, which apply across word boundaries only if they also apply across syllable boundaries. Therefore, we must limit this discussion to nonassimilatory feature-changing rules.

The suggested historical development of such rules can be stated as follows:

(16) Nonassimilatory rules originate at the highest phonological boundary, which is the phrase or utterance boundary, and later spread to lower boundaries in sequence, first to the word boundary and then to the syllable boundary.

Morpheme boundaries, which do not represent phonological units, appear to have no role in this process.

The hypothesis given in (16) will explain the fact that nonassimilatory rules apply at syllable boundaries only if they also apply at word boundaries, since, it is claimed, such rules only apply at syllable boundaries as a generalization of application at word boundaries. However, we must still explain why it is that these rules frequently apply more generally at word boundaries than they do at syllable boundaries. A second hypothesis about the historical development of these rules is required and is proposed in (17):

(17) The environment in which a nonassimilatory rule applies may generalize at a phrase or word boundary, but not at a syllable boundary.

The hypothesis in (17) will correctly constrain generalization of environments of nonassimilatory rules, like aspiration and deaspiration rules, to word-initial or word-final position, insuring that such rules cannot generalize independently at syllable boundaries.

In the case of an aspiration rule, then, it is suggested that a rule which applies in word-initial position may spread to syllable-initial position. The rule may later generalize at the word boundary, and that generalization may also spread to the syllable boundary, and so on. The process presumably could continue until all voiceless stops were aspirated in all word- and syllable-initial positions.

If this description of the historical development of aspiration and deaspiration rules is correct, and such rules apply at syllable boundaries only as extensions of rules which apply at word boundaries, then we can explain why such rules never apply more generally at syllable boundaries in word-medial position than they do at word boundaries. Further, if the environment of such rules generalizes only at word boundaries, we can explain why these rules may apply more generally at word boundaries than they do at medial syllable boundaries. Of course, at this level of "explanation," we are doing little more than merely describing the facts, and the explanation suggested here itself needs an explanation. We will consider explanations for (16) and (17) in Section 7.

6.1.3. In looking for additional support for the hypotheses stated in (16) and (17), we should consider two types of evidence. First, we would like to find that the claims made by the hypotheses are true for earlier stages of the languages we have examined. For example, (16) claims that aspiration in Type II languages once applied only to word-initial stops in stressed syllables, before it generalized to apply to all stops in stressed syllables. Unfortunately, however, the details of the historical development of aspiration in English, German, and Swahili are unknown, and we have no way of determining if such claims are in fact correct. The hypothesis also claims that in Type III languages, aspiration once applied only to word-initial stops unless they were preceded by a consonant, before it spread to apply to syllable-initial stops under the same conditions in medial syllables. Again, we do not know if this was in fact the case. However, the hypothesis also predicts that any generalization of the environment of the aspiration rule will take place in word-initial position. We have just such a situation in Tarascan at the present time, where aspiration applies optionally to word-initial stops that are preceded by a consonant. If the hypothesis is correct, aspiration in Tarascan should proceed to become obligatory in this environment as well, and later may spread to medial syllable boundaries under the same conditions. In general, however, we will not be able to find direct evidence of the stages of development predicted by the hypothesis, either, as in the case of Type II languages, because aspiration is an allophonic process and was not recorded or discussed in historical records, or, as in the case of the Type III languages considered here, because we have no records at all of the historical stages of the language.

The second type of evidence that would support the hypotheses is evidence that other types of nonassimilatory rules, in addition to aspiration and deaspiration rules, are consistent with the claims made by the hypotheses in (16) and (17). We do in fact find fairly numerous examples of differences in generality of application of other kinds of rules. This evidence is of two types: (1) rules which apply at boundaries of larger phonological units but not at boundaries of smaller units, and (2) rules which apply more generally at boundaries of larger phonological units than at boundaries of smaller units.

In the first category, there are rules which apply only at word and phrase boundaries but not at medial syllable boundaries, such as glottal stop insertion word-initially and phrase-initially in Finnish (Lehiste 1965) and the devoicing of liquids word-finally and phrase-finally in Central Cagayan Negrito (Oates and Oates 1958). There are rules which appply only at phrase or utterance boundaries but not at phrase-medial word or syllable bound-aries, such as the devoicing of certain phrase-final sonorant consonants in Northern Ostyak (Rédei 1965) and Maidu (Anwar 1974), lenition of phrase-final consonants in Maxakalí (Gud-schinsky, Popovich, and Popovich 1970), and the unrelease of phrase-final stops in Tagalog (Schachter and Otanes 1972) and Diola-Fogny (Sapir 1965).

There are also rules which apply at all phonological bound-aries (syllable, word, and phrase), such as the change from glides to affricates syllable-initially, including word- and utterance-initially, in Spanish (Bowen and Stockwell 1955), devoicing of obstruents syllable-finally in German (Moulton 1962, Venne-mann 1972), and velarization of /l/ syllable-finally in English. However, there are no nonassimilatory rules which apply at syllable boundaries but not at word or phrase boundaries, and none which apply at syllable and word boundaries but not at phrase boundaries.

Examples such as these, which show rules applying at higher boundaries without also applying at lower boundaries, and the lack of examples of nonassimilatory rules which apply at lower boundaries without also applying at higher boundaries, provide additional support for the hypothesis in (16), in that they illustrate the intermediate stages of historical development pre-dicted by the hypothesis.

In the second category, there are rules which apply more generally at higher boundaries than at lower boundaries. Most of the aspiration rules discussed above apply more generally at word and phrase boundaries than at syllable boundaries. In addition, there is evidence that, at least in English, aspiration is stronger, or more precisely, of longer duration, word-initially than it is in word-medial syllables. Umeda and Coker (1974), in their study of aspiration time for one speaker of English reading from a text, found that there was no significant difference in aspiration time of /t/ in stressed syllables phrase-initially, word-initially, or word-medially when preceded by a vowel. The aspiration time, or VOT lag in Lisker and Abramson's (1964) terminology, was approximately 60 msec in all these positions. However, the aspiration time word-initially was found to be independent of any preceding segments, but word-medially in stressed syllables it was only 40 msec if the /t/ was preceded by a consonant, compared to the 60 msec when preceded by a vowel. This difference is reminiscent of aspiration in Tarascan, which does not occur at all after a consonant.

There are rules which apply more generally at phrase boundaries than at word or syllable boundaries. Glottal stop insertion before initial vowels in English, an optional process, applies more frequently at phrase boundaries than at word boundaries, and more frequently at word boundaries than at medial syllable boundaries, where a glottal stop may occasionally be found in words like *theatrical*. Stops in Thai are said to be completely unreleased utterance-finally but "slowly released" word-finally in phrase-medial words (Noss 1964). Final-syllable lengthening in English, discussed by Oller (1971), is of greater duration at phrase and utterance boundaries than at word boundaries. Specifically, Oller found that syllables in utterance-final position are lengthened, as compared to syllables of similar segmental and stress characteristics in nonfinal position, an average of 135 msec. Syllables are also lengthened clause-finally an average of 110 msec, phrase-finally an average of 95 msec, and word-finally an average of 35 msec.

These examples, which show that rules apply either more frequently or more generally or with greater effect at phrase and word boundaries than at syllable boundaries support the hypothesis in (17), in that they illustrate the result of generalization of application at higher boundaries but not at syllable boundaries.

7

Given that the hypotheses stated in (16) and (17) will correctly restrict aspiration and deaspiration rules, as well as other nonassimilatory rules in natural languages, to the types in (12c) and (12d), while correctly disallowing rules of the types in (13c) and (13d), we turn now to the question of an explanation for the hypotheses in (16) and (17). The questions we must ask are:

(18) a. Hypothesis (16): Why do nonassimilatory rules originate at the highest phonological boundaries and spread to lower boundaries?

b. Hypothesis (17): Why does generalization of environment occur at word boundaries but not also at syllable boundaries?

7.1.1. To attempt to answer the first question, we must consider the nature of the nonassimilatory rules discussed above. The rules mentioned here which apply in initial position all seem to be strengthening processes. That is, aspiration, as well as glides changing to affricates and glottal stop insertion, seem to be strengthening processes in some sense. Further, the rules mentioned which apply in final position all seem to be weakening processes. Deaspiration, as well as devoicing of sonorant consonants, consonant lenition, unrelease of stops, and final-syllable lengthening (which Lehiste (1960:45) describes as "final drawl") all seem to be weakening processes in some sense. The difficulties of discussing strengthening and weakening processes in any meaningful way are many. Ideally, we would like to find some measurable articulatory or acoustic correlate of strength, which would provide an objective basis for claims about these processes, but none exists at the present.[6] However, it is not unreasonable to believe that someday such a correlate will be found, in which case it may be possible to characterize rules which apply in initial position as strengthening rules and those which apply in final position as weakening rules. In addition, it may at some time be possible to correlate the strengthening nature of initial processes with the inherent "strength" of initial position, as determined, for example, from rising subglottal pressure and fundamental frequency, and to correlate the weakening nature of final processes with the inherent "weakness" of final position, as determined, for example, from falling subglottal pressure and fundamental frequency in many languages. It should be possible to support the claim that nonassimilatory processes, which are either strengthening processes in initial position or weakening processes in final position, originate at phrase or utterance boundaries, because that is where articulatory strength and weakness are most clearly found. Later, as these processes become "phonologized," to borrow a term used by Hyman (1975) and others, they spread to lower boundaries, where articulatory strength and weakness are less clearly manifested, although they are likely present to some extent. That is, strengthening and weakening processes apply first in positions that are inherently strongest and weakest, respectively, and later spread to other positions, according to their relative inherent strength.

I am claiming, then, that once we have a better understanding of phonetic and phonological strength and weakness, we will be able to answer question (18a) and explain the hypothesis in (16). The explanation will most likely be in the form of a universal principle of language, like the one in (19):

(19) Strengthening rules originate in the position of greatest strength and spread to positions of decreasing strength. Weakening rules originate in the position of greatest weakness and spread to positions of decreasing weakness.

Given definitions of strengthening and weakening rules, and of strong and weak positions in an utterance, we will have an explanation for (16).

7.1.2. The universal suggested in (19) will also favor the generalization of nonassimilatory strengthening or weakening rules at word boundaries rather than at syllable boundaries, given that word-initial position is stronger than medial syllable-initial position that the word-final position is weaker than medial syllable-final position. However, another explanation for (17) can be found if we consider the function of the types of rules discussed above.

One effect of the application of these various types of rules at word boundaries is that certain types of segments either occur or do not occur at word boundaries, and their presence or absence can serve as an indication of the presence or absence of the boundary. Trubetzkoy (1969) proposed this view of "boundary signals" in his theory of "delimitative elements" or the "delimitative function of sound." In his terms, there are some phonemes or allophones, or groups of phonemes or allophones, that occur only at word boundaries, and therefore are positive signals for the presence of a word boundary.[7] There are others which do not occur at word boundaries, and therefore are negative signals for the presence of a word boundary. We can formulate this aspect of Trubetzkoy's theory as the universal principle in (20):

(20) Nonassimilatory feature-changing rules apply at word boundaries in order to signal the presence of the word boundary.

If we consider the historical development of nonassimilatory rules proposed in (16) and (17) in light of Trubetzkoy's theory, we see that before these rules spread to syllable boundaries, they apply only at word boundaries and provide just the type of boundary signals that Trubetzkoy mentions. However, after the rules spread, they no longer provide signals for word boundaries. If we assume that such signals serve a useful function in natural languages, which they most likely do in speech perception, then it appears that the reason the nonassimilatory rules generalize at word boundaries, after they have spread to syllable boundaries, is that by doing so some of their "delimitative function" is restored.

7.1.3. The explanations we have considered here, then, indicate that there are two principles of language relevant to the generalizations about aspiration and deaspiration rules noted in (12) and (13), a principle of strength and weakness, stated in (19), and a principle of the "delimitative function of sound," stated in (20). The interaction of these two principles can be outlined as follows. First, nonassimilatory rules, which are strengthening or weakening rules, originate at phrase boundaries, because phrase-initial position is the strongest position in an utterance and phrase-final position is the weakest. Second, these rules spread to word boundaries, both because word boundaries represent the next strongest or weakest positions and because the application of such rules at word boundaries serves the function of marking or signaling the word boundaries. Next, the rules spread to syllable boundaries, because syllable boundaries represent the next strongest or weakest positions in an utterance. However, by this spread to syllable boundaries, the delimitative function is obscured. Finally, the rules generalize at word boundaries, in order to recapture some of their function of the marking of word boundaries.

8

In summary, in this discussion of aspiration and deaspiration processes, I have considered various types of languages and the analyses of these languages with respect to their aspirated and unaspirated voiceless stops. I have noted several generalizations that can be made about the aspiration and deaspiration rules that are found in these analyses and have shown that the same types of generalizations appear to be true for all other types of nonassimilatory feature-changing phonological rules. I have discussed several current theories of phonology that partially explain these generalizations and have proposed two constraints on the historical development of such rules, given in (16) and (17), to further explain the generalizations. In considering an explanation for these proposed constraints, I have claimed that it is the interaction of two universal principles of language, given in (19) and (20), that fully explain both these constraints and the generalizations in (12) and (13).

NOTES

1. Stress is on the penultimate syllable in Swahili (Polomé 1967).
2. This problem could be avoided for English, and possibly for German, by analyzing the other series of stops, which are usually considered to be voiced, as voiceless unaspirated stops, which are voiced in certain environments. English, then, would have two series of voiceless stops in underlying representations, one unaspirated and one aspirated. Phonological rules would voice the former and deaspirate the latter, under certain conditions. This analysis would not be totally unsupported, given that in English the "voiced" stops are frequently voiceless in word-initial position. In fact, all 20 subjects in an experiment by Zlatin (1974) produced such "devoiced" stops at least some of the time. However, it would be quite difficult to argue for such an analysis of Swahili, where word-initial voiced stops apparently are not only fully voiced but also are frequently prenasalized (Polomé 1967).
3. Since deaspiration rules appear to differ from aspiration rules in that they are conditioned only by the following boundary, and not by the types of preceding or following segments, the generalization in (12d) can be stated more simply than the one in (12c).
4. It is frequently claimed that stops in languages like German, Northern Ostyak, and Keresan are aspirated in word-final position (Moulton 1962, Rédei 1965, Spencer 1946). However, without a clear definition of aspiration in final position and without instrumental analyses of final stops in these languages, it would seem to be impossible to determine whether the stops are actually aspirated or simply "released." A clear example of a language with word-final aspiration would be a language like Hindi, with a contrast between aspirated and unaspirated stops, but

in which the contrast is neutralized word-finally in favor of the aspirated series. In a language like this, if there were no perceptual difference between the two series of stops, then there would be no doubt that the neutralization was the result of an aspiration rule. However, to my knowledge, there are no examples of such languages.

5. Sapir (1965) suggests such a rule for Diola-Fogny. He reports that labial and dental voiceless stops are "slightly aspirated" in stressed syllables, except when these stressed syllables are in word-initial position. He does not report any aspiration of the palatal or velar stops. Aspiration rules of the types we have been considering apply equally to the whole series of voiceless stops, regardless of their place of articulation. Therefore, I would claim either that Sapir failed to notice the aspiration of palatals and velars or that aspiration in Diola-Fogny is different from the type of aspiration under consideration here. It seems unlikely that Sapir would have failed to notice aspiration of palatals and velars, given that Lisker and Abramson (1964) found that the duration of aspiration, or of lag in voice onset time, is greater for velars than for stops of any other place of articulation. This indicates that if velars are aspirated in Diola-Fogny, their aspiration would be more noticeable, and more likely to be reported, than would the aspiration of, for example, labials and dentals. Therefore, aspiration in Diola-Fogny, if it exists at all, is quite unusual and does not constitute a clear counterexample to the generalization in (13a).

6. For further discussion, see Hooper (1974) and Houlihan (1975).

7. Trubetzkoy claims that there are boundary signals for morpheme boundaries, as well as for word boundaries, but morpheme boundaries have not been included in the present discussion.

REFERENCES

Anwar, Mohammed Sami (1974) "Consonant devoicing at word boundary as assimilation," *Language Sciences* 32:6–12.

Bowen, J. Donald and Robert P. Stockwell (1955) "The phonemic interpretation of semivowels in Spanish," *Language* 31:236–240; reprinted in M. Joos (ed.), *Readings in Linguistics I*, pp. 400–402. Chicago: The University of Chicago Press, 1957.

Chao, Y. R. (1947) *Cantonese Primer*. New York: Greenwood Press.

Chomsky, Noam and Morris Halle (1968) *The Sound Pattern of English*. New York: Harper & Row.

Collinder, Björn (1969) *Survey of the Uralic Languages*, 2nd ed. Stockholm: Almqvist & Wiksell.

Foster, Mary LeCron (1969) *The Tarascan Language*. Berkeley: University of California Press.

_____ (1971) "Tarascan," in Jesse Sawyer (ed.), *Studies in American Indian Languages*, pp. 77–111. Berkeley: University of California Press.

Friedrich, Paul (1971) "Distinctive features and functional groups in Tarascan phonology," *Language* 47:849–865.

Greenberg, Joseph H. (1969) "Some methods of dynamic comparison in linguistics," in Jaan Puhvel (ed.), *Substance and Structure of Language.* pp. 147–203. Berkeley: University of California Press.

Gudschinsky, Sarah C., Harold Popovich and Sarah Popovich (1970) "Native reaction and phonetic similarity in Maxakalí phonology," *Language* 46:77–88.

Harms, Robert T. (1968) *Introduction to Phonological Theory.* Englewood Cliffs, N.J.: Prentice-Hall.

Hooper, Joan B. (1974) *Aspects of Natural Generative Phonology.* Bloomington: Indiana University Linguistics Club.

Houlihan, Kathleen (1975) The role of word boundary in phonological processes. Unpublished Ph.D. dissertation. University of Texas at Austin.

Hyman, Larry M. (1975) *Phonology: Theory and Analysis.* New York: Holt, Rinehart and Winston.

Jakobson, Roman and Morris Halle (1971) *Fundamentals of Language.* The Hague: Mouton.

Ladefoged, Peter (1971) *Preliminaries to Linguistic Phonetics.* Chicago: The University of Chicago Press.

Lehiste, Ilse (1960) "An acoustic-phonetic study of internal open juncture," *Phonetica* 5 (supplement):1–54.

Lehiste, Ilse (1965) "Juncture," in *Proceedings of the 5th International Congress of Phonetic Sciences,* ed. by E. Zwirner and W. Bethge, pp. 172–200. Basel-New York: S. Karger.

Lisker, Leigh and Arthur S. Abramson (1964) "A cross-language study of voicing in initial stops: Acoustical measurements," *Word* 20:384–422.

McCawley, James D. (1968) *The Phonological Component of a Grammar of Japanese,* Monographs on Linguistic Analysis 2. The Hague: Mouton.

Moulton, William G. (1962) *The Sounds of English and German.* Chicago: The University of Chicago Press.

Newton, Brian E. (1972) *The Generative Interpretation of Dialect: A Study of Modern Greek Phonology.* Cambridge: Cambridge University Press.

Noss, Richard B. (1964) *Thai Reference Grammar.* Washington, D.C.: Foreign Service Institute.

Oates, W. J. and L. F. Oates (1958) "The phonemes of Central Cagayan Negrito," in *Studies in Philippine Linguistics,* ed. by members of the Summer Institute of Linguistics, pp. 34–46. Sidney, Australia: University of Sidney.

Oller, David Kimbrough (1971) The duration of speech segments: The effect of position-in-utterance and word-length. Ph.D. dissertation. University of Texas at Austin.

Polomé, Edgar C. (1967) *Swahili Language Handbook.* Washington, D.C.: Center for Applied Linguistics.

Rédei, Károly (1965) *Northern Ostyak Chrestomathy* (Indiana University Publications, Uralic and Altaic Series, Vol. 47. Bloomington: Indiana University). The Hague: Mouton.

Sanders, Gerald A. (1974) "The simplex-feature hypothesis," *Glossa* 8:141–192.

Sapir, J. David (1965) *A Grammar of Diola-Fogny.* London: Cambridge University Press.

Schachter, Paul and Fe T. Otanes (1972) *Tagalog Reference Grammar.* Berkeley: University of California Press.

Spencer, Robert F. (1946) "The phonemes of Keresan," *IJAL* 12:229–236.

Trubetzkoy, N. S. (1969) *Principles of Phonology,* trans. by Christiane A. M. Baltaxe. Berkeley: University of California Press.

Umeda, N. and C. H. Coker (1974) "Allophonic variation in American English," *Journal of Phonetics* 2:1–5.

Vennemann, Theo (1971) Natural generative phonology. Paper read at the Annual Meeting of the Linguistic Society of America, St. Louis.

—— (1972) "On the theory of syllabic phonology," *Linguistische Berichte* 18:1–18.

Whitney, William Dwight (1889) *A Sanskrit Grammar.* Leipzig: Breitkopf and Härtel.

Zlatin, Marsha A. (1974) "Voicing contrast: Perceptual and productive voice onset time characteristics of adults," *Journal of the Acoustical Society of America* 56:981–994.

12
A functional typology of elliptical coordinations

Gerald A. Sanders
University of Minnesota

1. INTRODUCTION

The study of reduced, or elliptical, coordinations has received a great deal of attention by linguists in recent years. Various facts and hypotheses about reduction have been presented, both for English and a number of other languages, in papers by Gleitman (1965), Schane (1966), Ross (1970), Postal (1968), Tai (1969, 1971), Sanders (1970, 1975), Dougherty (1970), Koutsoudas (1971), Pulte (1971), Sanders and Tai (1972), Hankamer (1973), Harries (1973), Rosenbaum (1974), and others. Quite a few of these studies, moreover, have been explicitly typological in their goals and orientation—that is, they have been concerned with determining the range of possible patterns of elliptical coordination in human languages, the range of possible combinations of these patterns in particular lan-

Lectures on this topic were also given in January 1976 at the University of Iowa, and in February 1976 before the University of Minnesota Linguistics Club. I am grateful to Linda Schwartz for helpful comments on the preliminary manuscript.

guages, and hence the general facts about the nature and variability of languages that underlie and govern the particular typological limitations observed.

Coordinations and coordinate ellipsis constitute a very natural and productive domain for such typological analysis, since we know with an exceptionally high degree of certainty that all languages have coordinations of full sentences or clauses, and that all have *some* type of reduced, or elliptical, coordination as well—with the particular types of reductions that occur varying widely but within limits from language to language.

I would like to take advantage of this (structurally and functionally) natural domain here, and of the fairly extensive research that has been carried out on it, to explore both the facts about elliptical coordination in natural language and the nature and function of typological analyses of language in general.

To carry out these explorations, I will first present a critical survey of four actual typologies of elliptical coordinations that have been proposed in the literature, pointing out some of the major factual and conceptual inadequacies of each, and drawing out by implication some of the primary goals, purposes, and criteria for evaluation of typological analyses in general. I will then present a fifth typological analysis of coordinate ellipsis that appears to overcome all of the various empirical and analytical inadequacies of the typologies previously proposed. Finally, taking the laws expressed by this typology to be (at least tentatively) true of human language, I will attempt to outline a possible explanation for these typological laws, and a general framework for the productive analysis of other such facts about the nature and variability of human languages.

Before proceeding, though, I would like to first define certain basic terms, concepts, and notational devices that will facilitate discussion of the facts at issue and serve as a uniform metalanguage for the expression of all the various typological analyses to be considered. The vocabulary of this metalanguage consists of the terms *coordination, conjunct, ellipsis,* and the several positional names defined in (1):

(1) In the following general schema,

$$[\ldots [A \ B \ C]_W \ \& \ [D \ E \ F]_W \ldots]_W$$

"ABC" is a *preceding conjunct;*
"DEF" is a *following conjunct;*
"A" and "D" are *initial sequences;*
"C" and "F" are *final sequences;*
"B" and "E" (where A, C, D, F are non-null) are *medial sequences;* and "&" is (possibly null) coordinating *conjunction.*

The terms *coordination* and *conjunct* I will take to be antecedently understood here, though, as suggested by the schema in (1), I consider a coordination to be any sequence of constituents which all have the same semantic function in their discourse context—for example, asserting, questioning, referring, predicating—and where this common function is also the function of the complete sequence as a whole.[1] The term *ellipsis* is somewhat less uniformly understood. I will say here that a constituent sequence XY is *elliptical*—or that there is an *ellipsis* or *ellipsis site* between X and Y—if and only if there is also a sequence XAY which means the same thing as XY, and there is a sequence A included in X, or in Y, or in both. (I will also be using the terms *reduced* and *reduction* here as synonyms for *elliptical* and *ellipsis*—although it should be emphasized that all of these terms are to be understood only in their purely relational senses, and not as the names for any process or set of processes.)

2. TYPOLOGY I

The earliest explicitly typological investigation of elliptical coordinations that I know of is that presented by Ross (1970) in his paper "Gapping and the order of constituents."[2] Ross's study is based on an arbitrary and grossly unnatural domain for typological analysis—ellipsis only of transitive verbs in clauses with noninitial verbs and subjects preceding objects—and makes a number of factual claims that are false, moreover, even within this narrow domain. Nevertheless, this was in many ways the first really substantive investigation of natural language carried out within the framework of generative grammar. By helping to redirect the attention of linguists to the primary linguistic goal of discovering and explaining typological generalizations about human language, Ross's paper thus served as an extremely valuable model and stimulus for further research by others, research which has resulted in important insights and raw materials for explanation in a wide range of areas concerning the structure and variability of human language. Moreover, in addition to its seminal values, Ross's typology, which will be referred to here as Typology I, provides an excellent illustration of the kinds of factual and conceptual inadequacies that typological analyses in general are subject to. We will thus consider this typology in some detail before proceeding to the much more general and more generally significant ones that followed it.

Typology I specifies three possible patterns of elliptical coordination and four possible types of language determined by the possible occurrence and co-occurrence of these ellipsis patterns. The specified reduction types and language types are given in (2), with ellipsis sites indicated by reference to the general coordination schema in (1).

(2) Typology I
    a. Reduction types
       SVO & SO: John ate steak, and Mary fish (E)
       SO & SOV: John steak, and Mary fish ate (C)
       SOV & SO: John steak ate, and Mary fish (F)
    b. Language types
       English-type:
          SVO & SO, *SO & SOV, *SOV & SO (E, *C, *F)

       Japanese-type:
          *SVO & SO, SO & SOV, *SOV & SO (*E, C, *F)

       Russian-type:
          SVO & SO, SO & SOV, SOV & SO (E, C, F)

       Hindi-type:
          *SVO & SO, SO & SOV, SOV & SO (*E, C, F)

2.1. Factual Inadequacies of Typology I

Typology I expresses factual claims only about that small subset of elliptical coordinations in which (1) the elliptical constituent is a superficially transitive or complemented verb, (b) subjects precede objects in both preceding and following conjuncts, and (c) the verb of the unreduced conjunct is noninitial. All of the factual claims that it makes about this domain are false.

2.1.1. Typology I claims that every language (with SVO and/or SOV clauses) has at least one of the three reduction patterns SVO & SO, SO & SOV, SOV & SO. This claim is false (see Tai 1969, Koutsoudas 1971, Sanders and Tai 1972). Thus, for example, in Lebanese Arabic, as shown in (3), there are SVO clauses, but none of the reduction types specified in (2).

(3) John darab il walad, wa Bill darab il bint (SVO & SVO)
     S   V   O   & S   V   O
    'John hit the boy, and Bill hit the girl'

    *John darab il walad, wa Bill il bint (*SVO & SO)
    *John il walad, wa Bill il bint darab (*SO & SOV)
    *John il walad darab, wa Bill il bint (*SOV & SO)

Parallel falsification data is provided by the facts about co-ordination in Chinese, Thai, and many other languages.

2.1.2. Typology I claims that if a language has SOV & SO reductions, then it also has SO & SOV reductions. This claim is false (see Pulte 1971, 1973). Quechua, for example, as shown in (4), has well-formed reductions of the former type but not of the latter (Pulte 1971):

(4)   Juanito aycata mik"un, Tiyucataq papasta mik"un
       S   O   V   S   O   V

    'Juanito eats meat, and Tiuca eats potatoes'

    Juanito aycata mik"un, Tiyucataq papasta (SOV & SO)
    *Juanito aycata, Tiyucataq papasta mik"un (*SO & SOV)

Actually, for all types of elliptical coordination in Quechua, including ellipsis of objects and subjects as well as verbs, the governing principle is simply that ellipsis is permitted in following conjuncts but not in preceding ones. Cherokee, according to Pulte (1973), is governed by this same general principle.

2.1.3. Typology I claims that no language has reductions of the form SO & SVO. This claim is also false. Thus in Zapotec, according to Rosenbaum (1974), there are perfectly well-formed coordinations of this type:

(5) xwain been jumE, ne makU been yuu (SVO & SVO)
     S   V   O   &   S   V   O
    'Juan made a basket, and Marcos made a house'
    xwain jumE, ne makU been yuu (SO & SVO)

2.2. Analytic and Conceptual Inadequacies of Typology I

The purpose of a typology, of course, is not to specify some merely arbitrary classification of objects, or some arbitrary set of true generalizations about them. The purpose, rather, is to provide a *significant* classification of a *natural* class of objects by isolating those true generalizations about them which highlight *essential* characteristics of the class, and those limitations on the possible variability of its members that are most amenable to principled explanation. An adequate typology, in other words, must provide a revealing, or conceptually useful, systemization of data, a coherent subset of interacting generalizations that raise interesting and important questions about the nature of some natural class of objects and thus serve as a productive basis for further inquiry and analysis. A typology can be inadequate, therefore, because of what it suggests as well as what it asserts. This is particularly well-exemplified by Typology I, which presents a quite distorted and misleading conceptualization of natural language structure, and would be inadequate, therefore, even if its particular factual claims were all true rather than false.

2.2.1. By its choice of domain, for example, Typology I suggests that facts about *verb* ellipsis in coordinations constitute a natural domain for analysis, that the principles governing ellipsis of this type of constituent differ in some way from the principles of ellipsis for subjects, objects, and other types of constituents. But this is clearly false (see Sanders 1970, 1975; Koutsoudas 1971; Tai 1971; etc.). The data in (6), for example, show that the patterns of coordinate ellipsis in English are precisely the same for numerous different types of constituents and constituent-sequences in the language.

(6) [S PRED] [~~S~~ PRED]   John sang and ~~John~~ danced   (D)
  *[~~S~~ PRED] [S PRED]   *~~John~~ sang and John danced   (*A)
  [DET N] [~~DET~~ N]   The king and ~~the~~ queen arrived (D)
  *[~~DET~~ N] [DET N]   *~~The~~ king and the queen arrived (*A)
  [S ~~PRED~~] [S PRED]   Bill ~~carved the meat~~ and
        Tom carved the meat   (C)
  *[S PRED] [S ~~PRED~~]   *Bill carved the meat and
        Tom ~~carved the meat~~   (*F)
  [S V ∅] [S V O]   I wrote ~~the letter~~ and you
        sent the letter   (C)
  *[S V O] [S V ∅]   *I wrote the letter and you
        sent ~~the letter~~   (*F)
  [S V O] [S ~~V~~ O]   Betty likes beans and Rhoda
        ~~likes~~ rice   (E)
  *[S ~~V~~ O] [S V O]   *Betty ~~likes~~ beans and Rhoda
        likes rice   (*B)
  [S AD V] [S ~~AD~~ V]   Jack often sings and Jill
        ~~often~~ dances   (E)
  *[S ~~AD~~ V] [S AD V]   *Jack ~~often~~ sings and Jill
        often dances   (*B)

The governing principle here is simply that ellipsis is permitted only in the final positions of preceding conjuncts and the nonfinal positions of following conjuncts. The category-independence that obtains for this general principle of ellipsis in English obtains also for the positional constraints on ellipsis in all other languages whose patterns of coordination have been carefully studied thus far.

It is not the case, however, that there are no nonpositional factors at all that have effects on ellipsis. Thus, there are constituency constraints, like the Immediate Dominance Condition (Sanders and Tai 1972), and various antiambiguity functions, of the sort discussed by Tai (1969) and Hankamer (1973) that impose limitations on ellipsis, which are evidently independent of the particular order of ellipsis sites and their antecedents. Moreover, as noted by Harries (1973), there are also certain factors involving the scope of grammatical relations which may determine apparent category- or relation-sensitive deviations from the standard, positionally defined patterns of reduction in a language. For example, in English, which normally excludes F-position ellipsis (*John runs fast and Mary swims ~~fast~~, *Fred cooked the meat and Helen ate ~~the meat~~), ellipsis in this position is nevertheless possible for certain sentential adverbials of time and place (John sang yesterday and Mary danced ~~yesterday~~, Fred saw a fox at the zoo and Helen saw a hamster ~~at the zoo~~). Such deviations are always systematically limited, however, and appear to involve only those types of expressions which function as operators (or predicates) of whole clauses or whole predications.[3] Since this formally heterogeneous class of sentence adverbials constitutes a semantic rather than a syntactic class of constructions, its special behavior in ellipsis would be fully consistent with the generalization that all constraints on ellipsis in any language are insensitive to any differences between syntactic categories of constituent types. In any event, though, it seems clear that there is insensitivity at least to all differences between predicates and their nominal arguments and between one argument of a predicate and another.[4] There seems to be no empirical basis, therefore, for distinguishing, as Typology I does, between the ellipsis of verbs in coordinations and the ellipsis of verbal arguments.

2.2.2. Typology I suggests that English and Japanese are *different* from each other with respect to coordination reduction. This is false (see, for example, Sanders and Tai 1972). Thus, as indicated by data of the sort given in (7), these two languages have exactly the same patterns of elliptical coordination.

(7) [ABC] [DEF]   John hit the boy, and Bill ~~hit~~ the girl (E = V)
                  John ga syonen o nagutte, Bill ga ~~syonen o~~ ∅ ketta (E = O)
    *[ABC] [DEF] *John ~~hit~~ the boy, and Bill hit the girl
                  *John ga ~~syonen o~~ ∅ nagutte, Bill ga syonen o ketta

[AB~~C~~] [DEF]   John hit ~~the boy~~, and Bill kicked the boy (C = O)

John ga syonen o ~~nagutte~~, Bill ga syozo o nagutte (C = V)

*[ABC] [DE~~F~~]   *John hit the boy, and Bill kicked ~~the boy~~

*John ga syonen o nagutte, Bill ga syozo o ~~nagutte~~

Since both languages also exclude ellipsis in position A, English and Japanese are seen to be governed by exactly the same general principle of coordinate ellipsis, reductions being permitted in both languages only in the final positions of preceding conjuncts and the nonfinal positions of following ones.

2.2.3. By its choice of domain, Typology I also suggests that intransitive verbs are either not subject to ellipsis or are governed by different principles of ellipsis than those governing transitive verbs. This is false too, of course, as shown clearly by numerous facts of the sort indicated in (8).

(8)

	Japanese	Russian	Hindi
Transitive	SO~~V~~ SOV	SO~~V~~ SOV	SO~~V~~ SOV
	*SOV SO~~V~~	SOV SO~~V~~	SOV SO~~V~~
Intransitive	S~~V~~ SV	S~~V~~ SV	S~~V~~ SV
	*SV S~~V~~	SV S~~V~~	SV S~~V~~

Thus for all three of these languages, the patterns and principles of ellipsis are precisely the same for transitive and intransitive verbs, ellipsis being permitted in F position only for Russian and Hindi, but in D position for all three languages. Similar category-independence is exhibited by the ellipsis patterns of all other languages investigated.

2.2.4. Typology I suggests that positions C, E, and F are the only possible sites for verbal ellipsis. This is false. Zapotec, for example, as shown in (5), has verbal ellipsis in position B. As seen in (9), it also has D ellipsis, as does Quechua, and many other languages as well.

(9) been xwain jumE, ne b̶e̶e̶n̶ abel bizie (VSO V̶SO)
     'Juan made a basket, and Abel made a well'

2.2.5. Typology I suggests that the relative order of subject
and object must be the same in all conjuncts of a reduced
coordination. There is no really clear evidence concerning the
truth or falsity of this implicit claim; its status must still be
considered uncertain, therefore, on the basis of presently available data. I know of only one explicit factual claim that is
relevant to this question. This is in Pulte (1973), where it is
asserted that "Quechua allows any order of subject, object, and
verb in simple sentences, and exhibits gapped sentences of the
following types: SVO + SO, SVO + OS, SOV + SO, SOV +
OS, VSO + SO, VSO + OS, VOS + SO, VOS + OS, OVS + SO,
and OVS + OS" (p. 100). But no actual examples of reductions with
nonparallel ordering of subjects and objects—or of any other
pairs of constituents—have been given either by Pulte (1971,
1973) or by anyone else in the standard literature on reduced
coordinations.

My own judgments about nonparallelism in English are notice-
ably unclear, but incline, nevertheless, toward the conclusion
that nonparallel reductions are at least generally if not always
ungrammatical in English. Consider, in this regard, the examples
of nonparallelism in (10).

(10) a. John will have the steak, and the fish Mary (SVO &
         OS)
      b. The steak John ate, and Mary the fish (OSV & SO)
      c. I bought the steak for John, and for Mary fish (SVOD
         & DO)
      d. For John I bought steak, and fish for Mary (DSVO &
         OD)

Although some reductions of this sort can be quite easily and
unambiguously understood, and are much more acceptable than
others, I lean toward the belief that they are all grammatically
ill-formed. In any event, though the question must obviously
remain open, I will assume for present purposes at least that the
conventional exclusion of nonparallelism is warranted and that,
for nuclear constituents at least, parallel ordering is a necessary

condition for fully well-formed elliptical coordinations in all languages.

3. TYPOLOGY II

Typology II, which is presented in Sanders and Tai (1972), has a more general domain than Typology I, and classifies languages on an entirely different basis—a basis which involves the grouping, or constituency, relations of conjunct components, rather than their relative order or position. Three positionally definable reduction types are, nevertheless, specified, along with a governing nonuniversal constituency constraint on ellipsis. These, and the two language types they generate, are given in (11).

(11) Typology II
    a. Reduction types
        C-type: ABC & DEF (e.g., S & SVO, S & SOV)
                 ABC & DEF (e.g., SV & SVO, SO & SOV)
        D-type: ABC & DEF (e.g., SVO & VO, SOV & OV)
                 ABC & DEF (e.g., SVO & O, SOV & V)
        E-type: ABC & DEF (e.g., SVO & SO, SOV & SV)
    b. Nonuniversal Constraint: The Immediate Dominance Condition
        A conjunction of (WXY) and (UZ) is an elliptical alternant of a conjunction of (WXY) and (UXZ) only if X is an immediate constituent of (WXY).
    c. Language types
        IDC type (Chinese, Thai, Lebanese Arabic, etc.):
         *SO & SOV, *SOV & SV, *SVO & SO, *SV & SVO, etc.
        Non-IDC type (English, Japanese, Russian, Hindi, etc.):
        (SO & SOV and SOV & SV) and/or (SVO & SO and SV & SVO), etc.

Typology II thus claims that there is a covariance relation in natural languages, for example, between the ellipsis of transitive verbs and the ellipsis of nonsubject arguments. It claims, in other words, that there are no languages that permit coordinate ellipsis for one of these types of constituent but prohibit ellipsis for the other. This has been confirmed with respect to a fairly large sample of languages (see Koutsoudas 1971; Sanders and Tai 1972), and I know of no clear evidence to the contrary.

3.1. Inadequacies of Typology II

By failing to take explicit account of the positional factors in ellipsis, Typology II fails to distinguish the various subclasses of the non-IDC language type, which differ only in their respective positional constraints on ellipsis. Thus, for example, while it suggests that English and Russian are the same with respect to coordinate ellipsis, they are actually not the same: Russian permits F-ellipsis, while English does not. Moreover, though Typology II makes no explicit claims at all concerning positional factors, it *suggests* by its choice of examples that position F is not a possible ellipsis site in any language, and, like Typology I, that positions A and B are also not possible sites for ellipsis. But all of these suggestions are false. Ellipsis in F-position has already been seen to occur in Quechua, Russian, and Hindi and can be found in many other languages as well. An example from Russian is given in (12).

(12) Vanja vodu pil, a Masha vino p̶i̶l̶ (SOV & SOV̶)
    'Vanja drank water, and Masha drank wine'

Ellipsis in B-position also occurs, as was shown by the Zapotec example in (5). Finally, there are also languages which permit ellipsis in A-position, the initial position of a preceding conjunct. Thus in Tojolabal Maya, according to Furbee (1974), there are perfectly well-formed reductions like the one given in (13).

(13)   y̶i̶'̶a̶   b'ak'et Hwan, sok yi'a   tek'el Mangwel
    (V̶OS & VOS)
    took   meat Juan   and took   fruit   Manuel
    'Juan took meat, and Manuel took fruit'

Actually, therefore, there is *no* position in coordinations that is *universally* excluded as a site for possible ellipsis.

4. TYPOLOGY III

Typology III, which is presented in Harries (1973), specifies the possible reduction types and language types given in (14).

(14) Typology III
    a. Reduction types:

C-type:	A~~BC~~ & DEF	⎫
	A~~BC~~ & DEF	⎪
D-type:	ABC & ~~D~~EF	⎬ = Typology II
	ABC & ~~DE~~F	⎪
E-type:	ABC & D~~E~~F	⎭
F-type:	ABC & DE~~F~~	
	ABC & ~~D~~E~~F~~	
(B-type:	A~~B~~C & DEF)	

    b. Language types
    Type *A-*B-*F (English, Japanese, Chinese, etc.)
    Type *A-*B-*C (Quechua, Cherokee, etc.)
    Type *A-*B (Russian, Turkish, etc.)
    Type *A (Hindi)

Typology III overcomes most of the inadequacies of Typologies I and II. However, it explicitly claims that position A is not a possible site for ellipsis in any language. This claim, as shown by (13), is false. Typology III also equivocates concerning the existence of B-type reductions and Type *A languages. Thus, though Harries reports the occurrence of B-ellipsis of objects in Hindi, she explicitly excludes any B-ellipsis of verbs in any language—a type of ellipsis that actually does occur in Zapotec, as seen in (5), and in other languages as well.[5]

5. TYPOLOGY IV

Typology IV, which is presented in an unpublished paper by Harvey Rosenbaum (1974), is defined over the same restricted domain of transitive verb ellipsis as Typology I. It is based on a much more representative set of facts about this domain, though, and accommodates the patterns of verbal reduction that obtain for clauses with initial verbs as well as medial and final ones, and with objects preceding subjects as well as following them. In contrast to Typology I, therefore, Typology IV generates factual claims about transitive-verb ellipsis in all human languages, and not just an arbitrary subset of such languages. The possible reduction types and language types that are specified by this typology are given in (15).

(15) Typology IV
    a. Reductions types
        VNN & V̸NN (D)
        NVN & NV̸N (E)
        NNV & NNV̸ (F)
        V̸NN & VNN (A)
        NV̸N & NVN (B)
        NNV̸ & NNV (C)
    b. Language types
        Chinese-type (IDC languages): No (verbal) ellipsis.
        English-type: (only E)
      ?Mam-type: (only D)
        Japanese-type: (only C)
        Hindi-type: (C, F)
        Russian-type: (C, F, E)
        Quechua-type: (D, E, F)
      ?Quiche-type: (D, E, F, B)
        Zapotec-type: (D, E, F, B, C)
        Tojolabal-type: (D, E, F, B, C, A)

The two language types prefixed by question marks are highly dubious and may be the result of simple reporting errors in the primary or secondary sources upon which the typology was based. Thus, concerning Mam (the only claimed member of this language type), Rosenbaum notes that while Koutsoudas (1971) classifies this language as an IDC language—a member of the Chinese-type—Furbee[6] classifies it as a non-IDC language which permits reduction, however, only in position D. The latter could be the case, though, only if Mam were a strict verb-initial language—that is, a language in which nothing but verbs can occur in clause-initial positions. But as noted by Greenberg (1963), there is no known instance of a strict verb-initial language, and there are good reasons for believing that natural languages of this type are in fact naturally excluded. I will thus assume that Rosenbaum's classification of Mam is simply erroneous, and that this type should be excluded rather than included in the set of possible language types specified by Typology IV. I will assume the same thing for the Quiche-type since Quiche, its only claimed member, is explicitly asserted by Furbee (1974:301) to belong to the Tojolabal-type with respect to verbal ellipsis.

Because of its unnaturally restricted domain of transitive-verb ellipsis only, Typology IV shares all of the analytic and conceptual inadequacies of Typology I except for that based on the omission of verb-initial reductions like (9). However, aside from its presumably erroneous claims about Mam and Quiche, Typology IV has no presently known factual inadequacies. It thus could serve as an empirically defensible systematization of the facts about at least one kind of elliptical coordination in natural language.

6. TYPOLOGY V

Typology V generalizes the domain of Typology IV to encompass all kinds of elliptical coordinations in all languages. It specifies six reduction types and six possible language types, as given in (16).

(16) Typology V
   a. Reduction types
      ̸ABC & DEF (A)
      A̸BC & DEF (B)
      AB̸C & DEF (C)
      ABC & ̸DEF (D)
      ABC & D̸EF (E)
      ABC & DE̸F (F)

   b. Language types

	permitted	excluded
Chinese-type (AB⟨C D⟩EF)[7]	D, C	A, B, E, F
English-Japanese-type (AB⟨C DE⟩F)	D, C, E	A, B, F
Quechua-type (ABC ⟨DEF⟩)	D, E, F	A, B, C
Russian-type (AB⟨C DEF⟩)	D, C, E, F	A, B

(16) b. Language types (*continued*)

Hindi-Zapotec-type (A BC DEF)	D, C, E, F, B	A
Tojolabal-type (ABC DEF)	D, C, E, F, B, A	

Typology V specifies every position of every conjunct as a possible site for ellipsis, and thus correctly asserts that there is no coordination position that is universally excluded as an ellipsis site in natural language. There are sixty-four logically possible combinations, or subsets, of these six ellipsis sites, including the null set. Typology V makes the claim—which is evidently correct—that only six of these sixty-four combinations actually occur as possible ranges for permitted ellipsis in actual human languages. Thus, as can be seen from (16), there are strong dependency relations between the occurrence or nonoccurrence of ellipsis in certain positions and its occurrence or nonoccurrence in certain others. If a language exludes ellipsis in position F, for example, the final position of following conjuncts, then it will also exclude ellipsis in position B, the medial position of preceding conjuncts. Or if a language permits ellipsis in position A, the initial position of a preceding conjunct, then it permits ellipsis also in all other possible positions. Some of the more important positional generalizations of this sort are explicitly expressed by the set of typological laws about coordinate ellipsis given in (17).

(17) a. No language has *D.
　　b. If a language has *E, then it also has *F.
　　c. If a language has *C and/or *F, then it also has *B.
　　d. If a language has *B, then it also has *A.

Given these laws, the principles of elliptical coordination in all languages can be expressed by the universal rule of natural language grammar given in (18).

(18) Rule for Elliptical Coordination:
Any pair of conjuncts of the form [[XWY] [UWZ]] can be understood to mean the same thing as a pair of adjacent conjuncts of the form [[XWY] [U∅Z]] except that the site of ∅ cannot be
a. E in Chinese, etc.
b. F in English, etc.

c. C in Quechua, etc.
d. B in Russian, etc.
e. A in Hindi, etc.

It will be observed with respect to this rule that each of the six
language types generated by Typology V is uniquely and sufficiently identified by reference to a single unique position where
ellipsis is excluded, including the null position for languages of
the Tojolabal type. Given one of these distinctive exclusions, in
other words, all of the other excluded ellipsis sites for a language
will be derivable as theorems from the typological laws of
ellipsis in (17). Take English for example. All that needs to be
(axiomatically) known about this language with respect to
coordinate ellipsis is that it does not permit ellipsis in position
F, the final position of a following conjunct. From this it
follows by (17c) that it also prohibits ellipsis in position B, the
medial position of a preceding conjunct. And from the exclusion
of B-ellipsis it follows by (17d) that A-ellipsis is also excluded in
this language, that is, ellipsis in the initial position of a
preceding conjunct. It thus follows correctly that English permits ellipsis only in positions C, D, and E, the final positions of
preceding conjuncts and the nonfinal positions of following
ones.

The factual generalizations of Typology V are expressed also
by the more graphic schema in (19).

(19)

*Degree of positional
resistance to ellipsis*

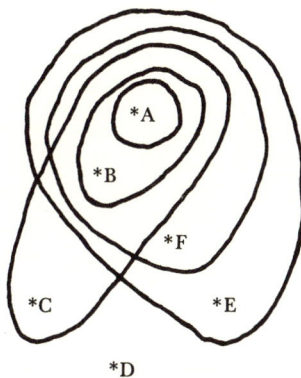

Here the possible sets of excluded ellipsis sites for languages are
enclosed by continuous lines, and the laws of (17) are thus

directly represented in the form of graphic set inclusions and intersections. Thus, for example, position D, which is a possible ellipsis site in all human languages, is included in none of the represented exclusion sets. The set that contains *E also contains *A, *B, and *F. This is the set of exclusions for languages of the Chinese type, which generally permit ellipsis only in positions C and D. Similarly, the sets that include *C, for languages of the Quechua type, or *F, for languages of the English type, also include *A and *B. But there are languages like Russian that exclude *B without excluding either *C or *F. Similarly, if *B is excluded, so is *A, but not vice versa—Russian, for example, excludes both B- and A-ellipsis, while Zapotec excludes A- but permits B-ellipsis.

The schematic representation in (19) also indicates, for each of the six coordination positions, its relative degree of positional resistance to ellipsis, as determined by the typological laws represented here and in (16) and (17). Thus position D, which is a permitted site in all languages and thus has no resistance to ellipsis at all, is assigned a zero degree of resistance. Positions C and E, which are each excluded in only one of the six possible language types, are assigned one degree of resistance to ellipsis. Position F, which is excluded in two of the six types, is assigned two degrees of resistance. Position B, which is excluded by four of the six types, is assigned three degrees of resistance. And position A, finally, which is excluded by five of the six types—all but the Tojolabal type—is assigned four degrees of resistance. It should be noted that this scale of relative resistance—or, inversely, favorability—to ellipsis in coordinations is derived solely from facts about the observed patterns of elliptical coordination in natural language. It thus constitutes a specification of linguistic structure that is derived and expressed independently of any facts about the functions of human languages or the social and psychological environments in which they are used, facts which are thereby rendered eligible for purposes of possible linguistic explanation here.

7. TYPOLOGY EXPLANATION

The function of typological analysis is to generalize and systematize natural classes of true and perspicuous law-like generalizations that are maximally useful as the raw materials for principled inquiry and explanation. A typology is adequate, therefore, only to the extent that it generates significant questions that are clear, explicit, and likely to be productively answerable. Typologies are constructed, in other words, to serve as the raw materials for explanation, the most refined and most manageable raw materials that are available concerning the nature of the objects they typologize.

The explanatory questions that are raised by any typology are of two distinct types. The first question is, Why is the typology as a whole the way it is? Or, in other words, Why do the objects in its domain have the particularly limited range of variability that the typology asserts them to have? The second type of question is, for each particular object in the domain, Why does this object belong to the particular typological class that it does belong to? Thus with respect to our typology of elliptical coordinations, it is appropriate now to ask, first, why natural languages are the way they are in their patterns of ellipsis, why every language is of just one of the six types specified by Typology V, why there are no languages of any of the fifty-eight other logically possible types that are excluded by this typology? It is also appropriate to ask why English, for example, is an English-type language with respect to coordination reduction, or why Russian is a Russian-type language.

Concerning this latter question, involving the explanation of type memberships of particular languages, I have nothing concrete to suggest in the way of answers or significant steps toward them. The natural strategy, of course, for all attempts at type-membership explanation is to seek some additional common distinguishing property or set of properties of all members of a given type, and then to try to find some causal or functional link between these independent characteristics and the defining characteristics of that particular type. On the basis of what I know about the representative languages on which Typology V is based—which is very little for quite a few of them—I can find no correlating characteristics for any of the types that are independent of the given facts about elliptical coordinations in each type. Thus in their nonelliptical characteristics, the members of each type appear to be structurally, as well as genetically, quite diverse. English and Japanese, for example, are both members of the same type class, although they are radically different in their basic ordering of clause constituents, and in most other aspects of their grammars as well. Quechua, Russian, and Tojolabal all have relatively free ordering of subjects, verbs, and nonsubjects in clauses, yet they belong to three different typological classes with respect to coordinate ellipsis. Russian and Japanese have comparable degrees of morphological marking of case and role relations, but they belong to different ellipsis types; Japanese has a much more extensive marking system than English, yet both languages are the same with respect to ellipsis.

What one might naturally expect to find here, of course, is some correlation between freedom in ellipsis and rigidity in other aspects of syntax—highly restricted word-order, well-developed systems of agreement and case-marking, etc.—since, other things being equal, ellipsis serves to increase the difficulty of determining the intended grammatical and semantic relationships of constituents.[8] But I am unable to find such a correlation here. Thus, for example, Tojolabal, which has the most freedom in ellipsis, is also completely free in its ordering of predicates and arguments and seems to have little if any morphological marking of verb-argument relations. Similarly, Chinese, which is extremely restricted as to constituent ordering, is also the most restricted type of language with respect to ellipsis. In short, then, I can find no significant correlations with ellipsis type, and thus no explanation for the particular typological class membership of particular languages.

Turning finally to the other and more important type of explanatory question expressed by Typology V, we must now ask what it is about natural language that restricts its range of variability in just the way that this typology specifies. Why, in other words, are the typological laws of (17) true of the set of natural languages? Why is language like this rather than like something else? Here, I believe, we can take some real steps toward an answer to the questions, still tentative and somewhat speculative perhaps, but nevertheless serving as an empirically vulnerable basis for a real theory of coordinate ellipsis in human languages and of the essential properties of such languages that govern and determine this kind of ellipsis.

In approaching this question of explanation for Typology V,

it will be useful to express the typology in yet another schematic form, the form represented in (20).

(20) *Possible ranges of ellipsis sites*

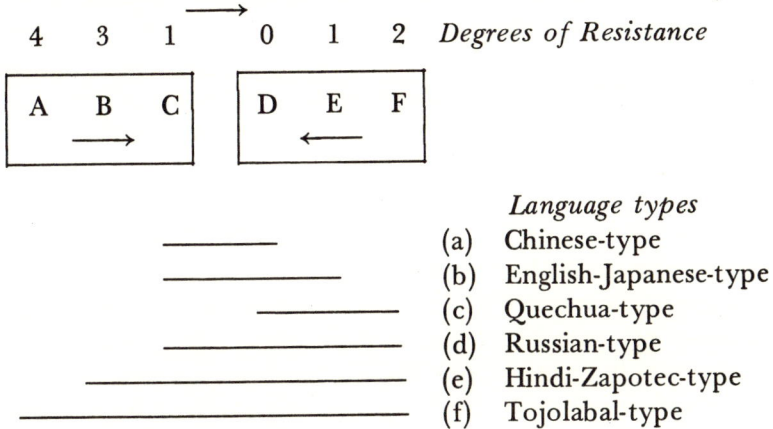

$$\xrightarrow{}$$

4   3   1   0   1   2   *Degrees of Resistance*

| A   B   C | D   E   F |

$\xrightarrow{}$ (in A B C box) $\xleftarrow{}$ (in D E F box)

Language types

 ————— (a) Chinese-type
 ——————— (b) English-Japanese-type
 ——————— (c) Quechua-type
 ————————— (d) Russian-type
 ——————————— (e) Hindi-Zapotec-type
 ————————————— (f) Tojolabal-type

This representation, which expresses the same factual generalizations as are expressed in different forms in (16), (17), and (19), serves to highlight the complete range of permitted sites for ellipsis in each of the six language types and the general character and relationships of these ranges. It can be readily seen from this schematization, for example, that each of the six possible ranges for coordinate ellipsis constitutes a continuous subsequence of the sequence of six coordination positions A B C D E F. It can also be seen that—with the exception of the ranges for type (b), the English-Japanese-type, and type (c), the type for languages like Quechua, which permit ellipsis only in following conjuncts—the ellipsis ranges for different types of languages are related to each other by proper inclusion—with the range of a language with relatively free ellipsis properly including the ranges of all languages with lesser degrees of freedom in ellipsis. These are facts about natural languages which are not logically necessary, of course, and which thus must receive an adequate explanation by any possibly adequate theory about such languages.

The schematization of Typology V in (20) also indicates degrees of resistance to ellipsis for each position in a coordination, and, by the arrows, the relative favorability of these

various positions as sites for possible ellipsis. Following conjuncts are thus more favored sites for ellipsis than preceding
ones, and, within each conjunct, favorability to ellipsis increases
toward the center, or the boundary between conjuncts. These
very general properties and relations constitute what I feel are
the most central and most significant facts about coordinate
ellipsis in human language, the facts that are most appropriately
subject to further analysis and explanation.

The general outlines of a quite straightforward explanation
here are directly suggested by the communicative functions of
ellipsis in coordinations and the functions of constraints on such
ellipsis. Ellipsis itself, of course, is of value chiefly if not wholly
with respect to the transmission of messages, since it provides a
systematic means for the abbreviation of complex messages,
permitting complex bodies of information to be adequately
conveyed by expressions of less than proportional complexity.
The efficiency and economy values of ellipsis with respect to
transmission must be weighed, of course, against its concomitant
countervalues, or counterfunctions, with respect to the reception
or decoding of messages. Thus because it contains fewer redun-
dancies and more discontinuities between related constituents,
an elliptical construction, other things being equal, will always
be harder to decode than its corresponding nonelliptical paraphrase. Ellipsis, in other words, while contributing to the
functional goal of economy of expression, works against the
equally important goal of clarity, or ease of decodability. To
achieve the appropriate balance, therefore, and approach the
optimum effectiveness for instruments of human communication, it is natural for human languages to have both ellipsis and
some constraints on ellipsis. The real question, though, of
course, is why they have the particular constraints and sets of
constraints that they do have. This question is quite amenable to
investigation, I believe, and the outlines of a possible answer at
least can be readily indicated.

The special, or distinguishing, task involved in the decoding or
understanding of an elliptical coordination is the task of recover-
ing by inference from its context the meaning and meaning
relations of the elliptical constituent or constituents of the
coordination. Success in this task requires, first, that all sites of
ellipsis be correctly located and, second, that the meanings and

meaning relations expressed by each ellipsis site be correctly determined. If we assume that there is at least some temporal component in the linguistic-decoding, or meaning-determining, processes employed by human beings—so that the meanings of the beginning parts of utterances are at least partially determined before the final parts are heard or received—then it is fairly easy to explain the directionality of the top arrow in (20), that is, the fact that following conjuncts are more favorable sites for ellipsis than preceding ones. Thus, the only way to recover an elliptical constituent is by determining what its antecedent is, the constituent which governs or controls its ellipsis. When ellipsis occurs in a following conjunct, all of the possible antecedents of the elliptical constituent have already been received and presumably understood, and they are all available in prior memory when the site of ellipsis is first encountered or perceived. When an ellipsis site is encountered in a preceding conjunct, on the other hand, none of its possible antecedents are available in memory at that time, and the decoding processes for the preceding conjunct must be suspended—with all previously obtained results being held in storage—until an appropriate antecedent is encountered in the following conjunct. Then it is necessary to go back and complete the decoding of the preceding conjunct. Therefore, other things being equal, the task of decoding will be much simpler and more efficient if ellipsis occurs in following conjuncts rather than preceding ones. Quechua-type languages, from the point of view of this two-conjunct effect, have an exceptionally natural constraint on coordinate ellipsis, since they permit ellipsis only in following conjuncts. From the existence of the other language types, however, it is clearly *not* the case that human beings are *incapable* of decoding sentences with ellipsis in preceding conjuncts. Moreover, the distinction between preceding and following conjuncts is not the only positional factor that is relevant here. There are also the positional-resistance differences *within* conjuncts, the effects symbolized by the conjunct-internal arrows in (20). These effects can also be understood, however, in terms of the distinctive decoding tasks for elliptical coordinations.

Success in this task can be achieved only to the extent that the antecedent of each elliptical constituent is correctly, easily, and rapidly identified. Since a search must be made for each antecedent among the set of nonelliptical constituents of sentences, it should follow that antecedents which are more prominent in memory should be more readily identifiable than those which are less prominent. This would in fact be fully consistent with the observed scale of positional resistance or favorability to ellipsis—given the language- and coordination-independent serial position effect for sequences of objects or events, and the assumption that no natural language can have sentence types that are relatively hard to decode unless it also has all those structurally related types that are easier to decode.

The serial position effect, which has been experimentally and observationally noted for a very wide and diverse range of sequential phenomena, involves the greater memory prominence of the beginnings and ends of sequences as opposed to their middles. Thus, beginnings and ends are learned faster and recalled more accurately and over a longer time than middles, whether the sequence involved is a poem, an arbitrary string of numbers, letters, or shapes, or whatever. Under experimental controls, in fact, the curves for errors or difficulties in serial learning and remembering, for all types of content or conditions, show a single remarkably distinctive serial position contour—lowest at the beginning, next lowest at the end, highest at the point two-thirds of the way through the sequence.[9]

With respect to coordinations, therefore, the serial position effect predicts that the initial position of a preceding conjunct and the final position of a following conjunct should be the most prominent parts of a coordination, and thus the best possible antecedents for ellipsis sites—that is, the most rapidly and most efficiently identifiable ones—and that the initial position of the following conjunct, which is two-thirds of the way through the coordination, should be the least prominent of its parts and hence the very worst of all possible antecedents for ellipsis. These predictions are in fact fully consistent with the laws about elliptical coordination expressed by Typology V.

Thus, position A, the initial position of preceding conjuncts, is the antecedent of ellipsis in position D—assuming parallelism, of course—and position D is the most favored of all possible sites for coordinate ellipsis—ellipsis in D position, with zero degrees of resistance, being permitted in all of the six language types of Typology V, that is, in all human languages. Position F, the final position of following conjuncts, governs ellipsis in position C, which has one degree of resistance and is thus more favored than positions A and B, with antecedents in the nonfinal positions of following conjuncts, and position F, with antecedent in the final position of preceding conjuncts. The ellipsis sites with coordination-marginal antecedents are thus found to be consistently more highly favored in languages than those with coordination-medial antecedents. Moreover, the fact that C-ellipsis and E-ellipsis have the same degree of resistance is precisely what would be expected from the fact that the characteristic curve for serial position effects is shaped so that the final position of a sequence (corresponding to F-position, the possible antecedent for C-ellipsis) is at the same height as the second position (corresponding to B-position, the possible antecedent for E-ellipsis). It seems clear, furthermore, that there is complete compatibility throughout between the serial position effect, favoring marginal antecedents over medial ones, and the previously mentioned two-conjunct effect, which favors antecedents preceding their governed ellipsis sites rather than following them.

The combined force of these two effects can thus be seen to determine precisely that scale of positional resistance or favorability to ellipsis that obtains in natural language. First, each position in the following conjuncts of coordinations is a more favored ellipsis site than its corresponding position in the preceding conjuncts. And, within a given conjunct, those sites with coordination-marginal antecedents are more favored than those with medial antecedents. Position D, the most favored of all, is optimal according to both effects—the antecedent precedes the ellipsis site, and the antecedent is at the initial margin of the coordination. Positions A and B, which are the most resistant of all to ellipsis, are disfavored by both effects, their antecedents being in the following conjunct and not at the margin of the coordination. The other positions—C, E, and F—are relatively favorable according to one of the effects but relatively disfavorable according to the other—which would account for their intermediate ranks on the universal scale of positional resistance or favorability. The serial position effect alone, nevertheless, is sufficient to generate the complete ranking of positional resistance, since it specifies for any sequence of six positions that the first (A) will be most prominent, followed by the second and last (B and F), followed by the third and fifth (C and E), and finally by the fourth position (D), the least prominent of all. The respective ellipsis sites governed by these positions are D, followed by E and C, followed by F and B, and finally by A—which corresponds exactly to the observed ranking from most to least favorable for ellipsis as expressed by Typology V.

None of this, however, constitutes an *explanation* of the facts provided by Typology V. The only thing that has been shown so far is that there is some kind of *correlation* between the occurrence and co-occurrence of ellipsis sites in natural languages and the relative ease or difficulty involved in the decoding of sentences with ellipsis sites in various positions, according to a particular hypothetical model for the decoding or understanding of linguistic messages. To note this correlation is at best to merely point out a fact. It says nothing at all about why natural languages are the way they are, with respect to ellipsis or anything else.

To proceed toward such an explanation, it would be necessary first to make the noted correlation fully explicit and fully law-like. This could be done as follows: First, we can define a scalar property of relative ease or difficulty of decoding, as determined by the temporal decoding model outlined, and the hypothesized processing interactions of the serial position and two-conjunct effects. On this basis, each coordination position is assigned a typologically independent rank of decoding ease or difficulty relative to all other positions. Then we can express a law-like generalization which correlates the language-independent decoding ease of a position with its decoding-independent degree of resistance to ellipsis, a property which is derived solely from facts about the actual occurrence and nonoccurrence of different types of languages.

A further and more general law can then be asserted on the basis of this correlation and the typological generalizations of Typology V, namely:

(21) For any natural language L, L does not permit coordinate ellipsis in position X unless it also permits ellipsis in all positions easier than X.

We would then, of course, have to ask for the explanation of this correlational law itself. Such an explanation would be provided if it were the case that for *any* type of difference in relative ease of decoding, with respect to *any* sets of structurally related linguistic expressions, no language permits use of an expression that is harder to decode than another unless it also permits use of the easier one.

I am inclined to believe that this law, in a more refined and developed formulation, has a reasonably good chance of being true. If this is the case—and particularly if it is true more generally that humans or human cultures are *incapable* of doing *any* hard thing unless they can already do all things that are easier[10]—then we will have a strong and sure foundation for the construction of a real, fully developed theory about elliptical coordinations in natural language, and about the essential principles of linguistic structure and function revealed by them.

NOTES

1. It will be observed that a sentence like *John and Bill left* will be assigned *two* coordination analyses by this definition: (1) the analysis [[[John] and [Bill]] left], where the coordination *John and Bill* and its conjuncts *John* and *Bill* share the semantic function of agentive argumenthood in the context of utterance with the predicate *left*; and (2) the analysis [[John] and [Bill left]], where the coordination *John and Bill left* and its conjuncts *John* and *Bill left* share the function of assertion in the context of utterance as a whole by a single speaker. It is a significant virtue, I feel, of the definition suggested that it will indeed generate such appropriately double analyses in all cases like this.

    It should also be noted that the terms *coordination* and *conjunct* are intended here, as defined by the schema in (1), and throughout the present paper to refer only to *conjunctive* coordinations (*and*-coordinations), and not to any other types of coordinative or quasi-coordinative constructions, like disjunctions (*or/nor*-coordinations), or adversatives (*but*-coordinations). Constructions of the latter types, whose patterns of anaphora and ellipsis are known to be characteristically quite different from those for conjunctive coordinations, thus lie completely outside the present domain of inquiry and analysis.

2. Although not actually published until 1970, Ross's paper was widely distributed earlier in its 1967 duplicated form.

3. Harries (1973:189) reports that in Russian a nonsentential manner adverbial (like *žadno* 'greedily' in the sentence *Ivan žadno el pirog, a*

Boris žadno pil vino 'Ivan greedily ate the pie and Boris greedily drank the wine') "can be deleted independent of its position in the sentence." Other sources, however, indicate that this is not the case, but rather simply that Russian prohibits B-ellipsis in such sentences while permitting E-ellipsis, which is exactly the same principle that governs the ellipsis of verbs, nominals, and other nonadverbial constituents in this language.

4. The actual range of nonpositional constraints on ellipsis may nevertheless prove to be quite diverse. For example, in Koyo, a Kru language of the Ivory Coast, as noted by L. Stigler (personal communication), ellipsis is possible only in C or D positions, but subject also to the additional condition that a predicate is elliptical if and only if one of its arguments is elliptical. According to Stigler, a similar dependency condition also holds for Tamašaq, a Berber language of Mali.

5. Like Typology II, Harries's analysis deals with nonpositional as well as positional constraints on ellipsis. She proposes here, in particular, that there is a general condition requiring that all semantic-scope relations must remain invariant under ellipsis, and that at least some positional constraints may be relaxed or overridden on the basis of such relational factors. Scope relations are assumed to vary fairly widely, however, both within languages (e.g., Chinese direct objects are assumed to have predicate scope in some sentences and propositional scope in others) and between languages (e.g., manner adverbs are assumed to have sentence scope in Russian but verb scope in English), and the range of typological variation determined by these differences is not specified by Harries.

6. Rosenbaum cites on this point an unpublished mimeographed paper by Furbee dated 1973 and titled "Gapping in Tojolabal-Maya: Problems of direction and identity."

7. Given the Immediate Dominance Condition, as specified in (11), a language like Chinese could alternatively be assigned to the English-Japanese type rather than the Chinese type, with its absence of E-ellipsis following from the IDC rather than from any positional constraint on ellipsis. It thus might be the case that there are actually only five positionally based language types with respect to ellipsis, rather than the six that will be accepted here. With respect to the Quechua type, Pulte has suggested that Cherokee would perhaps be a better exemplar of the type than Quechua since, for at least some speakers of the latter language, certain types of ellipsis in C-position are at least marginally acceptable. See Pulte, W. (1973) "Some claims regarding gapping: The evidence for Cherokee," in J. H. Battle and J. Schweitzer (eds.), *Mid-America Linguistics Conference Papers, 1972,* pp. 255–260 (Stillwater, Okla.: Oklahoma State University).

8. This is of course not to say that elliptical sentences are generally harder to produce or understand than nonelliptical ones, or that they are generally judged to be any less normal, acceptable, or grammatical. In fact, as pointed out by Sidney Greenbaum (personal communica-

tion), there are many contexts in which it is the nonelliptical member of a paraphrase set which would be found anomalous or difficult rather than the elliptical one. But observations like this merely show that the communicative facilitation effects of ellipsis—like brevity, for example—can sometimes totally outweight its inhibitory effects.

9. Typical serial position experiments are described, for example, in Baker (1960) and Millward (1971). In summarizing their findings Millward says: "The serial-position function plots some measure of the number of errors against the items according to the position of the items in the list. It has been found that the curve rises to a maximum point just past the middle item of the list and then declines again. Usually the last item causes more errors than the first—about the same number of errors as for the second item" (1971:101). In similar fashion, Baker reports that "items standing in the third quarter of the list are the most difficult ones to master. All people seem to perform in a similar manner. The item that is most difficult to learn, other factors than position assumed to be under control and equal, stands about two-thirds through the list. There is also stability in this for lists of various lengths extending at least from those as short as five or six items to those of eighteen" (1960:327).

10. The truth of such a law would appear to be a necessary precondition also for explanations of typological generalizations about the sounds of human languages, including in particular all phonological or morphological facts standardly described in terms of the notions of markedness, naturalness, or the relative strengths and weaknesses of sounds in various syllabic or lexical contexts. In fact, even more generally, it might perhaps be argued that unless some such law of obligatory easiness is true, linguistic facts can have no possible extra- or supralinguistic explanations at all.

REFERENCES

Baker, L. M. (1960) *General Experimental Psychology*. New York: Oxford University Press.

Dougherty, R. C. (1970) "A grammar of coordinate conjoined structures." *Language* 46:850–898.

Furbee, N. L. (1974) "Identity in gapping and the lexical insertion of verbs," *Linguistic Inquiry* 5:299–304.

Gleitman, L. R. (1965) "Coordinating conjunctions in English," *Language* 41:260–293.

Greenberg, J. H. (1963) "Some universals of grammar with particular reference to the order of meaningful elements," in J. H. Greenberg (ed.), *Universals of Language*, pp. 58–90. Cambridge: The M.I.T. Press.

Hankamer, J. (1973) "Unacceptable ambiguity," *Linguistic Inquiry* 4:17–68.

Harries, H. (1973) "Coordination reduction," *Working Papers on Language Universals* 11:139–209.

Koutsoudas, A. (1971) "Gapping, conjunction reduction, and coordination deletion," *Foundations of Language* 7:337–386.

Millward, R. B. (1971) "Theoretical and experimental approaches to human learning," in J. W. Kling and L. A. Riggs (eds.), *Experimental Psychology*, 3rd ed., pp. 905–1017. New York: Holt, Rinehart and Winston.

Postal, P. M. (1968) "Coordination reduction," Section III, Report 2, *Specification and Utilization of a Transformational Grammar*. Yorktown Heights, N.Y.: IBM.

Pulte, W. (1971) "Gapping and word order in Quechua," in *Papers from the Seventh Regional Meeting of the Chicago Linguistic Society*, pp. 193–197. Chicago: Chicago Linguistic Society.

—— (1973) "A note on gapping," *Linguistic Inquiry* 4:100–101.

Rosenbaum, H. (1974) Toward a nonuniversal analysis of identical verb deletion. SWRL Educational Research and Development, Los Alamitos, Calif. Manuscript.

Ross, J. R. (1970) "Gapping and the order of constituents," in M. Bierwisch and K. E. Heidolph (eds.), *Progress in Linguistics*, pp. 249–259. The Hague: Mouton.

Sanders, G. A. (1970) "Constraints on constituent ordering," *Papers in Linguistics* 2:460–502.

—— (1975) *Invariant Ordering*. The Hague: Mouton.

—— and J. H.-Y. Tai (1972) "Immediate dominance and identity deletion," *Foundations of Language* 8:161–198.

Schane, S. A. (1966) A schema for sentence coordination. Information System Language Studies No. 10. Bedford, Mass.: Mitre Corp.

Tai, J. H.-Y. (1969) Coordination reduction. Ph.D. dissertation, Indiana University; Indiana University Linguistics Club Bloomington: Mimeographed.

—— (1971) "Identity deletion and regrouping in coordinate structures," in *Papers from the Seventh Regional Meeting of the Chicago Linguistics Society*, pp. 264–274. Chicago: Chicago Linguistics Society.

AUTHOR INDEX

SUBJECT INDEX